Deep Are the Roots

Gordon Heath

Deep Are the Roots

Memoirs of a Black Expatriate

Introduction by
Doris Abramson

Afterword by
Ekwueme Mike Thelwell

THE UNIVERSITY OF
MASSACHUSETTS PRESS
∾ AMHERST

Copyright © 1992 by

The University of Massachusetts Press

All rights reserved

Printed in the United States of America

LC 92–181

ISBN 0–87023–778–0

Designed by Edith Kearney

Set in Berkeley Book by Keystone Typesetting, Inc.

Printed and bound by Thomson-Shore, Inc.

Library of Congress Cataloging-in-Publication Data

Heath, Gordon, 1918–1991.

    Deep are the roots : memoirs of a Black expatriate / Gordon Heath; introduction by
Doris Abramson.

      p. cm.

    ISBN 0–87023–778–0 (alk. paper)

    1. Heath, Gordon, 1918–1991.   2. Afro-American actors—Biography.   I. Title.

PN2287.H39A3   1992

792'.028'092—dc20

   [B]   91–181

                                                         CIP

The horizons of an artist should be as wide as his talents can encompass.
A whole artist is everything his open hands can hold.

—GORDON HEATH

Circle One **(for Gordon Heath)**

Nothing happens only once,
Nothing happens only here,
Every love that lies asleep
Wakes today another year.
Why we sail and how we prosper
Will be sung and lived again;
All the lads repeat themselves,
Shore for shore and men for men.

—OWEN DODSON

Contents

～ Introduction

Doris E. Abramson

IN THESE PAGES we meet a man, meet him as a child, an actor in training, an actor in performance. We meet a black man born in the United States in 1918 who fashioned a life for himself that kept him mostly abroad, mostly in Paris. Gordon Heath can be counted among such distinguished black expatriates as Ira Aldridge, Paul Robeson, Richard Wright, and James Baldwin. Their names have been written larger than his in the record books, but with the publication of his memoirs Gordon Heath moves from footnote status to deserved inclusion in the text itself.

Looking back on the support given to Negro artists by England and Europe, Paul Robeson once wrote:

> A century ago it was not possible for the Negro actor to appear on the American stage—not even as a buffoon. (Such parts were reserved for "whites only" in the days of the black-face minstrel shows, and only toward the end of that era was "progress" made to the point where a Negro face was permitted to appear in the traditional burnt cork of that happily now-dead form of American theater.) Hence, there was no place on our stages for one of the greatest actors in theatrical history—Ira Aldridge, a Negro. Still generally unknown to Americans is the enormous stature he gained in England and elsewhere in Europe as one of the most distinguished Shakespearean performers ever seen. . . . The door that was open to me in 1930 to play Othello in London was open to Aldridge in 1830 when he played the part at the Royalty Theater in that city.

By the time Gordon Heath played Othello in Great Britain in 1950, first on stage and then for BBC, only eight years after he had seen Robeson in the role on Broadway, much had happened to change the Negro actor's condition. Much, but not enough. Heath's own career is a case in point.

Owen Dodson, his boyhood and forever friend, reciting "The Highwayman" at summer camp, gave him the initial impulse to go into the theater. Other influences come clear as he reminisces. By his twenties, he was doing what aspiring young American actors usually do: he held odd jobs, got an education in and out of school and college, acted a variety of rôles in New York's little theaters, and held himself ready for his big chance. It came in 1945 with *Deep Are the Roots* by Arnaud d'Usseau and James Gow. His account of being cast, being directed by Elia Kazan, of living with this problem play in which he played Brett Charles, the young Negro lieutenant (more than one critic called him a "colored hero") returning from World War II to the Deep South, enables us to witness Gordon Heath coming of age under a set of unusual circumstances. Here he was *on* Broadway, in a hit play (Burns Mantle chose *Deep Are the Roots* as one of the ten best plays of the 1945–1946 season),* with a largely experienced cast and a director he respected, playing a role that had a very special meaning for him. "Playing the role of Brett is the most satisfactory kind of experience I could have in the theater," he told Frank Harriott in 1946. "He expresses the ideals, the frustrations, the hopes and bitterness of the Negro minority." On other occasions he has said that the audience reaction to seeing a black man with a white woman on stage—Gordon Heath and Barbara Bel Geddes—brought home certain facts about American racism. He has credited Elia Kazan with teaching him that "acting was where I *had* to be" and also, in a way, for helping him to acknowledge his blackness. Not that he had to learn about blackness from being in a play about the South for, as he told Harriott, "You go around with an insecurity whether you're living in the North or the South. You always have it, whether you want it or not." In the same interview he took some time to speak thoughtfully about Negro insecurity:

> In the North it isn't so much the fear of violence as the fear of insult or hypocrisy. When you're about to forget, when you have a certain sense of security, something happens to make you remember that the Negro is a very special case.
>
> You might answer a want ad that doesn't specify race. You might walk into a restaurant—you're never sure. You might visit white friends in an apartment house or hotel, and some friendly fool of a doorman will insist on trying to help you find the delivery entrance.

And finally, bringing it back to himself and the role of Brett Charles, he said: "Three critics wrote that I'd played the part with great *sincerity*. But that *sincerity* hasn't come only from playing the part well. It comes from having been a Negro for 27 years."

Harriott asked him what kind of roles he would like to play in the future. His answer was that he'd have trouble getting parts he'd like to do. "Let me put it

* The others were *State of the Union, Home of the Brave, The Magnificent Yankee,* Katharine Cornell's *Antigone, O Mistress Mine, Born Yesterday, Dream Girl, The Rugged Path,* and *Lute Song. Deep Are the Roots* was the first play selected by Mantle for his record of the theater season.

this way," he said, "if a Negro actor speaks English he has a hell of a job finding a part. But if he is a low comedian, a dialectician, he gets more chances." There it is again, that shadow of the buffoon that haunts all black actors. "But about the roles I'd like to do," he went on, "assuming that a decent part won't come along every season, I'd like to play the classic repertory." He had played Hamlet the previous summer (1945) at Hampton Institute, under Owen Dodson's direction—"Owen was the greatest influence and Elia Kazan the second greatest"— and he had now decided that Broadway would welcome the idea of Negroes playing the classics. Or so he said, flushed with success in 1946.

Gordon Heath played the role of Brett Charles for fourteen months on Broadway and then went to London's West End to play it for another six months. Then, after a short visit to America, he made the crucial decision to live abroad. By 1948 Paris was his home. Why? Why didn't he stay in New York and build on his success in *Deep Are the Roots*? Black theater historian Loften Mitchell believes that his time in London "made Gordon Heath take another look at the Statue of Liberty and the plight of the Negro theater artist in America; he packed his bags, went back to Europe and settled in Paris." *The plight of the Negro theater artist in America.* While Heath was performing in *Deep Are the Roots* in 1945–1946 at the Fulton Theater, there were only three other Broadway shows employing black performers. Two of them were musicals—a revival of *Show Boat* (his friend Pearl Primus was a featured dancer) and *St. Louis Woman*, with the Nicholas Brothers, Pearl Bailey, and Juanita Hall, to name names still recognizable—and one was a problem play about an attempt to integrate housing, *On Whitman Avenue*, with Canada Lee and Abbie Mitchell as a Negro veteran and his wife. Two musicals and two straight plays* in one Broadway season; all of them, by the way, by white playwrights. To be sure, what we now call Off and Off-off Broadway provided occasional work for Negro actors, but not enough to pay the rent.

James Edwards, who played Brett Charles in the touring company of *Deep Are the Roots,* was given the starring role in the 1949 film version of *Home of the Brave*, a role that might have been Heath's had he stayed home. But there seems little point in speculating about what roles might have been his and not James Edwards's or Sidney Poitier's. There never have been enough to go around. The fact is that Heath chose to be an expatriate, and he seems never to have regretted that decision. On one of his visits to New York, he told Loften Mitchell that he was glad he had moved to Paris, especially after taking a look at the 1965–1966 theatrical season. He had, Mitchell reported, "walked out on the first act of most of the season's hits, and he charged that the American theater

---

* *Home of the Brave* from that season is not listed because in its original form it was about a Jewish, not a black, soldier.

was going no place at a remarkable pace." As much as Mitchell was sorry to see him go back to Paris—"with him flew many dreams that could have made a great contribution to black drama and to the American theater"—he certainly understood his disenchantment with the American scene.

Like many another black artist before him, Heath found Paris a congenial place. In 1949 he and Lee Payant became co-owners of a nightclub called l'Abbaye. The two men had met in American in 1947 and were to become devoted companions and business associates for the next thirty years. (L'Abbaye closed when Payant died of cancer in 1976.) In 1952 *Ebony* did a feature about Gordon Heath that began: "Smallest and most talked-about night spot in Paris today is L'Abbaye, operated by Negro Gordon Heath, 34, and white Lee Payant, 28, two young American actors turned guitarists." They sang American and French folk songs—Heath sang spirituals too—and in their audiences over the years, in addition to the inevitable tourists, were Hollywood stars, French existentialists, and diplomats. *Ebony* mentioned seeing Lena Horne, Elliott Roosevelt, and Rita Hayworth there. Heath is quoted as saying, "I like it more each day. Paris has been kind to me."

In the sixties, Heath also became director of an English-speaking production company, Studio Theater of Paris,* where in its ten-year lifetime he produced such plays (new to Paris) as *The Glass Menagerie, After the Fall, The Skin of Our Teeth, Telemachus Clay,* and *Kennedy's Children,* among others.

He acted in French as well as in English in Paris and appeared quite regularly in London, both on stage and in films. He frequently returned to the United States in February, the month when l'Abbaye was customarily closed. In 1970, Heath was invited by New York's Roundabout Theatre to play Oedipus, and in 1977 the same theater invited him to play Hamm in *Endgame.* Edmund Newton wrote of his performance as Hamm:

> Every night at the Roundabout Stage Two, this tall, striking actor, brimming with Old World grace, changes magically into a human wreck. . . . Even at the edge of the void, he's a throbbing presence with the deep, resonant voice of the classic tragedian (which he is), frosted beard, sensitive eyes behind the smoked lenses of a blind man.

Heath's comment on Beckett, whose *Endgame* he had seen in Paris when it first opened, was: "There is no straight line in Beckett and you cannot pretend that any one point is a final truth."

No one point in Gordon Heath's life says it all, but a description of one moment says much about him as actor and man. Onstage he just played classical and contemporary roles, played them with grandeur and passion and intelligence. In his club, each night at the stroke of midnight, anyone who was

---

* Lee and Ruth Breuer, JoAnne Akalaitis, David Warilow, and Fred Neumann, who were to become Mabou Mines, were among its earliest members.

ever there will tell you, he performed a ritual that seems in retrospect to capture the essence of the theatrical Heath who knew how to build a scene and, most assuredly, how to hold an audience. At midnight a candle was lit on the table of each group requesting a special, final song. As each request was granted by the singers—Heath, a baritone, and Payant, a tenor—the candle was extinguished. At the final table, after the last song, Gordon Heath snuffed out the last candle— and the evening's entertainment was over.

GORDON HEATH DIED on August 28, 1991. He had been ill for the past few years, in and out of the hospital—continuing to work on his memoirs all the while—in his beloved Paris. He had been in a coma for two weeks before his death, his devoted friend Alain Woisson reported in letters and phone calls to American friends; he left instructions to be cremated "without any ceremony" and to have his ashes scattered in Provence.

During his illness, Heath had continued to write to many friends in the United States, apologizing for his "hands behaving badly" but nevertheless writing charming if brief notes on improvised notecards decorated with his own drawings. "Paris is lovely," he wrote to me in the spring of 1988. "The chestnuts along the Seine were proud and lush." Owen Dodson once said that Gordon Heath made ordinary songs sound extraordinary. He did the same with ordinary words in describing what might have been an ordinary day.

At memorial occasions—one in Paris on his birthday, September 20, one at the American Place Theater in New York City on October 14—friends had a chance to pay homage to the actor, to the man. In New York we were encouraged to applaud by snapping our fingers, the customary way to applaud at l'Abbaye. (Originally done so as not to disturb the neighbors, it became part of the evening's ritual.) I doubt that friends in Paris had to be instructed how to applaud their departed friend. On both sides of the Atlantic, the snapping must have started vigorously in recollection of times past, and then slowed to a quiet sound reflecting present loss.

Clive Barnes was quoted in the *New York Times* obituary (August 31, 1991): "A man born to play the prince, Mr. Heath has an instinctive nobility and moves and talks with all the natural authority of a classic hero." Put into past tense, it can serve as a worthy epitaph for Gordon Heath.

Sources

Bishop, Helen Gary. "Gordon Heath—American Actor between Two Continents." *The Soho Weekly News,* 21 April 1977.
Dodson, Owen. *Powerful Long Ladder.* New York: Farrar, Straus and Co., 1946.

"Gordon Heath." *Ebony,* December 1952.

Harriott, Frank. "Gordon Heath Explains Perpetual Insecurity." *PM New York,* 6 January 1946.

Heath, Gordon. Interview with Camille Billops. 18 February 1975. Hatch-Billops Collection. Present: CB, Owen Dodson, Gordon Heath.

Mantle, Burns. *The Best Plays of 1945–1946.* New York: Dodd, Mead & Co., 1946.

Mitchell, Loften. *Black Drama: The Story of the American Negro in the Theater.* New York: Hawthorn Books, 1967.

Newton, Edmund. "'Endgame' Brings an Actor Home." *New York Post,* 21 May 1977.

Robeson, Paul. *Here I Stand.* London: Dennis Dobson, 1958.

∿ Columbus Hill and I Are Born

IN MY DAY—my childhood day, that is—Manhattan's far west side appeared on the map as a progression of coexisting districts where boundaries were really frontiers. The Battery, the Bowery, Hell's Kitchen—ancient charts would have noted in the margin, "Here Be Dragons!" The ingredients of the "melting pot"—races, colors, and nationalities—simmered, bubbled, and, from time to time, boiled over. These picturesque names were imposed on Manhattan's grid of intersecting numbered streets and numbered avenues. When you arrived in the Fifties and Ninth, Tenth, and Eleventh avenues, you were in, or on, San Juan Hill—so named as a tribute to the black troops who fought under Theodore Roosevelt in the prefabricated Spanish-American War, but suggestively and appropriately bellicose, summing up the enclaves of Irish railway workers, West Indian blacks, American blacks, Jewish and German storekeepers and landlords, and Chinese launderers.

Philanthropist Henry Phipps contributed a million dollars or so toward the construction of eight six-story, low-rent apartment houses, back to back, four on Sixty-third and four on Sixty-fourth streets between Tenth and Eleventh avenues. I was born in one of these buildings. They were meant to house "ex-slaves," meaning blacks who had immigrated to New York, not necessarily directly out of bondage but indisputable *there* and already spread out all over Harlem a couple of miles to the north.

Phipps Houses were completed in 1911. Only one building blocked them from a view across the Hudson River to New Jersey but that Firestone tire factory also diminished the force of icy winter winds blowing from the river. The project was the envy of the entire West Side. Sixtieth to Sixty-fourth streets between those avenues were solidly black. The east side of Tenth Avenue to Central Park West was starkly white—lower middle class, brownstone and tenement. Central Park West was upper-income white: high-rise apartment

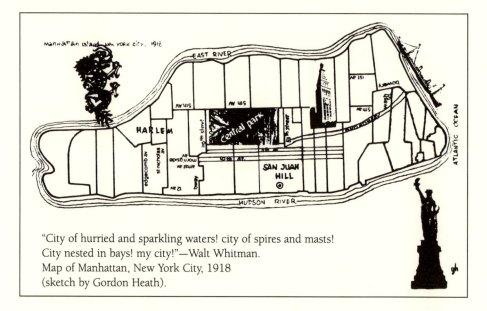

"City of hurried and sparkling waters! city of spires and masts!
City nested in bays! my city!"—Walt Whitman.
Map of Manhattan, New York City, 1918
(sketch by Gordon Heath).

houses, hotels, churches looking out snobbishly to the park all along its length.
Phipps Houses neither depressed nor inflated real estate values in San Juan Hill.
They simply gave Sixty-third and Sixty-fourth a leg up the ladder of gentility.
Sixtieth, Sixty-first, and Sixty-second remained slummy crowded tenements
and four-story boardinghouses made up of "railroad" flats—rooms off a cor-
ridor—buildings petering out downhill in grimy garages meeting Eleventh
Avenue and giving way to railroad tracks divided by a live and powerful "third
rail" children were warned against.

⌁ No one had been warned about the advent of Cyril Gordon Heath, late
of Barbados, British West Indies, a dapper, dark-haired Ronald Colman who
met, dazzled, and married Hattie Hopper, a second-generation American with
African and Indian bloodlines that culminated in a cream-colored, boldly
featured, and handsome woman. Hattie was born on Sixtieth Street. Cyril
announced his intention of taking her away from all that. All that being mother,
stepfather, and at least two siblings for whom Hattie was pulled out of school to
act as deputy parent. "Away" turned out to be Sixty-third Street and Phipps
Houses. I don't know how Cyril and Hattie met; possibly in the local dance hall.
They spoke often of prizes they'd won, but I never saw them. I don't know,
either, when I became aware of the unlikeliness of that union. He saw her as his
creature—a Galatea who would do him credit. She was biddable—in fact she
adored my father, which was probably the only attitude he would have accepted (what am I saying, "probably!"). That Edwardian monument never

wavered in his certain belief that all authority, the laws, and the prophets reposed in his bosom. When I saw *Mutiny on the Bounty* and heard Captain Bligh say, "You do your duty and we'll get along—but you'll do your duty!" I realized I had been walking that quarterdeck a good while myself. There we were—in those spanking new apartments: two businesses and two personal references required, no dogs, and preferably, if not practically, no children. Three rooms: kitchen (with two huge washtubs under the window), living room, bedroom, and bath. My father daringly demolished two closets to enlarge the living room that at night was my bedroom.

In the spring and summer my father worked on the "boats"—the Hudson River Night Line—making excursions up and down the river from Forty-second Street to Albany, the state capital. Dad was a "first hallman," a kind of uniformed steward dispensing service like a family retainer, with hair curling and a moustache trimmed to within an inch of its life. The pay wasn't bad and the tips were even better and my mother made all my clothes—pongees, silks, and corduroys exciting scorn and envy the length and breadth of San Juan Hill. My father and his genteel cohorts got *that* changed to *Columbus Hill*—a designation they considered more suitable to a housing project, a community center, two churches, a playground, and all the other refinements Sixty-third and Sixty-fourth streets began to boast.

Somewhere along the line it was decided that I was to be an only child. My mother was one of eleven children and my father one of six, which was quite a dose of "family." I remember asking for a sister or brother but I was pleased enough to be the center of the universe. My father had suffered in his youth at the hands of an autocratic schoolmaster parent who did not spare the rod. My father did not spare the strap and while he did not always beat his child in anger, he could, more frighteningly, conjure up his original anger when he got around to beating me for yesterday's misdemeanor. He had strong reactions to the phenomena of "liberated" women. "Tramps" smoked in the street, ladies did not drink, makeup was a visible proof of corruption. Mother never went to a hairdresser until she visited me in Paris when she was fifty. In her thirties she began to use a flesh-colored lipstick and gradually applied darker shades that my father finally accepted as "natural." But in spite of all those puritanical instincts vibrating, he did not relinquish his womanizing tactics. His swooping gallantry was always on top and he bowled them over like ninepins—from the cross-eyed songstress at Sunday teas who trilled "I Passed by Your Window" to the creaking pillars of the church to whom he would sweep off his hat, after the doxology, with a "Good morning, Girls!" He laid waste all about him. I knew my parents fought a good deal because of these women, these "cows" who were encouraged to hope. I should think that it was my mother's sense of her own rectitude that allowed her to launch spirited attacks on him—but always with a full sense of just how far she could go without a crisis. I watched my father, in a smouldering fury, take dishes out of the closet, stack them carefully in the dishpan, and smash them into bits with a hammer. There is a dent in the living room wall made by a flashlight he threw at my mother.

It sounds as if my father lived with us as a ravening beast seeking to devour, but of course that was by no means the entire story. He had a schoolboy sense of fun, he loved to entertain, he reveled in social occasions, he played with my toys much more creatively than I. He teased us both with great affection and he was volubly proud of any accomplishment or excellence that came to his attention. He strove to erect a facade of domestic propriety and well-being— a genuflection to public opinion and the accompanying hypocrisy. "What man has done man can do," he would say and believe fervently. His diatribes were always designed to lighten intellectual darkness. The Bible was his casebook, not primarily for its revelation of the hand of God and his loving presence but for the parables and proverbs complete with moralities. He was always "Dad" to me or "Sir" and my mother was always "Mother." I never talked back or ever dreamed of doing so.

Their respective families hated each other. My younger aunts were forbidden the house, having displayed entirely overt hostility to my father's airs and graces and his West Indian sense of superiority. He was every man's equal but they were not necessarily his. American blacks were a shiftless lot who lived supinely under the lash and accepted being second-class citizens in their own country. He was a British subject, by God, and proud as Lucifer. All that sat badly with the "natives." The West Indians, from the highest to the lowest, were convinced of their exalted origins.

My education began with my father's schoolmaster father. An austere, gaunt Barbadian, he looked like Abe Lincoln in middle age and George Bernard Shaw at its end. He taught me spelling and vocabulary—British style, of course. He "inculcated" (a word that always meant to me "with the end of a ruler") instruction. Grandpa was even straighter and narrower than his son. After fifty he walked with his hands clasped behind his back—a veritable symbol of uprightness. My grandmother* I remember only as an invalid in a dark stuffy bedroom, her head tied up with a kerchief, gasping perpetually for breath, racked with that asthma that looks and sounds like dying itself. But she retained enough force to drag Grandpa back to the Indies betimes. The Big City gave her husband too much scope with any number of intrigued ladies.

---

* She contributed the name I was christened—*Seifield!* I have no idea where she got it from or why my parents accepted it. They neutralized its effect by inserting *Gordon* in between. It was pronounced "Sea field" and was inevitably misspelled, mispronounced, and an invitation to mockery by my contemporaries. I started calling myself "Gordon" after most of the damage was done. There are perhaps three people left in the world who know me as "Seifield."

One of my paternal aunts, Ottie, gave me violin lessons when I was eight. Light-skinned, plump, opinionated: "only coarse people call it 'rosin'—it is 'resin'! Your sign is Pisces. You will have trouble with your feet." (My sign is Virgo but I *am* having grievous trouble with my feet!) Although easily categorized by blacks as "Negro" she married a Filipino gentleman, passed for white in a white neighborhood, and discouraged her brothers and sisters from visiting. They took umbrage and stopped speaking to her for five years.

My uncle Charleston looked a lot like my father but was smoother, younger, with an olive complexion and East Indian hair—a really handsome, really audacious, really unscrupulous rogue. I always suspected my mother of having a soft spot for him in spite of her blanket disapproval of his maneuvers, for example: driving a taxi without a license, practicing dentistry likewise, tapping the city's electric supply for heat and light in his own apartment. Later in life he went into the real estate business: charm and chicanery, inc. His children were my only playmates in the city.

The only other relative on my father's side to have an impact was a distant cousin from Trinidad, Valerie—Aunt Val, that is—who claimed blood ties with Dad more profound and binding than any by-the-way incident like marriage. A wife was only a wife, she informed my mother and an American wife, she implied, was even less than that. But my mother was, in the long run, acceptable as a fit enough mate for Cyril—as long as she remembered her place. My mother acknowledged the charm and directness of this imperious lady and, I suppose since Val owned a brownstone in Harlem and entertained and celebrated holidays lavishly, her house and her hospitality were lodestones for my parents and the clan gatherings.

Sunday afternoons we would get on a streetcar—those lovely vehicles on steel tracks with overhead electric cables, running boards down the sides, seat benches whose backs flipped over at the end and beginning of the run so passengers could always face in the right direction. The line began at Sixty-sixth Street and Columbus Avenue and the track curved and twisted at 110th Street where the Cathedral of St. John the Divine loomed up on a high hill and the car went on into Harlem. The elevated railway rose up on the same route to scenic heights saluting the cathedral. Both trips were an adventure. The conductor pulled the cord that rang the bell and glided acrobatically along the running board to collect fares and slide coins into the metal container on his belt, which then emitted a long ticket to the passenger. A Sunday afternoon treat of picnic proportions! The picnic motif was carried out to its ultimate at Aunt Val's: petit fours, cookies, cake, homemade ice cream and sherbert. I know because I was frequently enlisted to crank the handle of the freezer. Suppers, on the other side of the sliding doors leading to the dining room, were prodigal. West Indian specialties, five courses and wine withal. Toasts were part of the rites. "I drink now to Trinidad. Men may come and men may go, but Trinidad goes on—shall I say forever?" A whispered response from all present, "Oh yes, say it!" An upper-class Edwardian spread—a corner of a foreign field that would be forever England. I was totally incurious about how all this was put together. There were no servants. It was only much later that I realized Val's poor-relation sister, already a young old maid, and Val's aging aunt shared the burden of cooking, cleaning, and maintaining. Val's husband, Albert, would flee to our house to drink more than he ought to (he brought it with him; there was no drink in our house) and complain, tears falling on his bristling moustache, about Val's tyranny over the household and the immutable circumstance that she had married beneath her and he wasn't going to be allowed to forget it. The middle boy of their three children—Roy, Val's favorite—died suddenly of pneumonia and she was a screaming Niobe somehow blaming it all on her husband. We heard her at the funeral, at the cemetery, in the house. The younger element in our funeral coach tried to ignore the drama and sang "September in the Rain" all the way out and back.

Domestic infidelity seemed to abound among my immediate and once-removed family. There were my adulterous uncle, my adulterous grandfather, my adulterous father, and my squabbling, cantankerous maternal grandmother. She would open her windows to make certain the neighbors heard every word of her quarrels—possibly because her second husband wouldn't listen to her and consoled himself with enormous meals, bringing his weight to some three hundred pounds—and he a baggage handler at Grand Central Station! I never met the men my maternal aunts married but they were not much in evidence and disappeared entirely after a very short time. My father's sisters, except Ottie, married West Indians and managed, at least on the surface, to attain a family life worthy of the name and productive of offspring. In my early teens I was aware of all the domestic strife and pain visited upon my mother and my uncle's long-suffering wife. When I grew out of my father's jurisdiction I realized with a sinking heart that I was my father's son. I coined an aphorism that probably won't stand up to close inspection—"the fundamental difference between my father and me was that we were exactly alike!"—but you see what I mean. I knew I would be arbitrary, selfish, possessive, and overbearing and would make exactly the same mistakes as my father had with my mother and probably quite different but equally damaging mistakes with any children I was unlikely to have. I didn't see how I could play fair in a marriage with a woman. The childhood kissing games of "post office," "spin the bottle," and social dancing left me quite, quite cold. I didn't know what that was all about and I had no particular desire to find out. I liked some girls well enough but a book was more satisfying. I was still not bold enough to approach the boys and men I was

Cyril Gordon Heath and
Hattie Hopper Heath, 1942

attracted to. I had no idea that there were many in the world who would meet me more than half way. So much for puberty!

Looking backward from puberty I see mostly an ordinary succession of enjoyment. My mother was my nanny and comrade. She took me roller-skating in Central Park in the summer and sleigh-riding in the winter. She was home base on a bench never far away. We would watch the sailor-hatted kids sail boats on the lake and the kissing couples in rowboats. A bit later when I was considered old enough to go to the park alone I'd go fishing (strictly forbidden) in the lake with a crooked pole, string, and a bent pin with wet dough as bait and catch the tiny sunfish. I'd bring them home sometimes to fry and feed to my black-and-white cat, Buddy. I'd tie him to our round ball-and-claw kitchen table and tease him cruelly. Sometimes he would play; sometimes he was bored. I had to give him up because I inherited my grandmother's asthma. The ailment severely limited my activities, increased my bookishness, and widened the gulf between me and the kids on the block who had already decided I was a "sissy" and did impersonations of me calling "Mother" from the court to the fourth floor. I was trotted around from doctor to doctor to clinic. They pinpointed my allergies and I was injected all over, arms and backside, with no appreciable results. I could never run for a bus, run up or down stairs, jump rope, or play hopscotch. I couldn't even play handball in the court because it might endanger my fiddling "career." The asthma attacks were violent and exhausting but I seem to have been philosophic about them and intensely grateful that they were not crippling as in my granny's case. I had to be careful but I still had a good time. I even played marbles along the gutters and into the target—the center of the incised iron steam covers in the middle of the street. A most unhygienic sport but helpful in making a tenuous contact with those kids on the block.

The most exciting treat of my childhood was to make the trip from the pier at 42d Street to 125th Street on my father's Hudson River Night Line boat. He would welcome us aboard with formal ceremony, install us on deck, facing the New Jersey side, and "take our orders"—which always meant ice cream for Mother and me. The whistles would blow, the horns would hoot, smoke would rise from the funnels, "all aboard" announcements would resound all over the three decks, chains and cables would rap against capstans, the powerful engines would begin to pound, and the agitated river would foam as we slid into the middle. My father would take me down to the engine room to marvel at those incredible brass pistons that plunged and rotated and rose tirelessly over and over as the boat lunged on its way. This was the first lap in a voyage that went east to Poughkeepsie and ended at Albany. My father would show off his handsome family* to his colleagues and we would bask in their admiration like honored guests.

The religious holidays were outpourings of fun. I blush to recall how long I believed in Santa Claus. I wrote letters to him down-playing the behavior lapses during the year, making my modest requests, fearing to sound greedy, and ending with regards and best wishes rather like those flowery French complimentary endings: "Soyez assuré, cher Monsieur, de nos sentiments les plus distingués, etc." My father who always supervised my letters, demanding many rewrites and corrections, would not read this yearly scrawl but would take the sealed, addressed letter to be mailed on. I even had replies from S.C. who was all-knowing but tolerant.

On Christmas morning there would be a gaily decorated tree with last year's star on top and presents heaped around the base inscribed to my cousins, to me, from Mother to Father, from Father to Mother, all stage-managed by them

---

* Certain distinctions prevailed at home in this matter of looks. My father would regard me quizzically; "I don't know—your *mother* has good hair." My mother would, in the same manner, say, "Your father has the softest skin—eyelashes almost too long for a man, Indian (east) hair. . . ." They would both leave this kind of observation dangling—the implication, of course, being that I had not inherited those natural beauties and thus handicapped I would have to make my way in the world somehow. It was a corrective to vainglory—I was the ugly duckling. Privately, like any ordinary doting parents, they thought I was beautiful and gifted and headed for a brilliant future.

with infinite craft and tenderness. I rose helpfully to the occasion by being unsuspecting and taking it all as miraculous, year after year. Val and her kids and Charleston and his kids would come over furred and gloved and bearing gifts and we were all out of the pages of Dickens—clamor and good cheer, excitement, and peace on earth.

⌥ Camp Carlton

We are the boys of Camp Carlton you've heard so much about,
And everybody makes a fuss whenever we go out.
We try to be the very best in everything we do,
And everybody likes us—we hope you like us too!

If you want to have a good time just come to Camp Carlton,
by the light, by the light of the moon . . .

I MET OWEN and Kenneth Dodson at the summer camp of the Brooklyn YMCA, Camp Carlton, somewhere near Poughkeepsie, upstate New York. A hundred acres cleared on the west side of a man-made lake stuffed with perch, pike, sunfish, fifty-cent-piece turtles, emerald frogs poised on lily pads that flowered with a Monet insistence. Chapel was rows of benches and an altar made of white-washed stones. Tall trees made shade on both sides of the lake. One could hide or climb but would never be lost. Snakes crossed the dirt paths but seldom lingered and eels would end up on our fishing lines from time to time. There were canoes for the deft and boats for the rest. There was a square raft a ways out in the lake where we rested and posed and wrestled just like Bellows's "Boys on a Raft" painting. Discipline in camp was paramilitary: bugle calls for reveille, meals, roll call, inspection, flag raising and lowering, all the way to taps at bedtime. There was the Big House—counselors' quarters—and the sprawling, wooden mess hall. We wore khaki shirts and shorts, heavy shoes and long socks. We lived eight in a canvas tent with wooden two-tiered bunks. The blankets and sheets mere meant to fit without a wrinkle, our baggage and belongings were meant always to be in their assigned places. The wood floor was scrubbed daily. We marched, we saluted the flag, we did simple exercises. We were fit, young, male, and Christian. Carlton was a site of surpassing natural beauty with elms, oaks, apple trees, and rich farmlands surrounding it. There was an unused barn fifteen minutes out of camp, fragrant with the scent of rotting apples—ammunition for battles in the hay, with worm-eaten timbers under our feet and over our heads. The roads leading out of camp were bordered with blackberry and wild strawberry bushes. Wire fences did not entirely protect the crab apple trees. The cherry trees had been reckless with blossom but the fruit was small and acid. Grasshoppers, worms, caterpillars, and butterflies abounded. Crickets and fireflies shared our nightlife.

The personnel was black, the campers were black. Every prospect was pleasing and we took it all for granted, we basically citywise boys who could be lured into a "nature walk" and might just recognize daisies as not being buttercups. I think we loved every minute of it, although we complained all the time about the food, the strictness of the rules, the supervision, and certain personalities in authority. But on hikes we marched proudly through the villages singing like victorious troops. What mischief remained to be gotten into was tribal: feuds, foraging, secret rendezvous, bullying the new boys, and, of course, the long "lights out" sessions dedicated to fervent, obscene speculations on who did it to whom, how babies were conceived, and what sexual activities were the most fun; to the exchange of dirty jokes and rhymes and information on the myths of Santa Claus and God (unreal, both of them); and to discussions of who was best endowed of the campers (they knew, too)! The background for these passionate debates and assertions was usually a version of the "dozens," a ritual chant, sometimes rhymed, composed of lewd and scurrilous accounts of one's mother's sexual perversions, one's sister's availability, whatever, all told with a wealth of improvised and completely fabricated detail. It was a game—a duel with uncapped rapiers that drew blood or at least tears— surprisingly—from the less fluent boys on the defensive. I was ignored, baffled and passive, but somehow excited. All the elements my parents had tried to protect me from in the city—foul-mouthed, streetwise adolescents, knowing in the ways of bullying, blackmail, obscenity, and sex—surrounded me. I learned most of the facts of life at their crudest during those eight weeks. I was wretched and exhilarated by turns. I was stupid and cowardly, bullied, tricked, beaten, and raped. I was eleven years old. The first week I was invited to play Black Jack with a bunch who seemed friendly enough. We played for fun and then we played for desserts. I lost my desserts for the entire season in twenty minutes. Served me right. I was sent out to get a left-handed monkey wrench from the shop. Well, you see. I got demerits and received punishments from above. I didn't know how to defend myself against anything. The rape was painful, of course; but afterward the older of the two boys who raped me picked me up from the ground and hit me in the eye—I suppose to discourage me from reporting him. That was Jackson. He must have been all of sixteen. I sat and cried on the wooden toilet seat. The other boy came back, sympathetic and solicitous—that was Bell. "Did he hit you?" I nodded between sobs. "Let me see. Where?" and then he hit me in the other eye. It didn't make the headlines. The only person I felt I could tell was Owen. He advised me to do nothing about it, stick closer to him, and take boxing lessons. I wrote nothing to my folks. I longed to ask them to come and get me, but the kind of freedom I was being offered—hazards and all—seemed preferable in the long run. Besides, my sexuality stirred and would not be quieted. Although sodomy and sadism were

"Feeling protective"
—Gordon Heath (*center*)
at Camp Carlton, 1929

not ideal introductions to adolescent manhood, the casual obscenity, the absence of affection, the dirty jokes, the sniggering schoolboy confidences, and the prevalence of promiscuity were much more real than responses in the Ethical Culture prayerbook or the ceremony of confirmation. I did not struggle to conciliate the warring elements. I was evidently going to be Earnest in the city and Jack in the country and the twain might never meet. My only concern was to find someone with whom I could—in E. M. Forster's word—"share." I was unformed, ignorant, and innocent. Freud would have made short work of me.

I was attracted to men and boys and that was that. The weeks to follow were so crammed with hikes, excursions, fishing trips, swimming competitions, and civic duties like cleaning the johns and scrubbing the mess hall floors, I hardly had time to consider what had happened to me.

On the traditional "camp fire night" that took place every two weeks, we huddled up with blankets for warmth, told ghost stories, and sang songs around the giant camp fire. Owen and Kenneth said poems: "The Highwayman," "The Ballad of the Harp Weaver," funny dialect poems by Paul Laurence Dunbar. They were both great theatergoers in New York and they described and mimicked scraps of scenes as they remembered them. The Dodsons were Carlton's star performers. They had already spent two summers there. They shared a tent, had a trunk(!), kept house efficiently. They worked for their board and keep like scholarship students. Owen was round-faced and cheerful. Kenneth, the elder, expressed a kind of weary patience and authority beyond his years. They must have been in their late teens but they were foster parents to many of us. It was natural to take my eleven-year-old troubled self to Owen for advice and equally natural that I was stagestruck from camp-fire night on—and that Owen was my hero, my loved one.

The new boys were warned that all accounts would be settled on the steamer trip back to New York City. The counselors would be involved with logistics and therefore inattentive to our welfare. The big boys would busy themselves with what Saki called "reconstructing the punishments." The threat was ingeniously cruel, hanging over our heads those last weeks. Some of the littler ones begged their parents to provide some other form of transportation but couldn't explain why. We were trapped. The tents came down. The flag was wrapped up. We were driven to the dock and boarded the boat, sacks on our backs, sticking together for dear life. Nothing whatever happened. Everybody wept with nostalgia, overflowed with remembrances, and cast longing looks in the direction of Poughkeepsie. For all our parents knew, we had had the time of our lives. There was never a cloud in the sky. Could we—oh *could* we—go back next year? Owen and Kenneth met my father and invited me to visit them at Christmas. They lived with their two older sisters in a Brooklyn brownstone. My cup was full. My father even thought it was possible I could go back to Carlton for eight weeks the next summer!

The Dodsons were not there the next summer but I had seen a good deal of them and their sisters during the year. The way they lived! Venetian blinds at the windows, Swedish modern furniture, books from floor to ceiling, a splendid Dynaphone record player, pottery for plates, cups, and saucers, conversations about art, poetry, theater, people. Unending hospitality offered with grace, ease, and openness. They were emphatically not rich but they had style without clutter or pretension. Owen became and remained the strongest influence in my life.

I went back to Carlton the next year, a sophomore but also a veteran and two inches taller. I was no longer a victim, at least not often, and I even protected and advised some of the new boys with my newfound, if ill-digested, worldly wisdom. I have thought since that city parents could do worse than send their children into the streets instead of school for a while and then ask them "What did you learn today in the streets?" These wise parents would consider and discuss the reality of the crudities and relate them to what the children were taught at home and school without condescension or condemnation but as a necessary part of their education. I see that today's splintered childhood has no place for this kind of discrimination. Ah well.

But the best and happiest thing for me was finding someone to "share" with me and the summer was an idyll in sylvan surroundings. We never saw each other again, but the summer was—indeed—cloudless.

> We're going to leave old Carlton, we're going to leave you now.
> We're going to leave Lake Placebo, the lake we love so well.
> Our boat is on the river, the hour is drawing nigh.
> And when the sun goes down tonight, we're going to say "goodbye."

∾ Music Appreciation

IN GRAMMAR SCHOOL—that dim period of conforming education—we were introduced to "classical music." Attendance at this "music appreciation" course was compulsory. We were fed snippets of concert music played on the phonograph that we were meant to be able to identify forever after. There were follow-up exams at regular intervals—probably citywide, since Miss Goldstein, our keen music instructor, would cheat at exam time, bending her arm at the elbow and poising her hand like a beak to help us guess Saint-Saëns's "The Swan" and clumping about like a troll for "The Hall of the Mountain King" from Grieg's "Peer Gynt Suite." We knew von Weber's "Oberon Overture" because you couldn't hear *anything* for the first twenty seconds—a pianissimo to remember.

Miss Goldstein coaxed a boy soprano voice from me and assigned solos: "How Lovely Are Thy Dwellings," "I Waited for the Lord," at assembly without benefit of censers or candles. At graduation in 1931 she wrote in my autograph book: "Many many good wishes to you, Heath—Keep on with your music. Perhaps you'll make the world listen to you some day. Sincerely, Lilian Goldstein."

My voice had not yet changed.

In the meantime at home I was passed on from my Aunt Ottie's peremptory violin instruction to a soft-spoken, small, elegant, young Jewish gentleman who wore his hair just a little longer than ordinary and gave piano lessons to a next-house neighbor by the name of Thelonius Monk. Simon Wolf studied under the concertmaster of the New York Philharmonic at the time when Jewish boys with talent and European sensibilities were merchants of culture and Jascha Heifetz and Yehudi Menuhin were avatars in short pants. Mr. Wolf himself was warm but impersonal, conscientious, and correct. Once a week for three years I struggled through scales, Spohr studies, and exercises to the inevitable "La Folia."* He stood by—suffering undoubtedly but not visibly—every now and then taking up the fiddle and demonstrating what it should sound like. I despaired of ever being able to play with that sonority and authority.

My father, pragmatic as ever, cornered Mr. Wolf as he came out of the living room and I dried myself and the violin: "Well now, how is Seifield doing?"

Mr. Wolf temporized: "He works hard but I couldn't say if he has talent."

My father, convinced that his son was furnished with as much talent as was required for anything he undertook, swallowed hard but went on to ask about Thelonius. Mr. W: "I don't think there will be anything I can teach him. He will go beyond me very soon."

Two body blows to my father's solar plexus. I myself was a bit startled to hear that I worked hard! I was like most music students: lazy, resentful of scales and exercises, and indeed did work like a fiend—but only the day before the Friday lesson to try to make up for the sloth of the other six days. I wouldn't have thought that Mr. W would have been taken in. I had chosen the violin mostly because everyone else I knew was studying the piano. I only loved my violin when Mr. W played it.

Mr W was offered a cup of coffee, which he accepted and my father needed: "And what do you think of Rubinoff, Mr. Wolf?" Rubinoff was a radio-celebrity fiddler—fine tone, no taste, or at least willing to pander. His specialties included "Flight of the Bumble Bee" twice as fast as Paganini, imitations of human conversation, and the like. He was a shameless showman. Mr. W was noncommittal. Dad plunged: "Can you play like that?" Mr. W shrugged without emphasis and said equally without emphasis: "Who would want to?"

The irony went past my father. Of course Mr. W understood him very well but Dad had no background to cope with this supersubtle article. I continued to study with Mr. W for three more years.

My spare time in those days was devoted to reading "all the books in the world" like the child in Kipling's "Ba Ba Black Sheep" (he almost went blind; I began to wear glasses!) and drawing movie stars in pencil from the lush photos in movie magazines. I used a variety of pencils; every eyelash, every strand of hair was painstakingly rendered—the eyes were glassy, the teeth were ivory, the hair was silky, the flesh was porous, the likenesses were unmistakable. I proudly tacked the drawings to the wall in the kitchen. Mr. W would pause without comment in front of them before adjourning to the living room, but one day he

* "La Folia" is a piece by Corelli (1653–1713) that happens to violin students (like "Für Elise" to piano fledglings). The melody inspired Bach, Pergolesi, Vivaldi, Lulli, and others to compose works with it as the theme.

asked in his unemphatic way: "Why do you insist on drawing those made-up faces? Why don't you draw people—or *anything* else?"

I had just won a prize in a city-wide competition, drawing Shirley Temple (who at eight wore little or no makeup and almost looked like a person) but it was Mr. W's remark that, paradoxically, made me feel I was an artist and worthy of serious consideration as such. I began to draw anyone who would sit for me and to make caricatures of the glamour queens.

One of those years my father gave me a ukulele as a birthday present. A collection of songs with diagrams for the accompanying chords came with it. I was not ready to adjust to a new fingering principle and I didn't really take to the instrument. My father, impatient with me, picked it up, figured out two or three of the chords and we—mother, father, and son—sang those standard ditties in the evening around the kitchen table like a black version of a Norman Rockwell magazine cover: "The Old Oaken Bucket," "Long Long Ago," "In the Gloaming." My father's favorite from the book was "Jenny Jones":

"We've come to see Miss Jenny Jones and how is she today?"
"Blooming!"
"We're right glad to hear it, to hear it and how is she today?"
"She's dead!"
"We're right glad to hear it, to hear it, etc."

At Camp Carlton I worshipped a boy named Johnny because he could produce a harmonic line for whatever we sang—plaintive and lovely and entirely intuitively. It was taken for granted among whites that any four Negroes made a quartet but he was my introduction to this particular talent which in fact I never found equalled until I did a revue with Tony Newley twenty years later. Tony's flair was slightly less intuitive but entirely sublime. I imitated Johnny under my breath against singers in life, from the radio, whatever and whenever. When we sang "In the Evening by the Moonlight" at home I tried out my harmonies unabashedly and was not displeased. From the book I played melodies on the violin and sang a harmony at the same time. I did this vaudeville turn for Mr. Wolf one Friday after my lesson. He was impressed to the point of acknowledging that I indeed had talent! He was not prepared to say what kind or where it might lead but he was frankly admiring. Praise from Sir Hubert was approbation enough!

Dad was a radio enthusiast from the crystal set period on (not quite in character for a man who rejected the telephone until it was proved a necessity and scorned the motor car and television when they came along). We had several radios and I was quickly made familiar with that body of vocal music referred to as "semiclassical," which strictly speaking means nothing but covers cherished items soon to become the hoariest of chestnuts: "Old Man Noah,"

Myrna Loy (sketch by
Gordon Heath, 1937)

"Many Brave Hearts Are Asleep in the Deep So Beware," "The Bells in the
Lighthouse Ring Ding Dong," "On the Road to Mandalay," and into the operatic
field with "Habañera" from *Carmen,* the Bell Song from *Lakme,* "One Fine Day"
from *Madame Butterfly,* Caruso singing "Che Gelida Manina," all the way to the
other end of the spectrum with early jazz (not approved of in our house),
Gershwin, and Cole Porter. My folks would whirl around the kitchen when
waltzes went out on the air and settle down breathlessly into cheerful remembrances of times past. Dad would say wickedly: "Remember when I'd meet you
coming from the corner bar taking home your little bucket of beer?"

My mother was always outraged, possibly because it wasn't so, but certainly
because it clashed with the genteel image she had of her adolescent home life.
She herself never drank and she hated that corner bar on Sixty-fourth Street
and her two elder brothers who were steady patrons, juvenile delinquents, and
jailbirds. So far as I know Dad never set foot in the bar. It was a very hard tease
but she bridled, cuffed him, and let it ride as a joke—blamed it on the waltz!

I was a prodigious if indiscriminate consumer of music in those early-teen
years and when the Columbus Hill Center organized an orchestra I was
accepted as a first violinist. We played a repertoire of "Over the Waves," Strauss
waltzes and Sousa marches. My high school orchestra made me concertmaster*
quite unexpectedly and, I thought, undeservedly. I never played to my own
satisfaction and there was a striking colored boy in the orchestra—light brown

---

* The first violinist of the first violins who establishes the pattern of the bowing for the first violins,
takes the violin solos occurring in symphonic works, leads the curtain call, and is generally
responsible for orchestral discipline.

with freckles and cinnamon hair—who not only played masterfully but did so with an impeccable left-hand position that has a poetry of its own and does not come easily to boys with big hands. Simmons was medium-sized with medium-sized hands and I envied and admired him, but we hardly exchanged a dozen words during the one and a half years of Beethoven's Second Symphony, Schubert's Unfinished, Mozart's "A Little Night Music," Grieg's "To Spring," and Bizet's L'arlésienne Suite.

I was in the hospital recovering from an appendix operation at graduation time (1934). Simmons visited, bringing me the High School of Commerce music medal and murmuring congratulations.

I started to teach myself the viola, having a strong desire to organize a string quartet from my high school orchestra personnel. I dreamed over the Budapest Quartet's romantic versions of the Schubert oeuvre and the late Beethoven quartets that contained such "profound human utterance." I struck up a friendship with a raw-boned Swedish boy who played second violin in my high school orchestra. Werner was not really attached to music or violin playing but I persuaded him to work with me on the Bach Double Concerto—which we were not quite equal to. His real enthusiasm was reserved for the reruns of the previous night's radio episode of "Amos and Andy." He retained all the dialogue and launched into scenes with me as more or less straight man. We did not get very far with the Bach and I was not encouraged to carry out my project.

In the period when my father was out of work he spent afternoons playing cards with Mr. Watts, a monosyllabic Barbadian, father of Enid, one of my neighborhood playmates. Mr. Watts and my father hardly conversed. They grunted from time to time and the slap of the cards and "Who dealt that mess?" was all that was on the sound track those tedious afternoons. They had no need to communicate. Their backgrounds and fixed values were identical. Their reaction to events, fatherhood, and the church went literally "without saying." Mr. Watts died and my father asked me to play a violin solo at his funeral in St. Cyprian's Church. I played Massenet's Elégie, sweating so profusely that my finger slid all over the place. I was ashamed. I gave up the violin entirely and didn't attempt to play it until thirty years had passed (by which time I had forgotten how to *hold* a violin).

〜 FOLKSINGERS WERE the thing. We went to their Town Hall concerts with almost religious devotion. Burl(y) Ives, who lived and wandered like a hobo, played his um-plink accompaniments on the guitar and sang the songs of moonshiners, railroad workers, sailors, pirates, farmers, and pioneers so unadornedly that the Library of Congress fastened on him to represent and record American folk songs from the Pilgrims to the American Federation of Labor.

Carl Sandburg, Chicago poet, collected grass-root versions of well-known folk songs, put them in a book and appended his own comments like a cracker-barrel gossip and philosopher, and sang the songs with his own toneless, speak-song midwestern tang. His life's work was a three-volume biography of Abraham Lincoln. The southerner John Jacob Niles not only researched the existing repertoire but also wrote his own and slid them between traditional examples of the genre, indistinguishable from the real thing. He sang to a dulcimer with a swooping voice that soared into a heart-stopping falsetto, draining the last drop of drama from the ballads. Then there was the formal Richard Dyer-Bennet who tucked his tails under him, played his own musical and individual settings, and sang, in his slightly spindly tenor, American and British folk songs and ballads, calling himself a "troubadour." Josh White had learned his trade from a blind black blues singer, and he added a large dollop of big-city sophistication and sex to his work songs and blues, aided and abetted by his flashy and insinuating guitar technique. Josh was a nightclub performer, selling his personality along with the songs—more entertainer than ethnic.

Susan Reed took her cherubim charm, her bird voice and her Irish harp to Café Society Uptown and sang the plaintive songs that were part of her Irish heritage.

All of these performers were "recording artists" and their songs—texts and music—were in print. Indefatigable scholars had published collections tracing the origins of this body of folk-song literature, orally transmitted and transmuted in the process. The songs were in the "public domain"—available to all. In the forties these singers had large followings and were very much "in."*

Badly bitten by the bug, I picked up a guitar and was amazed to learn how friendly and sympathetic it was to the touch. (I always had to *wrestle* with my violin!) Guitar sounds, chords, lay waiting to be uncovered. I had been offered scholarships to the David Mannes Music School and the Dalcroze Institute. I attended the Dalcroze school just long enough to be introduced to what they called "imbroglios"—key and chord shifts in harmonic composition. I dropped out and never really learned what music was all about. (An "imbroglio" was, as the dictionary had it, "a confused misunderstanding." I left it at that.)

On the other hand, the chord structure to accompany the bulk of the folk songs I wanted to sing for my own pleasure was encouragingly simple, like the folk songs themselves. The combination of my voice and the guitar pleased me a lot. Surprisingly, it pleased my friends also and I was invited to parties and gatherings with the proviso that I would be accompanied, so to speak, by my guitar. My painful adolescent shyness was locked in my guitar case and I achieve an acceptance I could never have had on my own. I don't know how I

---

* Add Woody Guthrie, Jean Ritchie, Ed McCurdy, and others.

Hudson River Night Line (sketch by Gordon Heath)

arrived at my singing style but my guitar "technique" was a feeble imitation of Josh White's. I achieved a certain amount of "originality"—coming about, as if often does, as a result of not being able to copy exactly. Owen was an early admirer of my ministrelsy. He encouraged me to broaden my repertoire and was the first to present me in concert—a quite unexpected turn of events.

While my father was floating up and down the Hudson River in his excursion boat a fourth of the year, my mother occasionally would take me out to Columbus Circle at night. In those days it *was* a circle and hospitable to soapbox exhorters, fulminating against whatever inequities they felt most strongly about or touting whatever politics or projects were closest to their hearts. Most of them were cranks and some of them were mad. My mother and I stood with the uniformed members of the Salvation Army Band—tamborines and cornets at the ready, opposing their beatitudes ("What a friend we have in Jesus") to the virulent outbursts and violent tirades going on around them. My mother would sing the hymns under her breath while I glanced about furtively. The Circle's activities attracted hecklers. The Army attracted drunks and bums full of mockery and hate. I felt like an early Christian martyr. My mother would take my hand and lead me to a little "rescue mission" holding perhaps forty (white) people. In this glaringly lit shabby room, just off of the Circle, we would sit, well toward the back, singing their minatory and exulting hymns.

Almost persuaded, Christ to believe
Softly and tenderly, Jesus is calling

The down-and-outers testified to their sinful lives and claimed their redemption, and the service would become a kind of free-for-all confessional. I don't know what my mother got out of all that. She was never deeply religious; she was not a student of "human nature." I think it must have been a love of spectacle as spectacle. She claimed to be ready to view dispassionately any grisly phenomena like a public execution. "Nonsense" said my father. I wondered. Tyburn and public floggings drew huge crowds of spectators in the not-that-dim past. I was certain my mother's mother would have made up a lunch for those occasions had they occurred in her lifetime!

I remember Sunday afternoons in the theater that was the RKO Colonial movie house, around the corner on Sixty-third and Broadway, where my mother listened, open-mouthed, to the revelations of spiritualists from Conan Doyle on, who had made contact with the Other Side and collaborated with explorers in the field. The table-tappers, the Ouija board communications, the spirit writing, the slide photographs of ectoplasm and white shadows emerging and vanishing before our eyes on the cinema screen. There was not a hint of skepticism, just plain documentary testimony from those who had twitched the curtain and glimpsed the Hereafter. I was terrified; my mother seemed unaffected. My father may have overrated his civilizing influence? On Sunday afternoons on the radio there was a broadcast from a rescue mission in the Bowery (5 and 7 Doyers Street—now why do I remember that?) presided over by a jaunty radio evangelist, an earnest but jocular gentleman called Tom Noonan. Tom sang the songs he loved—secular and religious:

For it was Mary, Mary—
Sweet as any name can be

There's a rainbow shining somewhere
There's a light across the skies
There's a rainbow shining somewhere
Like a gleam from Paradise

My folks were captured by his cheerful personality and believed him to be all he claimed—God's shepherd in the most disreputable and criminally minded part of Manhattan. I regret to say they were equally taken in by the silver-tongued radio priest, Father Coughlin, reactionary, anti-Semitic, and persuasive. Mother sent for his literature but I don't think my folks read it and they certainly didn't recognize his soft-pedaled fascism for what it was.

I understood very well my mother's pilgrimages to the Abyssinian Baptist Church in Harlem. Before Sunday service began, the Amen Corner, consisting of a handful of the older, most fervent supporters, gathered and delivered one-line texts out loud.

I was glad when they said unto me, "We will go into the house of the Lord."

Jesus is my help and my redeemer.

The Lord is my light and my salvation.

Loud protestations of "Yes, Lord," "Thank you, Lord," "Bless His name," "Oh my Jesus"—antiphonal and rhythmic. They would sing the best-known hymns—the ones they knew the words to—a capella, as the congregation streamed in and settled itself in the rows of velvet-covered pews. At eleven o'clock the choir, in splendid robes and tasselled caps, would come down the aisle and proceed to the choir loft, with full organ accompaniment, in their syncopated 1-2-*and* walk, followed by the formally dressed ushers, all with one white-gloved hand behind their backs while the other arms swung in perfect unison. The choir was bubbling and black; the ushers were solemn and black. When everyone was in place, the minister, robed over a tailcoat and striped morning pants, cravat, and pearl tiepin, made his way to the centrally placed pulpit as the women in the congregation waved white handkerchiefs to show their respect and love. For them he was God's representative every bit as much as the pope was to Catholics.

He made the week's announcements with a beaming rhythmic informality. He talked a little about the community concerns and announced the next hymn to be sung by choir and congregation, all standing. After the hymn an "offering" was taken up by those white-gloved ushers with their felt-covered plates (no unseemly clinking coins) while the organ played soulfully with only a hint of jagged gospel song, as if the right hand refused to be responsible for whatever the left one was doing. The sermon followed: variations on "remove your sins from out of your bosoms," lessons culled from Bible stories, testimony about the minister's own relation with God and his wrestling matches with Satan, chanted reiterations of faith, deliverance, and eternal bliss, each paragraph rising higher and higher in intensity and speed. The sweat came pouring down and most of the congregation was on the edge of hysteria and ecstasy. Some clapped, some wept, some danced, some shouted, a few fainted. White-clad nurses came down the aisles with smelling salts and comfort.

The sermon concluded, the minister subsided heavily into his carved chair, wiping his head, face, and neck with a silk handkerchief and a display of ceremonial exhaustion. The choir sang the offertory hymn, seated, and a second collection was taken; folded bills in envelopes were produced and proudly deposited in the vessels. The minister, restored to himself, rose, thanked everyone present, and, almost as an afterthought: "Now I want you to look in your pockets and see if you have a dime—one thin dime—I will ask the ushers to pass among you and collect the dimes. They will be consecrated here and now and you will have made your bid to be counted among the saints. The Lord loves you. Tell him you know it and show Him you love Him. Give with a full heart, for the Lord loveth a cheerful giver."

With the organ frankly swinging this time, the choir spread its wings and two-stepped out. I looked on, fascinated, and even produced a dime at the required moment. The show was worth it! It must be said that this and other churches all over Harlem not only met the spiritual needs of the community but also defined its social life and unified its identity. Ministers were community leaders and had to be taken into consideration at election time. As Martin Luther King so effectively proved, ministers created public opinion and held that the quality of life should be radically improved here on Earth. Heaven was the destination but it could wait while black people fought to be treated, as the Constitution stated, "equal." The "show business" element of the ceremony stemmed directly from the histrionic instincts of the sons and daughters of Africa. They sang and danced and praised the Lord. That's what Sundays were for!

❧ Growing Pains

I WAS AS DELINQUENT a juvenile as could be. I stole, lied, forged my father's signature on at least two report cards from grammar school. The marks weren't bad but the cards documented my entirely too frequent absences and late-nesses. I wasn't clever about my little crimes. I lied badly and my first thefts were pennies from an uncouth black lady who kept a newspaper stand off the corner of Sixty-third and Tenth Avenue. She sheltered in a tiny hut, the newspapers were stacked almost to the edge of the sidewalk and there was a little wooden box for the money on a horizontal pulley arrangement that she sent out and pulled back when the pennies accumulated. She spotted me and reported the thefts to my father who was outraged because it meant he had to speak to her—something he would never have considered doing otherwise. The school got in touch with my father directly and he had a conference with the principal. My art work was admired but I was in the soup. My father beat me (bare bottom with a strap) until his arm got tired. I squirmed, screamed, and cried. None of that touched him. He beat me very often but it didn't make me a "better boy"—only more careful. I didn't hold the beating against him—I had been warned. My mother stayed mutely by, closing the windows to muffle the sounds. She interfered only once, when my father dropped the strap, picked it up, and went on with the buckle uppermost.

School was fourteen blocks away. I used to hitch rides on the great taxi back bumpers and the horse-drawn ice and milk wagons and street cars. One afternoon I came home forty-five minutes after let-out time. My father said "Where have you been?" I protested that this was normal walking time. He said "Put your coat back on" and he put on his. "We will walk to school and if it doesn't take forty-five minutes I will beat you when we get back." We walked together leisurely, stopping for traffic lights and clusters of pedestrians. We arrived in front of the school in twenty minutes. When we got back he beat me for twenty minutes. "A beast, but a just beast." I continued to steal—now from Woolworths. I also continued to loiter and play on the way home and when I was sent on errands. My folks wondered if it was the influence of "evil companions." I resented that—I didn't have "companions." I would have influenced *them* if I had. I had been enrolled in the Ethical Culture Society's School at Sixty-third Street and Central Park West. It was a private and progressive school. They had one colored boy already, who, from all accounts, was a paragon. My father used his influence with a board member to get me in on a kind of scholarship when I was six. I seem to have been a restless and disturbing factor and detailed reports were sent home. "He could be a very good student but he is always in some kind of mischief and he teases the other children." Obviously I was not going to be a model child reflecting credit on my race and justifying my father's strenuous efforts. All I remember of those years is a four-wall mural we made of the Greek islands and the battle of Thermopylae: Spartans, Trojans, myrmidons, and all. I was, however, introduced into the Ethical Culture Society's Sunday school and the Sunday grown-up meetings held in the beautifully designed curving oak auditorium in the adjoining building. Rough-hewn, ten-feet high wooden statues of shepherds kept watch on either side of the balcony, and the horizontal platform itself was carved with bas-reliefs in wood depicting the pilgrims at Emmaus. Over it, the legend in gilt Gothic lettering: "The place where men meet to seek the highest is holy ground." The services were austere. First there was an organ prelude: Vidor, Reger, as well as Bach and Buxtehude. Each service was built around a discussion of what was happening in the world: "Can Freedom Survive?" "Rediscovery of Citizenship," "Can We Lick Fascism?" "Scottsboro Five Years On," "The Forty Days of Musa Dagh." Ethical religion, they called it. The emphasis was on ethical behavior, recognition of world community, protest against injustice and the taking up of arms. The set of responses led by the speaker did not ask for God's help or blessing. "My children, love ye one another and if thy brother do thee a wrong, remember that he is thy brother." "Hereafter shall come a new heaven and a new earth. On that day all men shall speak a pure language and no one shall hurt another anymore and no one shall wrong another anymore but the earth shall be full of goodness and truth as the waters cover the sea." In my teens I was very affected by being exposed to this rational and sober idealism. This was the way the world should be I thought: Bach, contemplation, and a meeting of minds. It all unfolded without religious or political shrillness. The speaker who reached me most directly was Algernon Black, an educator gifted with Jewish suavity and irony, who hoped to reach the heart by way of the brain. The Sunday school was on the top floor of the Sixty-fourth Street building, a very schoolroom kind of room with a raised platform in front, large enough to hold an upright piano and a piano stool, folding chairs in rows, and a company of just under high-school aged boys. The lady who played for us had gray hair, gathered into a bun at the back. She was generally impatient with us, rapping exasperatedly on a piano key to pull us back on pitch. The thin hymnbook contained only the words of the songs. "If there breathe on earth a slave/Are you truly free and brave?" "Our common mother rests and sings/Like Ruth among her garnered sheaves." "Like the lark would I were winging/Over azure plains on high." We were taught with a combination of boy-scout respect for nature, patriotism, and an insistence on individual freedom. The songs were set to existing hymn tunes and melodies from Brahms and Mendelssohn. Some of the settings were brand new and, "like the lark," could only be sung properly (as has been observed of our national anthem) by boys whose voices are changing! It was a song service, spaced out with storytellers recounting tales like Oscar Wilde's fables with Victorian envoys. On great occasions one of the spokesmen from the auditorium would come up and chat with us man to man. John Lovejoy Elliot, one of the founders, empire-builder British in appearance, would puff in and tell us improving stories with a twinkle and a folded smile under his colonel's moustache. It was an informal but disciplined Sunday school. Again I was the only Negro. Now and then a black soloist or vocalist performed during the offertory downstairs in the auditorium. I remember Ruby Elzy* singing a soaring "On Ma Journey" behind the curtains that draped the organ site. The Ethical Culture Society was my first experience of a cult of stoic, quietist militancy, requiring people to consider each other as neighbors concerned primarily with the "Do onto others as you would have them do onto you" section from the Sermon on the Mount. Predominantly Jewish, founded by philosopher-teacher Felix Adler, it aimed at creating—exactly as its name indicated—an ethical society. It began my drift toward socialism. Humankind could only play the game if everyone had an equal amount of counters.

I was, nevertheless, at fifteen not the kind of son my father had envisaged and had so sedulously trained to be an extension of himself. It was also that teen-age moment when children begin to react against parental authority. My mother and father quarreled, about money for one thing. She was incapable of keeping to a budget. My father was a rigid planner. They fought about women. Neighbors were quick to tell all they knew and more. I very slowly realized my folks were jealous of me—if that's the way to put it. I chose as my best friend a girl who lived "up the street." Very black, very tall, very homely, angular, and proud. Beryl lived with her mother and two brothers. They were all repectable enough. The parents were West Indian. The father was absent. My father considered "fatherlessness" a sure indication of fecklessness and social inferiority. Besides, she was *so* black, and black men were supposed to direct their

* Ruby Elzy, a soprano, played Clara in the original *Porgy and Bess*.

attentions to women lighter than themselves. Skin whitener and hair straightener sold very well in black communities. My father often compared me with Thelonious Monk. "This boy—no father—his mother scrubs floors to pay for his music lessons and look at the progress *he* is making." I held my peace. I thought I knew Thelonious better than he did and Dad wouldn't for a minute have approved of him. I resented the comparison and my friendship with Beryl deepened and defied my father's prejudices. Beryl was an avid concert-, theater-, and museumgoer and probably the only young person on Sixty-third Street with whom I could share my "highbrow" interests. She had strong gaunt opinions as a spectator. Music reached her most poignantly. You could see ecstasy pulsing through her. Her concert and theater programs were covered with notes and exclamation points—sometimes in shorthand, which we had both studied in high school. We were surprised to discern the same kind of intensity in each other. I kept a file of clippings, book reviews, theater critiques, interviews, and newspaper photographs of the artists I admired. Newspapers, magazines, and books began to pile up. My father called it "junk" and of course the accumulation was a nuisance in that small flat. Beryl followed suit and made problems in exactly the same way in her mother's even smaller flat.

I got my first part-time job handling the athletic and games equipment at the community center across the street. I was paid eight dollars a week and of course made plans for spending it long before the week was over. My father—who had probably gotten the job for me in the first place—insisted on collecting my pay and giving me an allowance. I suppose that arrangement was fair and appropriate but I thought the pay was *my* money. I was also expected to be home not later than eleven at night. In my father's mind sin flourished after eleven and nighttime was sinister and dangerous. I managed to sin in broad daylight easily enough but having to leave an after-concert/theater-kaffee klatch or party in time to get home by his deadline irked me increasingly. I was late often enough to be beaten and threatened with eviction if the lateness continued. I was working with amateur theater groups as well and their activities recognized no fatal difference between eleven in the morning and eleven at night. I couldn't decide to my father's satisfaction what I wanted to do or be. I chose to go to a commercial high school and learn typing and shorthand and languages. When I was awarded the music medal my folks were prey to mixed reactions. Perhaps I wanted to be a musician? I won that drawing prize—perhaps I had talent as an artist? But how was I going to make a living? I won the first prize in a city-wide drama competition playing a seventy-year-old man—perhaps I wanted to be an actor? I was confirmed in St. Cyprian's Church and sang in the choir. Was I interested in the ministry? That would have pleased my father especially since he often considered it for himself—not as a "calling" but as a well-paid occupation with built-in perquisites like hosts of adoring women. Money in those years of the Depression was a grim preoccupation. My father was out of work. My mother took on piece-work sewing in a factory. My father kept house, shopped, and cooked. He was much better at it than my mother. He kept to a budget and organized our lives. Day-old bread and muffins from Horn and Hardart, vegetables from itinerant peddlers, clothes bargained for on Fourteenth Street where the shop owners stood in the door-ways of their stores luring customers in. My father bargained ruthlessly and ended up paying half what was asked (and probably only twice as much as their minimum). I though of him when I first visited the souks (markets) in Morocco. He would have been in his element. I would go with him shopping at the outdoor vegetable and fruit markets on Tenth Avenue. He would pick out two pounds of string beans, a lemon, three pounds of potatoes, a half-pound of tomatoes. "How much will that be?" he turned to me. I would be struck dumb—reach for a pencil and paper. He would have totaled it in his head long before. "What do they teach you in your school? You need a pencil?!" Unfortunately his digestion did not allow him to invent and experiment in his cooking with all the food he dearly loved, the spicy West Indian dishes he was raised on: the black puddings, stuffed sausages, heavy breads, and plantains were forbidden. Our cuisine remained bland and predictable. No sea food, no wine, fish on Friday, liver and bacon on Saturday, simple gravies, custards. On the outside I ate junk food, drank too much coffee, and Coca Cola and was an ice cream addict.

My day-to-day closeness to my father only emphasized the furtiveness of my life away from him. I observed, censoriously, his bigotry, his snobbishness, and his built-in hypocrisy. When he went out on the street he behaved like a country squire—feudally gracious, gallant to the females, ready to assist, advise, arbitrate. I couldn't help admiring his intellectual dexterity, his balanced judg-ments, his ability to see two sides of a question when dealing with other people. He was also a very graceful man with beautifully shaped hands and contained gestures. I was six feet tall at sixteen with big feet and hands, clumsy and self-conscious. When I was alone I worked—for years—at being "graceful"; sitting, standing, walking, downstairs, upstairs, reading, going to bed, getting-up—as if I were taking courses to be a department store mannequin. Walking, I threw my right leg way out to the right* to compensate for those knock-knees and to reproduce my father's breezy alderman gait and my grandfather's uprightness. My father's social ease and master-of-ceremonies talent may have been achieved with more tension than I realized, but in my teens I was shy, introverted, and bookish, hating and admiring his facility and fluency and perceiving the

---

* This mannerism justified Aunt Ottie's prophetic "You will have trouble with your feet." At sixty my foot doctor in Paris diagnosed a permanently deformed right foot traceable to my life-long insistence on shifting abnormal weight to my right leg and foot.

reactionary being, so carefully disguised in public but so manifest at home. I in turn exasperated him, I think, by having all the qualifications he demanded of his Dauphin: mind, talent, sensitivities, but stubbornly and perversely refusing to display them, aiming for irrelevant goals, drawn to unsuitable companions, secretive, sly, and delinquent. Besides—I looked just like him! The immediate question, however, was what was I going to do with my life?

❧ National Youth Administration

FRANKLIN DELANO ROOSEVELT, our father-image president, and Congress created the Works Progress Administration Act, known officially and affectionately as the WPA, to give employment to a large part of the unemployed and, especially, to the racial minorities. The WPA was nationally administered—as flagrant a socialist gesture as the country had ever known. Public works and the arts, social services, ecology (the Civilian Conservation Corps), and a junior branch, NYA (the National Youth Administration) employed and restored self-respect to those hundreds of thousands who would otherwise have been on "home-relief"—the 1930s version of "welfare." The government and the State were equal-opportunity employers; no color lines were drawn. A great step forward for blacks, as long as it lasted. Hitherto some blacks had avoided discrimination and the world of employers with "unwritten-agreements" by passing objective examinations for "civil service" jobs, becoming post office employees, school teachers in the system, and the like. It was a safe harbor: guaranteed employment, pensions, paid vacations, white collars or uniforms—in a word, security. To me it seemed like nine-to-five monotony and boredom, the height of middle-class ambition. I was eligible to work in the NYA set-up and at eighteen was assigned to be an "assistant case worker" in the black organization, the Brooklyn Urban League, which was at the time occupied with recommending families to be recipients of "home relief" funds in the government program. The "assistant case-workers" made the initial investigation at the homes of the supplicants. We, the assistants, were all about the same age and all appalled by the situations we had to report on. The abject poverty, the diet deficiencies, the shoeless children, the illiteracy, the hopelessness, the slum scene altogether. We had to pry to unearth the already obvious and sordid realities of their lives. We had read of such things. We knew the global statistics. We knew people who were poor and struggling, but outside of Charles Dickens's works we had no contact with people who lived without necessities or hope. We were part-time workers but we brought full-time dismay and shock to the job. Our boss, Mrs. Tempie Burge, a spare, neat, candid lady of the old school, had spent her life resolutely separating her work from her sympathies. She was superbly understanding, compassionate, and human, but when she locked the office door at 5 P.M. she went on to her own life with no overlap. We tried to learn from her. It was frustrating work. We were not allowed to editorialize, recommend, or even sum up our "cases"—just the facts, names, ages, schooling, sources of income (!), health problems, employability, other statistics. We were continually tempted to bring fruit, buy children's shoes, leave a carton of milk on the table, anything to ease our own pain and helplessness, to say nothing of the unacknowledged guilt—("If there breathe on earth a slave, are you truly free and brave?")—How can you sit down and eat three meals a day when, not a mile away, people live, having no idea where their next meal is coming from? Kafka said, "You can hold back from the suffering of this world. It is allowed. It is your disposition. But it may be that this very holding-back is the one evil you could have avoided." We were only half aware of the paradox. We were romantics. Tempie Burge was a realist. We were really too young to be doing this work. Sadie, Una, Regina, Alex, and I worked together. We were all under twenty and only Regina intended to continue in social work. Regina had been assigned to counsel and report on delinquent girls already in collision with the law. They very often got themselves pregnant or picked up going in the same direction as before. Regina remained hopeful and undiscouraged, lived with her successes and her failures, and grew up into her life's task as a social worker. Sadie and Una were, I think, undecided about their futures. Alex wanted to be a photographer. We all grew very close to each other—a band of culture vultures. Together we attended concerts, rejoiced in the stateliness of Marian Anderson's entrance from the wings, her increasingly elegant costumes and coiffures, her liquid Schubert, her contralto shifting to baritone when she sang the spiritual "Trampin'" and all the Negro spirituals she sang as if they were lieder, eyes closed, submitting herself to their profound faith and aspirations. She always ended with Schubert's "Ave Maria." It must have been in her contract. Her audiences would have felt unsatisfied if she omitted it. We were there in force when Dorothy Maynor sang "Depuis le jour" from Charpentier's *Louise,* letting it float like a breeze in a flower garden. She sang it with an unearthly perfection. The audience went mad, so she sang it again—with the same unearthly perfection. We wept and so did the rest of the audience. We heard the tenor Roland Hayes sing "Round About the Mountain" walking around the grand piano like Moses coming down from Sinai, the tablets in his arms. His "Little Boy How Old Are You," the child Jesus confronting the elders in the temple, led me to learn enough guitar chords to sing it for myself. We were there when Paul Robeson sang a Gretchaninov lullaby in Russian with that masculine tenderness that was his great and unique gift. We saw the baby ballerinas Petipa had brought into the world: Baronova, Riabouchinska Markova, Toumanova, and their cohorts, Anton Dolin, Leonide Massine dancing the repertoire of the Ballet Russe. We learned how absolute a ballerina assoluta could become. We watched Arthur Rubinstein bounce through de Falla's "Ritual Fire Dance" levitating from his piano stool. We fell in love with George Bellows, Edward Hopper, and Georgia O'Keeffe at the Whitney Museum, downtown then; with Picasso and Lautrec and Monet at the brand new Museum of Modern Art. Following Alex's interests we looked at the work of those distinguished photographers, Steichen, Stieglitz, Penn, and Cartier-Bresson, with newly educated eyes. We went to the Metropolitan Museum of Art for the free Saturday evening concerts, chamber and symphonic. I remember standing on the steps of the Met thrilled by the sight of people streaming from downtown and uptown on Fifth Avenue itself to foregather in a place "where men meet to seek the highest." We were greedy and insatiable and quick with opinions, especially me, the only performer in the lot. With my mother and Una at Lewisohn Stadium with Heifetz playing the Beethoven violin concerto, I said scornfully, "It's all scales and exercises!"* They didn't dare contradict. I was an incessant show-off in that company.

We treated the city as if it were ours alone, exulting in that marvelous double-decker-bus trip going all the way up Fifth Avenue from Washington Square to Fort Tryon Park, where Rockefeller money had transplanted, stone by stone, a French medieval cloister that now overlooked the Hudson River, its formal serenity intact and flowering. We took ferry trips to Staten Island, edging the Lady Liberty and being reminded that the mighty Atlantic Ocean was our natural boundary. We took church outing trips on steamboats like my father's to picnic sites like Bear Mountain on the New Jersey side. Alex and I would walk across the magnificent Brooklyn Bridge in the late summer, and the city belonged to us.

Alex was fascinated by Sadie, who teased and flirted but kept him at arm's length. I think we were all a little in love with each other but I was desperately and plaintively involved with Alex. I would write him violently compromising letters, sing the lyrics of popular love songs to him between bouts of lolling and wrestling on Central Park meadows where sheep safely grazed and were shorn in season. We would exchange the long, long thoughts of adolescence. My

* Diaghilev interview in the *Daily Mail*, 1920: "Beethoven, my dear Englishmen, is a mummy. Listen for yourselves and you will realize that in a work like the Beethoven violin concerto which goes on and on for three quarters of an hour, there is not today one spark of living interest." Before I made my own I had not read that statement, but of course, it was a bit of special pleading on Diaghilev's part since he was introducing *Russian* music to the British.

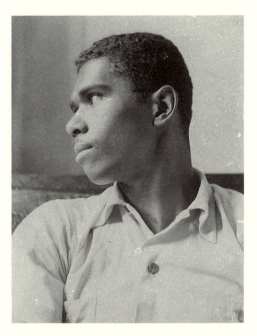

Alexander King, Jr.

thoughts were rather longer than his. He was gentle and sensitive and very impressed by my style and talents and he tolerated my demanding attentions with a combination of affection, admiration, and curiosity at how far his own sensuality would take him. Our wrestling in the park was a metaphor for our relationship. Alex was annoyingly certain that he would remain in control. He was equally certain that he would always be in charge of his life. He lived with his mother and his younger dwarf sister. He was devoted to both of them. His father was a hopeless drunkard whom his mother threw out of the house. She undertook to bring up her children by herself. She was a handsome, nut-colored, fine-boned, fox-faced woman, swarthy like a Gypsy, and Grace, her daughter, with black hair and dark eyes, had the same Gypsy look. Grace was animated and intelligent but always in precarious health. Alex's mother was an intensely practical, no-nonsense worker who suspected that there was a touch of the dreamer in her sturdy beloved son and she tried to keep in him an awareness of the reality and earnestness of life and survival. I would visit him in their Brooklyn house on weekends when more often than not he would be washing the household sheets. I hated to see him at it. His mother scraped and saved to keep out of debt. Every little bit, of course, helped, but I conceived a deep and abiding hatred for the influence and effect of alcohol on people's lives.

We saw Alex win the 200-yard dash in a city athletic competition. There was something of a finely bred horse in his tension and release. I thought he was a beautiful man altogether and made many sketches of his head and his body. We were said to look like each other—we were the same size and had the same coloring. We could, and did, wear each other's clothes. I was jealous of Sadie, of course, but annoyed with her for withstanding his half-serious pursuit.

One of the invited guests to a "surprise" party my parents were planning for my eighteenth birthday gave the game away to me a week before. All that concerned me was whether they knew enough to have invited Alex. Nothing would have comforted me for his absence. They knew enough.

Alex was the only fixed point on my horizon. My successes, achievements, even my conquests were "garnered sheaves" to be laid at his feet. This headlong infatuation was not comparable to the gratitude and hero worship I had for Owen. I never got far enough away from it to look at it—or myself, if it comes to that.

One evening Alex and I stood talking on a Fulton street corner with two girls—his friends. I was restive and slightly bored. I said, "I'm sorry but I'm too tired to stand up any longer. I'd better go home. Excuse me." I left them on the instant. When I saw Alex the next day, he said almost wonderingly, "I didn't realize until I looked at you that you were really tired!" He drew no conclusions but I realized I automatically gave dramatic form to whatever I felt or was persuading myself to feel. I screamed when my father beat me—not because I was in pain but to signal that I was being hurt. Well, I was an actor, wasn't I? But I became suspicious of myself for the first time and questioned how much of me was real. The habit of self-protection was leading me to deceive myself. I was prone to "stage" my emotions and create scenes with appropriate dialogue. I wasn't ready to admit any of this to myself at the time. I was to suffer most of my life from this professional deformation. I *had* to believe that Alex was my destiny and prove it by whatever means were to hand.

The NYA broadened its scope and created an arts project to train young people for careers in radio, theater, music, and dance. I got myself transferred to the project and left the Urban League.

In a gloomy building downtown on Mangin Street looking out at Manhattan Bridge, NYA created a kind of postgraduate course in the performing arts. Our drama instructor was a tall, young, fleshy black lady with a generous moustache. She was marked for spinsterhood, but she saw herself as the epitome of style, taste, femininity, and theatrical know-how. She was painfully genteel, almost totally without humor, and could hardly draw a spontaneous breath. Her endowments fitted her for the part of overseer in a children's playground— nothing more. She spoke carefully, preoccupied with assuming becoming postures, her mind running on her small suburban concerns and her unassailable gentility. She was fussy and old-maidish, in no way tuned into the way of life or theater in the late thirties. There were about twenty of us in the class, much more hard-bitten, street wise, and sophisticated than she could cope with on any level. I was indecently superior and snobbish about this bunch—I think because they frightened me. They were from Harlem and knew each other. They were really worldly and I only pretended to be. That winter I wore my father's Chesterfield coat over my shoulders like a cape—which they took for affectation. (My father's overcoat was too small for me. It was the only one I had and that was the only way I could wear it.) Our teacher fed us with acting exercises, probably out of a text written in Queen Victoria's time. She actually gave us an exercise she called "plucking a flower from a cranny"—high up, that is, which was meant to increase our grace in ordinary movements above our heads. This was academic crap and we all recognized it as such. We also recognized that we were not going to learn anything useful in these sessions and settled for teasing and diverting her. One day she called in sick and suggested that Eddie take over the class for the day. Eddie was Edmund Cambridge, a member of the class, a lithe black boy, quick in repartee, a natural mimic and comic with a shrewd appreciation of falsity, pretension, and eccentricity. He "took" the class as requested. He reproduced the instructor for one pitiless hour. He caught every tic, every flutter, every non sequitur, all of her gauche, overbred idiosyncracies, and her deplorable inability to instruct, explain, or inspire, all crowned by her immense self-satisfaction. The impersonation was cruel, exact, and definitive. We howled, beat on our desks, wept with joy: "Paulie, will you please close the window for me. I feel a draft on my back. Thank you, dear." He ended up with this petulant flourish. Our teacher was demolished and so were we—barbarians all—with stomachaches from laughing. Eddie had justified her existence and provided us with the only acting lesson we ever experienced in that room.

In the meantime my relations with my father were hardening into hostility. A girl a few years younger and a shade or two darker than I was introduced to me by my father as my sister, Bernice! I don't know what went on between my parents. I could only surmise that my father had bullied my mother into accepting the situation. I didn't understand how my father with his exaggerated respect for public opinion and his public high moral tone could have put himself in this position and presented this fait accompli to my mother. Bernice herself was rather fun and it was kind of exciting to find out one *had* a sister. My father said he had to tell me because we might meet and instinctively like each other "too much." I didn't believe him. I thought he was simply flaunting. I met Bernice's mother and understood even less. She seemed nice enough but nothing special—even her evident adoration of my father was no more than I had sensed and seen emanating from lots of women who were real sirens. Bernice was Bernice *Heath,* if you please, and I was once again dumbfounded. Nobody ever explained anything to me. I don't know, for instance, how much my father contributed to her support or how much time he spent with her and

Bernice Heath and
Sadie Browne

her mother. I only heard him say, off-handedly, that she was spoiled and had asked for a horse for Christmas! I introduced her to my gang and she got along with them well enough. She didn't seem to mind that I "had" her father and my mother managed to treat her with great tact and, I think, even affection, in the years still to come. She traveled to Washington, D.C. to see my *Dr. Faustus* and was proud of my careers. We were, however, never really close or confidants for each other. We fought now and then. She tore my sketch of her in half; I don't remember why. My respect for my father suffered badly and we squabbled all the time. I was furious about how he treated my helpless mother who had only me to confide in or complain to. Her family would gloat; they had been solidly against the marriage in the first place. She had no personal friends in or out of the neighborhood. My father talked to me—once—intimating that my mother was to blame but submitting no evidence that I could take seriously. He was King of the Mountain and if we didn't like it, we could lump it. Having summed up my father as "lordly" I might have, with detachment, admired his application of his droits de seigneur. He didn't really give a damn what anybody thought. He gave lip-service to the cause of middle-class morality but he didn't feel bound by it himself. I offered no opinions. I never dared to comment or accuse. We quarreled about me, never about him. I was getting too big to be beaten but not yet big enough to declare independence. Life at home was fraught. My mother was trapped and shrewish. My father was edgy and unwell, but he had gone to work at the Carlton YMCA in Brooklyn as assistant to the Boys' Work secretary, which meant supervising the sports and games provided for teenage and adult members. He was entirely at home with the boys—inventive, informal, inviting their confidences, maintaining order, and gaining their affection and respect. He even became a crack ping-pong player. There was a terrible irony in his successes with those boys and his failure with me. He all but adopted one of them who looked like him and had soft and wavy hair like him. My mother suspected he was making a play for the boy's mother but I thought the love between the boy and him was unambiguous and real, even if my mother was right. I had seen Dad on his own turf. I was envied by those boys who wanted my father for their very own. I was perfectly willing to give him to them. There wasn't enough room in our apartment for the hovering passions, jealousies, and repressions. I wanted out! I engineered my get-away by staying out deliberately till midnight and forced my father to carry out his threat. He said "Come in and we'll talk about it," but I ignored the gesture and the implication and left, promising to gather up my "junk" and my clothes "sometime soon." I ended up in a furnished room in a Brooklyn rooming house on Willoughby Street near the Urban League. My window looked out on the street. Two tramlines crossed at the corner. When the trams passed there was a shower of sparks from the overhead wires and an unholy racket as the wheels negotiated the juncture of the tracks but the neighborhood was prim and quiet otherwise and my landlady, Mrs. Bullock, was friendly. I had no money except my meager NYA salary but I was twenty years old, free—on very short rations, but free—and winging like the lark! My Brooklyn friends were, more than ever, daily companions. Alex's mother, certain that I ate badly and skimpily, fed me as often as I would let her and encouraged me to stay over on weekends. The resulting intimacy affected Alex more than he was prepared for and he revealed to me that he was engaged to be married to a girl I had never met and he had never spoken of before. It was a serious commitment, not a gesture to dislodge me, but my dream of our going through life hand in hand was irrevocably shattered. I had written to Owen about Alex and they had met each other in Brooklyn. In fact all of the "band" lived in Brooklyn and knew a little about Owen's career and his surviving family. The black people in the same striving middle class in Brooklyn tended to know each other much more than in Manhattan. Sadie, Una, and Regina were at Brooklyn College together. Owen was a local culture hero and Kenneth's death was front page news. But Owen was still at Yale and not, this time, the person to confide in. Alex and I remained the best of friends. My feelings were unchanged but I didn't inflict them on him. There was no visible evidence of shifting affections, in fact the girls didn't recognize or intuit how much passion was spent on our "friendship." What with leaving home and "losing" Alex I was demoralized and unbalanced. I had never stopped shoplifting, books, for the most part now, especially publications about photography. The luxurious monthly issues of *U.S. Camera,* for instance, were brought to Alex at spaced intervals so he wouldn't suspect their provenance. I was careless and reckless and one day in R. H. Macy's I was caught, arrested, and imprisoned for two days in the Centre Street jail, mostly because I refused to tell them my name or address. I called Alex who came immediately and said "You're out of your mind. You have to tell them—and get your father here." The prison officials were puzzled. "Stealing *books*? Nobody steals books!" The prison psychiatrist talked with me sympathetically and in five minutes summed me up: "Compulsive stealing often accompanies homosexuality." I neither confessed nor denied, but he was certain of his diagnosis. My father came to Centre Street, humiliated: "I've never even been in a *court house* in my life!" The police were, naturally, impressed with him, gave me a suspended sentence, and released me in his custody. He didn't tell them I had left home. I don't remember what he said to me in the way of reproof. It wasn't much and it wasn't angry. I think he felt he could no longer influence me and I could go to hell on my own. Two years later my draft board called me. The psychiatrist from Centre Street was the examining psychiatrist for the draft board. He recognized and remembered me. He said: "Do you want to get into this?" I said: "No, not really." And he inscribed my name in the 4F column—"unsuitable material for military service," shook my hand and dismissed me—a striking example of what my mother always called "the Heath luck" or "doing evil that good may come."

A music and dance unit was installed in the Mangin Street building in the persons of Alvin Bauman and Judith Martin, a keen, communicative, and crisp Jewish couple. Al had crinkly, dark hair, big front teeth, a rosebud mouth, blazing eyes, and a strong resemblance to a questing and highly intelligent chipmunk. Al set us to learning madrigals and rounds: Morley's "Now oh now we needs must part," Gibbons's "The Silver Swan"; rounds: "Heigh ho, Anybody home," "Signor Abbato"; folk songs: "The Boll Weevil," "Willie, the Weeper," and as major works, Randall Thompson's "Peaceable Kingdom" and Earl Robinson's "Ballad for Americans," a choral work about America's liberal, melting-pot tradition, with baritone soloist and spoken interpolations. Al, conductor-pianist, pointed out that although the work itself produced a certain euphoria and chauvinistic pride, it generalized and simplified America's history too facilely to add up to a really important statement. (It was the first time I had been exposed to vocal music approached dialectically and sprinkled with non sequitur Jewish humor.) He tightened "Ballad," directing us to explore a "subtext" and find new emphases within the work. I remember his straddling a chair, demonstrating the power of the foreshadowing introduction to Bizet's *Carmen.* He made us conscious of the tensions generated in putting words to music and music to words, and the added complication of conveying a "message." He would finish off a probing exegesis saying, "but really much more!" sending us to probe for ourselves. Paul Robeson recorded "Ballad" and it became very popular as an affirmation of America's devotion to the idea of freedom and the complementary observation that opposition and indifference and intolerance lived side by side with the American ideal. The soloist, anonymous at the beginning, tells the story of the nation's struggles to keep the freedom flag flying. The chorus challenges him to say who he is. He says he is Irish, Jewish, Polish, Czech, and double-Czech American, speaking for and as America. In the forties Robeson was told, with a maximum of viciousness, that he could not speak for America, and blacks told him he could not speak for them, either. Al, in his analysis, warned us that the conflict was both more subtle and less resolved than Robinson's cantata suggested. The ironies did not escape Al; flag-waving was all very well—but. . . . Al reminded us, without saying it, that the Negro and the Jew in America had more in common than the history books dealt with.

We loved him, of course. Our husky baritone soloist went further than that, puzzling Al greatly, until we, who had watched it all happening, told Al what was going on. He side-stepped gracefully and managed not to tread on the baritone's feelings. Al did not demand adoration.

Alex visited me at Mangin Street, partly to investigate the possibility that the NYA would be creating a photography unit. He spent the day with us observing the people I had often described to him. We had coffee together at the end of the day and, as the kids passed by to say "g'nite," he said, "What about Eddie?" I said, "*What* about Eddie?" He nodded energetically. "You mean. . . ?" "Yes, I do and, what's more, you're *it!*" I had never speculated about Eddie. He was the clown, the marvelously talented but cynical performer who would not permit himself a revealing or serious moment. He thought I was stuffy and superior and I was sure he had treated his buddies to rich mockery of me and my pretensions. But Alex's intuition was exact and Eddie, only a year younger than me, had been smitten almost from the beginning and was openly and exuberantly ready to respond to my much more tentative and unbelieving advances. His buddies were scandalized but not unsympathetic.

I had almost convinced myself that I should marry Regina, who was adorable, bright, beautiful—and not unwilling. There was an inviting symmetry about that. Alex would marry Alma, I would marry Regina, and we would have beach parties and evenings of whist and record playing. Alex thought it unlikely and unsound and, in my heart of hearts, I did too. Eddie's entrance onto the scene dissolved that dream and saved Regina from certain misery she could not have anticipated.

I spent a lot more time "sitting in" at Judith Martin's dance group sessions because Eddie was an active participant. Judy looked like a Martha Graham

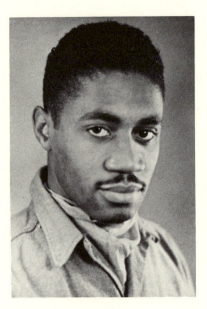

Eddie Cambridge

dancer—hair drawn tightly back from her forehead, a harsh downtown–New York voice and a general stripped-for-action look. She undertook to create a dance spectacle illustrating the forms social dancing took from the minuet to the Lindy Hop. Al's madrigal repertoire was joined with a group of folk songs and "Ballad" to make up a (free) entertainment to be presented at the city's settlement houses and cultural centers supported by the local authorities. Judy's dance panorama was also to be given. She came up against official objections to colored boys dancing with white girls. (This was New York in the late thirties.) Judy was incapable of thinking in those terms and kept her conception intact.* I don't know how this problem was handled finally because I left Mangin Street to work in radio under the NYA umbrella at the city station WNYC in a series called "Music and Youth." I wrote and narrated fifteen-minute potted sketches from the lives of great musicians of the past: Brahms, Berlioz, Schubert, and so on. For example, Beethoven to his landlord: "Ah, Herr Sturch, the wages of sin—they have not been paid" [second movement of the *Moonlight Sonata*]. Karl Maria von Weber's love life was summarily dealt with:

WEBER   Karoline, Theresa said I was blind . . . but *she* blinded me. Will you
           let me spend the rest of my days proving that I love you?
KAROLINE   Herr von Weber . . . Karl . . .

* In the fifties Judy organized and directed a touring company called "The Paper Bag Players," which presented skits and sketches, using unlikely workaday objects as props and approximating décor and costumes with the simplest of materials, just as children play house and tell each other stories using whatever comes to hand to illustrate.

WEBER   Will you, Karoline?

KAROLINE   *Yes,* my dear.

[Swelling music—"Spectre de la Rose"—up and out]

Eighteenth-century subjects but twentieth-century Warner Brothers treatment.

Anyway it was good practice and, I suppose, the research was valuable.

During most of this NYA period I worked at unlikely part-time jobs: counter boy at various hamburger heavens; wrapping books at the Gotham Bookshop; assisting the *Herald Tribune* society photographer, Stettner (I was allergic to developer fluid, though); errand boy for Flexostat, a firm that bent type to order; delivery boy for a prosperous Kitchen, Inc., who sent out three-course hot dinners in glass casseroles to the East Side affluent from Fortieth Street to Sutton Place. The cook's son became a friend. George was small, light, with a pitted skin, great, gray, myopic eyes, and camp sophistication. He changed all his clothes, twice a day, watches and rings included, and would have felt naked without a light street makeup. He was not really attractive but he was confident of his ability to seduce any man he fancied, and in fact he didn't believe in that category, "man." "They can be *had,* Heath, my dear—there isn't a real man in the lot!" He went into the Civilian Conservation Corps, composed, in theory, of the manliest men since Attila the Hun, building dams, laying bricks, and felling trees. He cut a wide swath in that population and proved his point repeatedly— at least to his own satisfaction. We would set out on our delivery service together. Once we encountered an outrageous transvestite type, flapping in the breeze. I said, "Lord, he's gay, isn't he, George?" "Oh no, Heath," he murmured, "*you're* gay. He's *queer!*"* On another occasion, apropos of nothing at all, he purred, "You know, Heath, what I like about you is that you don't give a damn *what* you wear!" Coming from Mr. Brummel himself that amounted to an accolade. He had the instincts of a pander and relished gossip, but he expressed great affection for the conjunction of Heath and Cambridge. He named the apartment "Heathridge"—the name stuck. George would "cater" our frequent parties with professional solicitude: ice in the bathtub, beer, cheese squares, diced fruit, and columns of Ritz crackers.

George was not a coiner of epigrams but his flat statements were timed to cynically undercut extravagances and cant and their effect was like wit. He was never at a loss. He knew what he thought and he seldom thought twice.

I had made application for a two-room apartment in Phipps Houses in 1938 and was awarded one that same year: fourth floor in 247, in the house next to

---

* I was in Europe when Alex wrote that George had invited a young butcher boy to his place one night who did a professional job on him with a knife and George's gaiety was quenched, with a hideous appropriateness—forever.

my parents. Bathtub in the large kitchen that had to be living room as well, tiny bedroom, just enough closet space, steam heat, indoor toilet, windows on the court, moderate rent (ridiculously low in the 1940s and 50s). I painted the kitchen a dark but lively green. Beryl's brother and Alex built dish closets, benches, and bookshelves covering one entire wall, brass chains looped on hooks served as handles and to attach a two-inch-thick plank covering the tub to the wall. Beryl and I laboriously brought six bricks at a time from the demolished building opposite to make a yellow brick-and-board set of shelves for the bedroom. My undersea nest was snug and functional like a ship's cabin; brass student lamps provided intimate lighting. I kept the flat for almost forty years. My father, furious and jealous, said, "You got it on the strength of my presence in these houses!" and never ceased to resent my apartment's existence. What is more, I invited a blacker-than-me, fatherless boy to live with me. You'd think I'd done it deliberately and defiantly, but the fact was I loved Eddie and it seemed natural to offer him a "home." (He played the "Boll Weevil" in Al Bauman's staging who was always "just lookin' for a home" and was irresistible in and out of the role.) The flat was really too small for two people, even if they lived in the utmost harmony and we were unknown quantities to each other.

Our first date was symptomatic. Eddie said, "Forty-second Street, corner of Seventh Avenue at 8 o'clock—Okay?" "Ok." I stood on Forty-second Street hopefully, fearfully, for a half hour, forty-five minutes—no Eddie. In class the next day, he said, "I missed you." We sorted it out finally. These Harlemites hardly ever said "a-hundred-and." He lived on 142nd Street. I finally saw a lot of 142nd Street. It was not unlike Sixty-second and Sixty-third streets, and it was a real "neighborhood"—a ghetto with lots of character and lots of characters, Eddie's mother among others. She was a large, black, looming lady, stately, almost immobile in her armchair and footstool—the disciplinarian, the fount of wisdom, and the hereditary monarch. The family was from Antigua, then a British island in the West Indies. Eddie's mother was proud, scornful, alien to American "culture"—whatever *that* was—and burdened with the responsibility of bringing up children according to her own standards in this ant heap of helpless, segregated poverty, demeaning jobs, and demeaning charity. The Antiguan assault on the English and American language produced a dialect with grammatical inversions that made occasional poetry and occasional gibberish. (Eddie used to do impersonations of his grandmother laying down the law: "Me no melly smarty atall atall—at from at leaves attimonious—so dat!"* A neighbor would say proudly to Eddie: "You keep on with your h'acting. You'll be a great h'actor some day. I know, I used to rig up pieces myself—oh yes!")

---

* I suppose that to mean "I have nothing to do with know-it-alls. They'll be found out," etc. (A very loose translation that I do not vouch for.)

They had folkway strength: "You can't outfrighten me. I from Antigua, too!" They had no longing to be integrated into the greater City of New York. They seldom ventured farther downtown than 110th Street. They were a tribe.

Eddie was a characteristic example of the young. He wanted to escape. He and his sister recognized their mother's rocklike integrity and they knew they were everything in the world to her. But his talent and his unwinking scrutiny of the hows and whys of people's behavior expressed itself in acute mimicry. He learned about the world by looking and listening. He directed a vaudeville troupe that contained many talented young people. Isabelle Sanford, whom we all called "Trouper" (the outraged maid in *Guess Who's Coming to Dinner* and a member of the Jeffersons' TV family), was the most accomplished farceuse I ever knew—even then in 1937. There was Clarice Taylor who played the nosey neighbor in my *Family Portrait* and the Bad Fairy in *The Wiz* and Moms Mabley in a one-woman show in the eighties. And they danced. How they danced! Once at a rehearsal break Eddie and Isabelle did a slow almost langorous Lindy Hop* that was as gallant and lyrical and dainty as any fifteenth-century minuet. Loretta, Eddie's special girlfriend, who was to play Mary's daughter-in-law in *Family Portrait,* sang for us her most recent class assignment "mi chiamano Mimì" from *La Bohème,* with a fresh innocence and modesty that years later I heard again in a recording of the same aria by Maria Callas. They were not "arty"; they were doing what came naturally, escaping into art. That was a step to detachment and a way of rejecting the implied limitations of color and background; their horizons were broad and their ambitions undefined but at the least they were going to belong to the aristocracy of performers. My snobbery melted away and my admiration grew. The one exception was Viv-ianne (pronounced "Vivi-Annie") the only poseuse of the lot. She assumed all the mannerisms of the unbearably talented and sensitive—the sighs, the clasped hands, the absorption in her own rendition of Debussy's "Clair de Lune," the out-of-this-world "swept-away" into her "vissi d'arte, vissi d'amore" vein (she had no other). A black version of E. F. Benson's magnificent fraud, Lucia, except that Vivianne fooled no one and was a made-to-order victim for Eddie, who would lead her on, send her up, and do her in. She arrived at Mangin Street one morning expressing a carefully preserved ecstasy derived from hearing on the radio the night before a symphony of Brahms new to her. It

* The "Lindy Hop" was a social jazz dance in which the boy almost never lets go of the girl's hand but flings her out to improvise her own movements as if flirting from a distance. He draws her back to him and they dance together until the next "fling" is decided on. The Savoy Ballroom in Harlem was probably its provenance and in the East, at least, it was the rage for decades. Named after Charles Lindbergh and his "hop" across the Atlantic.

My father loved to watch it—said it was a "clean" and "open" dance (because the dancers were not pressed up against each other). I thought that it was really sexy and it could be tender and tough at the same time.

was, she averred, Brahms's Fifth! That was the kind of luck she had. Vivianne married before the NYA was voted out of existence and subsided into a young matron role that pulled her back into comparative reality, but I never knew if she grew up finally. NYA perished along with WPA in 1940 as part of a shift to a wartime economy and of course the political maneuvers attacking all the liberalism it represented. *PM** launched a crusade to protest and unmask the villains of the piece, to testify that we had been robbed of means and training and employability, to say nothing of our livelihoods. *PM* wanted combative statements and anguished cries to be built into a sweeping attack on congressional stupidity and venality. I said I would get along, NYA or no NYA, that I was grateful for what it had offered but I wasn't going to starve if it vanished. I was not quoted but I questioned myself when I saw that my father approved of my attitude and I realized that I didn't understand political action and when it was necessary to close ranks, embrace collective action, and stop being a West Indian reactionary snob. My father had been a union organizer on the "boats" and he told me—when I was old enough to understand—how the ranks crumpled and retreated and left him holding the bag in the middle of employer-union crises. He no longer had faith in collective action. Eddie and company were rebels against the status quo but were not instinctively political animals. When I moved to the radio project I found myself part of another "band"—predominantly Jewish—the Village to Mosholu Parkway—who were left-wingers lined up with the liberals, Henry Wallace, union leaders, and the then-legal Communist party. Stanislavsky and Marx were their prophets. Sylvia Silberstein and her brother, Mori, were going to be the Lunts of their generation. Mori had a John Barrymore profile and was the leading debater, critic, and analyst. Sylvia and I played together in radio sketches at WNYC and amused ourselves working on scenes from Philip Barry's *Hotel Universe* and James Barrie's *Dear Brutus*. I learned a lot about Jewish family life, religion, and politics but was warned that I was very doubtful material for a party member—"too vulnerable" pronounced Sylvia, knowing all about me. I kept company with Epstein, Podolsky, Silberstein, and Kompaneetz. The latter, at eighteen, informed me dispassionately that Russia and communism would be the future of the East and Mittel Europa and everything else was of relative unimportance. In 1938 he knew it all. Sylvia and I on the way to the theater arm-in-arm walked past the Hotel Astor where a very fashionable lady standing on the hotel steps hissed "Communists!" at us. Sylvia hugged me more tightly. "If she knew I was Jewish as well she would really have had a case."

* *PM* was an afternoon reformist liberal New York tabloid newspaper published by Ralph Ingersoll.

❧ The Temple of Tranquility

IN 1938 I STARTED to perform with a loosely knit group of colored actors and actresses under the direction of a purposeful, fluent woman, Marian Wallace. She put on plays carpentered from Bible stories: "For He Had Great Possessions," "Cleophas," and so on. Racine it wasn't but the plays were serviceable and edifying and Harlem churches were happy to sponsor them. Their popularity and ours led Marian to consider staging scenes from Shakespeare. She called me up one day exulting: "Gordon, I want to do *The Merchant of Venice* and I want you to play the *title role*!" Thank you very much. Antonio, the merchant in question, borrows money from the Jewish moneylender Shylock to finance his dear friend Bassanio's courtship of the rich heiress Portia. Shylock requires that if Antonio fails to repay the loan by a specified date he must forfeit a pound of his flesh. We had all read the play in school and we considered Antonio the sad sack of all time—a born victim and theatrically an unrewarding, passive, colorless role. Shylock had juice and bitterness, Portia had charming eloquence, Gratiano had cynical humor—all Antonio had was resignation.

Obviously Marian saw herself as Portia—who is indeed bossy and manipulative—but not quite an executive in a cosmetics firm. Oh, all right, but who's going to play Shylock? Marian answered the unspoken question at the next meeting of the troupe. She presented us with a hefty, middle-aged six foot two, blue-eyed Scotsman with a flaring thatch of white hair like the orchestra conductor Leopold Stokowski. He was Hamish Cochrane of Aberdeen, purveyor of poetry and dramatic readings. Everything he said was a dramatic reading. He spoke with such vigor and precision that you had the impulse to dodge or back up out of his path, but Hamish would come close to you as if exchanging confidences head to head, his voice piercing the air. It is difficult to render his volume in small letters. MARIAN, I SAY, MARIAN, YOU MAKE THE BEST COFFEE IN HARLEM. I SAY YOU MAKE THE BEST COFFEE IN HARLEM!

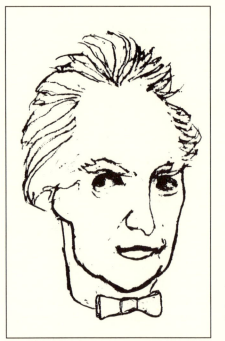

Hamish Cochrane of
Aberdeen (sketch by
Gordon Heath)

He spoke English English, of course, never slurring a vowel or softening a consonant or cheating on a dipthong. He had toured Great Britain doing his dramatic readings and poems and teaching speech during prolonged sojourns. He had "done" Canada, descended to New York, and quite by chance had found himself in our audience. He was immediately seized with the conviction that blacks were ideal interpreters of Shakespearean characters—YOU ALL HAVE SUCH PASSION AND COLOR! Color, certainly; passion, possibly; but what else? He would teach us to speak "beautifully" and, with our approval, would play Shylock in our proposed production of *Merchant*. He gleamed with friendliness and enthusiasm and we began to work at what earlier had been called "elocution." Hamish's instruction demanded a kind of athletic cooperation of tongue, teeth, and lips to give every word, every syllable, its full value: no slipping or sliding, no elisions, special attention to final consonants, exactly what our grammar school "English" teachers impressed upon us when we read poetry aloud in class. In real life, communication was established without that incisiveness and to persist in speaking well was considered priggish and artificial. Yeah for yes, yuh for you, tuh for two, a tutor who tooted a flute was a tooter who tooted a floot. [Ten years ago I saw a film called *The Duel*. The two American leading men, meant to be Austrian officers, insisted for the length of the film that they were going to fight a *dool*!]

As actors we already spoke rather better than the average American but

Hamish flung down a gauntlet. I WANT YOU, WHEN YOU GO TO THE GROCER'S, TO ASK FOR A LOAF OF BROWN BREAD AND A POUND OF BUTTER—there were at least three t's in *butter,* the *wh* whished in *when,* the *o*'s were open and the *f*'s were forthright. AND IF HE LAUGHS LET HIM LAUGH! YOU CANNOT SPEAK SLOPPILY AT HOME AND IN THE STREET AND EXPECT TO BE ABLE TO SPEAK CRISPLY AND FINELY WHEN YOU ARE FACED WITH SHAKESPEARE! Incontrovertible—but were we prepared to be the pariahs of the Western world? *Dared* we? Hamish spoke with the authority of those nineteenth-century barnstorming actor-managers whose diction pro-pelled the dialogue effortlessly to the back wall of castle, church, hall, or theater. It was the grand manner at its grandest. Hamish could not teach us techniques of voice production or the functions of speech organs. He could only exemplify the power and the glory of speech itself and stir our sluggish consciences. I don't think that we, any of us, confronted our friendly neighbor-hood grocer with an eye like Mars to threaten and command, but we turned down the volume and hoped our pretensions would be overlooked or at least not commented upon.

In spite of our cowardice, we progressed. *The Merchant* was our exercise book and Hamish exclaimed, twinkling and blinking rapidly, that we all had wonderful "ears" and were a credit to him. He himself spoke—I will not say "played"—Shylock with his usual brisk clarity cleaving the air. He used an upward inflection at the ends of sentences to serve as indications of Semitic utterance. He was, of course, the worst possible Shylock imaginable. We rented a hall called "The Temple of Tranquility," formerly the abode of the self-ordained prophet Sufi Abdul Hamid whose cult operations came to the atten-tion of the authorities and had to be discontinued. Hamish decided we were ready. Black suits, white shirts, black ties for the men, evening gowns for the women. We would do scenes from *Merchant.* I would recite Wilde's "The Ballad of Reading Gaol" (discreetly cut) and Hamish would recite Hood's "The Dream of Eugene Aram" (indiscreetly full-length) to round off the evening's enter-tainment. We were indeed speaking extremely well and we sounded as if it were our natural everyday speech. Hamish was euphoric: WE'RE GOING TO BE HOT STUFF TONIGHT, GORDON—I SAY, WE'RE GOING TO BE HOT STUFF! Obviously a cultural exchange had been effected.

The show went on. The six of us recited in an almost completely undramatic reading of the scenes. Owen said it looked like a ventriloquist demonstration. I did my dramatic reading. Owen said, "You cannot read the word 'mad' madly"—a first-rate observation. Hamish boomed his way through "Eugene Aram" complete with upward inflections held over from his Shylock. Intensely boring and long. The audience was politely receptive and uncertain what they should think of the evening's offering. Hamish loomed in the lobby radiating satisfaction and shaking hands all round. He was a dear lovable man, hopelessly old-fashioned, but true to his own priorities and dedicated to his craft.

In the middle of my submergence in iambic pentameter I got my first film role. *The March of Time* was making a documentary about how sections of the country were reacting to the new draft laws. My segment was shot on a set representing a cabin (in the cotton, naturally!) somewhere in the South.

> [Action: Mother sewing in a corner. Boy comes in, a newly opened letter in his hand.]

MOTHER   Is it from the Gov'mint?

BOY   Uh huh. Dey callin' me fur de draf'.

The End

Thank you, Hamish, for preparing me for this moment!

◑ Dream Days and Daydreams

I HAVE MET ALONG the way a number of contemporaries who had limitless dreams about roles they wanted to play, directors they wanted to work under, as well as companies they wished to belong to. Most of them were white; some of them had talent. I envied their certainties, their gradus ad Parnassum. I knew I wanted to be an actor but I didn't have the daring to proclaim it challengingly. If one loved and lost, the fewer people who knew about it the better.

Where do you go from there? To Professor Lee Strasberg, that's where. Straying momentarily from the frame of the almost defunct Group Theatre, Lee had been presented in 1943 with a play called *South Pacific* dealing gingerly with a racial situation and starring Canada Lee as a black American paratrooper brought down during the war into a brown-skinned island where he establishes himself as a kind of Emperor Jones, annexing the prettiest native girl who has been courted most correctly by a young native doctor, Oxford-trained (they were *always* Oxford-trained). The paratrooper wins the girl with Yankee know-how but loses the match against native cunning or some such.

Canada Lee, an ex-prizefighter much admired for his Banquo (Federal Theatre's *Macbeth*) and his role in Orson Welles's version of Wright's *Native Son* and a bête de théâtre, was a natural, forceful actor. He lacked real versatility and style but was effective and unique for that moment, which could boast only Robeson and himself as black leading men. We used to say you had to be big, black, and one-eyed (Canada had lost the use of an eye in a ring battle) to have original theater scripts proposed to you.

The play was by Dorothy Heyward (*Porgy*) and more cartoonish than its pretensions. Lee was going to search out its polemic strengths and give it body. A slightly Hollywood idea, like "get Faulkner to rewrite the last four reels. . . ." That Oxford-trained doctor—that was me (or *I*, as he would have said)—was really the second lead and, as these things go, a very important role and Lee was

Canada Lee (*left*) and Gordon Heath during the early stages of rehearsal for Dorothy Heyward's *South Pacific* (1943)

a most attentive midwife. We'd walk about the stage, his arm around my shoulder (which he could barely reach) while he reinvented the role with a wealth of detail, stopping just short of the doctor's toilet training. Canada was sniffingly suspicious and finally queried: "Lee, what is that Stanislavsky crap you and Gordon talk about all day?" Lee replied, "Don't worry about it, Canada. Stanislavsky saw you and wrote the book!" A brilliant rejoinder but it served inadvertently to increase Canada's scorn for discipline and training. After ten days of Lee's coaching, the management came to me apologetically: "We have two unknowns in this play and it's a gamble, but one of them is a beautiful girl [she was, too] and we think we'll get away with her but we need someone with more solidity and experience as the doctor, dear Gordon, and we propose that you help us out backstage as one of the (entirely unseen) native population. We will pay you your contractual salary for the play's run." The play was dismissed by the critics and praised only for Boris Aaronson's lush set. It came on at Christmas and came off at New Year's. I had been replaced by a shuffling, apologetic actor, too old to contrast with Canada and too crude to have gotten into, not to say come out of, Oxford. I had indeed loved and lost and quite a few people knew about it. Canada went on to play Bosola in *The Duchess of Malfi* in white face (more surprise pink from were I sat) and Caliban in *The Tempest* for

Margaret Webster. He also starred in *On Whitman Ave,* a play dealing with housing discrimination. He appeared in films: Hitchcock's *Lifeboat, Body and Soul,* and *Lost Boundaries.* He played Scrooge (I narrated) on radio for a Christmas program in 1950. In 1950 he also played the old father, touchingly, in *Cry, the Beloved Country,* filmed in South Africa. By that time, he was high on the list of "subversives" and the combination of ill health, blacklisting, and the experience of South African pervasive viciousness brought on collapse and in 1952 he died, at forty-five.

Anyway, with my *South Pacific* experience, I became a member of Actors' Equity—a giant step toward professional status, but not a guarantee of professional employment. Backstage, George Fisher (later known as Brock Peters) and I became friends and we came to know Juanita Hall. Juanita conducted her own chorus then and was responsible for the "music" these happy natives produced (offstage). George and I decided she was more ringmaster than choir master and there ensued a certain friction. She reminded me of my Aunt Ottie. She later created—appropriately—the "Bloody Mary" role in a much more successful venture called—as if Mrs. Heyward and her collaborator had never been—*South Pacific* (1949).

Nineteen forty-three gave way to 1944 and Pearl Primus, West Indian by birth but African by formation, got her act together with Alphonse Cimber and Norman Coker with their squat speaking drums and a crew of dancers that included Albert Popwell—long, black, sinuous—who could have wrapped himself around a tree a couple of times and proffered an apple to whatever luckless virgin happened to be passing. Pearl herself was an illustration of her ethnic studies—a whirling, leaping, protesting dervish—small, stocky, muscular, moving from earth to sky and back, and making them gasp at Café Society Uptown.

Closer to theater and show business was Miss Katherine Dunham who learned to exact full measure from her equally serious ethnic excavations: color, costumes, lighting, drama (hieratic and colloquial), African village to Harlem dives. She and her young troupe glittered on and off stage—the highest prancing camp in the business. The curtain calls were models of their kind: the modesty of the lowest bows in town, the glinting arrogance in the corner of the eye, the careful, reverent distance behind Miss Dunham, the inexpressible gratitude to the audience, so abject as to be mocking. A minute later, behind the curtain, hen-house chatter, high-pitched recriminations, screams of accusation and outrage.

Miss D was priestess of the dance rites. The discipline was stringent, her tongue was savage, and her will was iron. *Tropical Revue* succeeded because Miss D had flair and vision and the troupe had determination and the capacity for grueling, relentless work and training. Talley Beatty, Archie Savage, Claude

Marchant, and, later, Eartha Kitt laid the foundations for their celebrated careers within and without the troupe. Miss Dunham created a school, a vocabulary, and a technique for black dancers. Her audiences multiplied and her ballets satisfied and excited both dance and theater aficionados. Her success gave encouragement to would-be dancers who otherwise lived on very thin hopes.

I became aware that all I asked of life was to be a dancer! It was too late, of course. I was too old, too uptight, and too knock-kneed. Several years earlier, when open auditions for a black version of *Midsummer Night's Dream* (with Louis Armstrong as Bottom and Maxine Sullivan as Titania [1939]) were announced, my dance friends said, "you should audition, Gordon, they need someone to balance 6'2" or 3" Archie Savage—it won't matter that you're not a dancer." On that endless stage of the almost brand-new Center Theatre twinned with Radio City Music Hall, I presented myself and was told all I had to do was dance across the stage. With not one iota of a dance vocabulary I flung myself into some kind of locomotion and, hours later, ended up in the opposite wings, miraculously still on my feet. It must have been hilarious—a superb example of sheerest ineptitude. No one laughed that I heard. The management thanked me gravely. *Dream* did not work, even without me, and not long after the Center Theatre itself ceased to exist. Another love lost and quite a few people knew about it.

But in 1944 Pearl Primus asked me to narrate three poems she intended to dance to: Langston Hughes's "I've Known Rivers" and "Our Spring Will Come" and Lewis Allen's "Strange Fruit" (bearing the subtitle, "A Man Has Just Been Lynched"). Pearl's dance erupted with clenched hatred and searing terror—the poem needed no subtitle. When she was creating "Our Spring Will Come" she grunted and hummed, whispered, sang, and spoke as she gave herself to movement. John Cage came along to watch. When Pearl took time out, he opened the grand piano and affixed his pocketfull of clamps and assorted hardware to certain strings like a plumber installing pipe joints. The "composition" that resulted was an uncanny percussive equivalent of Pearl's dialogue with herself. I marveled and enunciated my narration warily.

Pearl and the company gave a series of concerts in New York on Sunday afternoons and evenings. It was a moment during which experimental dance groups were making "socially conscious" danced statements—usually downtown and usually on Sundays—short populist pieces influenced by Martha Graham and folk dancing. I remember one offering entitled "The Young Are Starving but Not for Food." You weren't quite sure *what* the young were starved for but its intentions were clear enough. The drought and poverty in the Southwest gave rise not only to Steinbeck's *Grapes of Wrath* but also to Woody Guthrie, folksinger and composer, with a sheaf of ballads about the Dust Bowl that along with Negro spirituals, gospel songs, and classic blues served as scenarios for dances. All were born of protest and witness to deprivation, and bigotry.

Pearl and company were invited to appear at Roxy Theater in that period when the ornate movie palaces featured vaudeville acts between showings of the film. Bernhardt and Pavlova, for instance, had gone this route. Our two-week engagement was shared with a tramp comic named Jimmy Savo, well known to cabaret- and musical-comedy goers. He sang "River, Stay Away from My Door," frantically trying to push the river back by main force, pleading as if catastrophe would overwhelm him. Which was pretty much the way recording and radio star, Mildred Bailey, the other headliner in the show, sang the blues—so full of "soul" that a large part of her public thought she was black! She was an earthy, raucous lady, beaming with show-business bonhomie. One of the women in our troupe showed up, battered and tearful, saying that the night before in Central Park she had been raped—twice! Miss Bailey, hands on hips, screamed, "Girl, you are a greedy selfish bitch. I can't even get a *half* a man these days!" The victim seemed to take comfort from Miss B's deprivation—as she was meant to.

I wrote and spoke—backstage on the house's microphone—an introduction to our spectacle, beginning, "The dance you are about to witness is really a prayer. . . ." Pearl demurred, wanting to be exact, ethnic, and educative but the management agreed the ethnology should be played down and the drama played up. They also wanted someone to sing the pop song to accompany the chorus line's number that opened the vaudeville portion of the program. I auditioned and was chosen (over my erstwhile friend, George Fisher) to croon, "There Goes That Song Again" at that selfsame micro—out of sight again, but amused by the incongruity of the whole bit: Pearl's ballet, drums, African costumes, frenetic but authentic African rituals, that cultured introduction, the spangled "Roxyettes" like trained horses at the circus and that pop song—"we fell in love while the organ played, over and over and over and over again"— three times a day for two weeks. The film was *Something for the Boys* with Carmen Miranda, garnished with fruit and cha-cha-cha. The audience applauded everything vigorously but they came primarily for Carmen. The two weeks went smoothly enough. The management asked the half-clad, black dancers and drummers to avoid proximity to the half-clad, white chorus girls but they knew without being asked.

Most memorable was our concert engagement in Detroit the day after a devastating race riot raged through the city. Tension was in the air like smoke but there were no incidents. We flew back to New York the next day—safe, but shaken. I did not give up my connections with the dance world after I no longer narrated for Pearl. I became the resident designer for another troupe that was in the process of being transformed from a workshop into a performing group by Wilson W. Wilson's intention, as nearly as I could gather, was to present African dancing in a modern context. I was too close to Wilson to begin with and when I got far enough away to observe the company's evolution I realized that Wilson's ego was riding roughshod over his dancers and that his compulsion to seduce and be made much of was much stronger than his ability to organize, create, or inspire. The troupe was heading for dissolution by way of disputes, jealousies, and intrigues fomented by Wilson and aggravated by his abusiveness. There was already too much brutality in the making of a dancer and the putting together of a company. Wilson did not have the selflessness and authority his ambition required. Perhaps in war and politics you divide to conquer but in dance and theater, at least, your effort must be to *unify*. I left Wilson and my logo designs and had no more to do with dance or dancers until 1987 when Pearl and I worked side by side to bring to life Soyinka's *The Lion and the Jewel* in Amherst, Massachusetts.

❧ Interlude: Icons, Idols, and Intimates

Cyril Gordon Heath

FIRST OF ALL, my lordly father, who was icon and idol but never, never an intimate. He never said what he was thinking, he said what he had thought. There was an awesome distance between us all of our lives and very little expressed affection. He cared deeply and possessively about me, I knew. He was quick to point at households where there was no father and the children "ran wild" in the street—a situation that obtained more often than not in our neighborhood—to remind me how fortunate I was to have him. I did not always agree with his summing up but it was easy enough to recognize the advantage of having a good-looking, fluent, and persuasive parent opening doors for one—protecting and defending. Easy enough to share his delight in crossword puzzles, in word games ("The mean mien of the man," and so forth), and his extraordinary card-playing sense. He taught us two- and three-handed pinochle. My mother, innocent of method and memory, won often enough to irritate him. He was something at the card table! He remembered unerringly every card that showed itself during a game. He'd gaze long and hard at the ceiling, putting together his playing strategy. He said his colleagues on the boats refused to play with him and he knew they would come to angry conclusions that he was cheating or dealing with Satan over his shoulder. I tried to cheat *him* once or twice. He looked at me pityingly with unbelief: "Come on, old man, you can do better than that!" He taught me a couple of versions of solitaire. Looking over my shoulder as I essayed my first game, he said like the river gambler he, indeed, was: "You put up fifty dollars for the pack. The house pays you five dollars for every card you get out. The house usually wins!" Years later I devised a different system of scoring that I thought added suspense and form to the game and, most important, gave the player at least a 50/50 chance of winning. I never played it in a gambling house but it has always been, in my version, a satisfying and calming pastime. My father became an authority on American baseball, forsaking cricket and rooting for the New York Yankees with batting and pitching averages tucked away for purposes of argument and analysis. It was in those glorious days of Babe Ruth, Bill Dickey, and Lou Gehrig when there was a great outcry to break up the New York Yankees, that combine no team could beat. He took me to Yankee Stadium often enough to make me care. Hot dogs with burning mustard and Coca-Cola, thumbs down for losers and violent altercations in the bleachers. He cared little for the theater or concerts but he could talk about current events—including cultural ones—unhesitatingly, feeling his way into the conversation even when he knew next to nothing about the subjects under discussion. (In my adolescence I would talk about books I had not read and plays I had not seen with that same airiness.)

One day toward the tag end of the Depression, my father came home from his part-time job, sat in a chair in the kitchen, and suddenly began to cry—loud, shaking sobs. My mother was appalled. "What happened, dear?" Still weeping he said, "A white man slapped me in the subway—for no reason. I was ready to kill him. And then I thought of you and Seifield and our life depending on me and how hard it is to get work and I just got out at the next stop." My mother said "Don't cry anymore, you didn't do anything wrong." My father said "That's why I'm crying" and poured himself a cup of coffee. My father knew the dice were loaded in America. He knew it every day of his life. That was the only time I saw my father cry when I was growing up. My mother said he cried during his long illness, he cried about his helplessness when he was in his seventies. He didn't cry when he learned his parents had died in faraway Barbados. He said he had wept for them just after they left America. He saw them dead in his mind's eye and knew he would never see them again.

My father's feelings were very close to the surface but that surface was a cement carapace—most of the time.

God

Then there was, of course, God, whose acquaintance one made through the auspices of St. Cyprian's Episcopal Church, off of Amsterdam Avenue and Sixty-third Street. I was baptized in that church, learned all the responses for the confirmation ceremony, sang in the choir, and was instructed most Sundays by the biblical annotations of the Reverend Samuel Grice, a large black man with splendid diction who made himself part of the community but who did not stir my imagination until the news of the manner of his death swept through Columbus Hill. He had taken a hot bath shortly after a heavy meal and his heart had stopped—like that!

Gordon Heath and his mother
dressed for church, 1948

My father's attendance at church was not exactly regular, but for him the standings, the sittings, and the kneeling were all reassuring Anglican high-church ritual. The text book, The Book of Common Prayer, was geared to the religious festivals—Easter, Christmas, the Second Sunday after Septuagesima, and so on, the length of the year. The Reverend Mr. Grice usually took his text from the assigned Gospels and I was required to learn the prescribed Collect for each Sunday by my father, so could safely predict the area from which Grice would choose his text. (The instinct proved useful when I played hooky. I could report on the sermon without having been anywhere near the place!) God was pretty far away from all this; icon and idol, surely: grace before meals, prayers at bedtime, and pressure to respect all ten of the Commandments. The Book of Common Prayer contained all the services for passage through life and into death and all the contingencies thereof—"for those lost at Sea." The General Confession, to be intoned "all kneeling," covered sins in generalities. The Communion service was more to the point but that old white man with a long beard was never much in daily evidence.

My mother, who was slightly repelled by the formality and bloodlessness of the Episcopal service, found fulfillment in the Baptist establishment on *our* side of Sixty-third Street. There the Reverend Mr. Sims shouted, wept, and exhorted God and the congregation to collect enough money to pay for the organ's repair, the church's roof, and the uninterrupted maintenance of his personal household. The robed choir strutted into the choir loft as if on parade, sang with thrilling unction, strutted out at the end of the services, beaming and sweating in passionate participation. Glory shone all 'round. Foot patting and hand clapping and rhythmic response to the minister's evangelic fervor were the order of the day. One entered automatically into the Kingdom of Heaven every Sunday. We were all hand in hand with God. All participants—no spectators. Passion and ritual, my introduction to the nature of theater.

The most moving celebration I experienced in the Baptist church was the New Year's Eve "Watch Night" service at Abyssinian. An hour before midnight the minister would read psalms of praise with perhaps bits of Ecclesiastes thrown in, to a somber well-dressed congregation that filled the church to bursting. They went on their knees as one. The tradition had it that if God found you on your knees the first morning of the new year, you would be blessed for the year's length. The minister would intone appropriate prayers. The congregation would remain kneeling, sending out whispered and unspoken prayers. At midnight all fell silent for a moment; the chimes struck the hour and the bells would ring joyfully (as they did all over the city) announcing the new year's arrival. The worshipers, rising, would shake hands with their neighbors. Husbands and sweethearts would kiss their loved ones and, led by the triumphant organ, everyone would sing,

> It's a happy New Year.
> It's a happy New Year.
> It's a happy, it's a happy,
> It's a happy New Year.

The song rang out like the bells. Some wept as they remembered those who were there last year, but were no more. But jubilation was uppermost. My father pulled my earlobe, kissed my mother, and shook hands heartily with everyone in reach.

> Let the heavens rejoice and let the earth be glad! (Psalms 96.11)

Owen Vincent Dodson

Owen was all three of the categories to infinity. He wrote to me almost every day from Bates College and, later, from Yale University, even sending special deliveries so I would find a letter in the box on Sunday. The letters were idiosyncratic—fanciful: "Spring is here with poets and bathtubs." His latest poems with their latest corrections kept company with diary jottings and schoolboy fun. Theater celebrities would lecture and be interviewed at Yale: "Basil Rathbone spoke to us yesterday. He was wearing a huge ruby ring on his little finger (?). Harold Clurman talked about the Group Theatre last week and Robert Lewis will probably tell us about his fantasy life next week." Owen drank at many wells—not very deeply perhaps because so much was being offered and tossed about and he was intensely pragmatic, taking what was of use to him. He was passionate about Greek drama and about the poetry and pith of Negro dialect. "Chile," he would say, "you better get yo'self together. We gonna dig Proust tomorrow." He extracted the color and the flavor first—the grammar and the core were for later. He absorbed the atmospheres without reading the weather reports. He was a romancer rather than a reporter and his letters were allusive and quirky, and—of course—loving.

He wrote a bitter play, inspired by the dangerous success and influence of the black "Father Divine" who fed the multitude with fried chicken in lieu of loaves and fishes, claimed divinity and immortality, and baffled the IRS, living high and owning nothing in his own name (which, in fact, was revealed to be George Baker). Owen's play, *Divine Comedy,* half in blank verse (influenced, I thought, by Greek drama forms—chorus, strophe, and antistrophe, and by T. S. Eliot's early playwriting), exposed the plight of the easily seduced minorities, the have-nots, the blacks and the poor and even the guilt-ridden rich, lulled into a false sense of security as they worshiped with heart, hand, and pocketbook at the shrine of a flamboyant charismatic fraud. The play anticipated Hitler and this very moment of today's corrupting and corrupt televangelism. *Divine Comedy* was performed at Yale as part of Owen's thesis for his fine arts degree.

His play about Medea, Jason, and the Golden Fleece, *Garden of Time,* placed the protagonists in the Deep South centuries later (black Medea—white Jason) after a first act laid in Colchis, Greece. Jason is bored with Medea and her magic and plans to leave her for another (white) woman. Medea calls upon her witch goddess and her magic to visit a cruel revenge upon Jason—as in the original legend. Owen invited me to Yale for a weekend to see the play performed with an all-white student cast. It was a noteworthy occasion. Owen was laurel-crowned. In life I was cast—not unwillingly—as his consort.

Owen "glittered when he walked"—with a blinding glitter of multiple talents and personal ease and charm. To me he was parent, adviser, teacher, and director. He was acquisitive and I was a part of his collection. His series of apartments—really the same apartment—in Virginia, in Washington, in New York displayed his talent for creating interiors—juxtaposing furniture and objects. The inexpensive and the rare lived next to each other in a perfect symbiosis of styles and provenances that showed the instinct of a stage de-signer: no crowding, generous space for entertaining. I remember a wrought-iron sofa with cushions, brass candelabra standing sentry, a full wall wood carving in bas-relief dramatically spotlighted, framed posters and paintings; a square Victorian piano stood under the bas-relief, a porcelain bird cage hung from the ceiling, African statues shelf-high dotted the filled floor-to-ceiling bookshelves, and a gaily colored carousel horse was the base for a circular table. It was a relaxed apartment; nothing demanded your attention in a store-window fashion, but one's eye was pleased wherever one stood or sat, paused or walked. Owen had already made me conscious of a "life-style" and the aura of the apartment sifted into my subconscious and affected my choices and dispositions permanently. I didn't copy directly and my apartments didn't look like Owen's—but he was always there.

When Kenneth, not yet thirty, died in 1940, Owen lost a part of himself. Owen was already acquainted with grief; father, mother, and now his comrade, his brother, his dearest and most understanding friend. I went to the funeral in Brooklyn. The service was notable for its dignity and the despair expressed openly and unashamedly by everyone who had known Kenneth. People wept, holding hands and calling Kenneth's name over and over as if to deny death. The organ played Sibelius's "Finlandia" as the pallbearers shouldered the mahogany casket.

Owen wrote:

My chief citizen is dead
And my town at half-mast:
Even in speech,
Even in walking,
Even in seeing
The busy streets where he stood
And the room where he was host to his friends
And his enemies, where we erased the night to dawn
With conversation of what I had seen and he had seen
And done and written during the space of time we were apart.
We will not talk again with common breath.
His voice has gone to talk to death.

I hadn't known Kenneth well. Owen didn't talk about him. He didn't talk about his losses or his continuing struggles to earn a first-class education or the part his sisters played in keeping the family afloat in their worst of times. He was possessed of relentless courage and determination to achieve. He handled his life like he directed plays: detail upon detail—noted, attended to, crossed off, and on to the next item. He didn't talk about his goals. I don't know who helped him along the way or how he and his sisters conceived and carried out their graceful life-style. Lillian, the eldest, taught school but was always in poor health. Nevertheless, their collective hospitality was unstinting and Owen maintained personal and professional friendships on a wide and generous scale.

I sat in on some of his drama classes at Hampton and Howard. He made his students see what their life experiences had to do with acting—how necessary it was to observe, to be curious, to work at understanding the lessons art and life could teach them. He took examples from their own behavior patterns. He attacked their passivity.

"All over the campus two days before Ma'ian [Marian] Anderson was expected you heard and saw the excitement and anticipation growing. Ma'ian Anderson—Ma'ian Anderson! She came. She sang Schubert. You sat back, almost indifferent. She sang Brahms. You were intimidated—you shuffled your feet. She sang spirituals. You sat up and clapped your hands. Ma'ian Anderson. You didn't let her take you any further than you had already gone. Who was Brahms? Who was Schubert? What were those songs all about? You didn't know—but worse than that, you didn't care. You've got to reach out and seize every moment. You've got to store up experiences. You've got to watch and listen and find out how things came to be. Did you see how they depended on each other—Miss Anderson and her accompanist?—the respect they had for each other? Did you notice how Miss Anderson stood in front of you and waited for your concentration and gathered her own? Did you notice she closed her eyes when she sang the spirituals?

"When you take communion in church, you are meant to be in a state of grace. When you are confronted with art you should be in a state of grace. Something—some part of what you see and hear—will become a part of you. It will abide with you, like the Holy Spirit. It is not enough to say "Ma'ian Anderson" and expect her to do it all for you!"

These mostly rural youngsters were not startled by the vivacity of Owen's impersonations. It was known that "Mr. O" was *dramatic*. Taking his classes was going to be a show—but they got the point.

In 1943 Owen was drafted into the Navy Station at Great Lakes and was busy at work turning out montages about black participation in the war effort and producing plays with and about the servicemen themselves. I stayed at Hampton long enough after he left to play a southern, hard-drinking playboy soldier—a kind of Mercutio (played on Broadway by Jimmy Monks; we became great friends much later) surrounded by less spirited but sympathetic northern buddies soon to go overseas into the reality of war. The play was *The Eve of St. Marks*, Maxwell Anderson's musing on America's youth preparing to join the crusade. I took on the southern drawl I loved so much and the indigenous students played the northerners.

After his discharge from the navy in 1944, Owen returned to Hampton. He invited me to come back as a student-teacher and directed me in Shaw's *Pygmalion*. I had seen the quite perfect Anthony Asquith film a dozen times and dreamed of doing the Leslie Howard (later Rex Harrison) part of the overbearing Professor Higgins. I went about the town with Owen, borrowing classy furniture from classy people to furnish Mrs. Higgins's drawing room (Chinese Chippendale chairs, one of which was broken and had to be very expensively repaired). Owen's production organization was a lesson in technique. Yale really trained them! In his sprawling handwriting, Owen scribbled notes covering every detail on his omnipresent clipboard. He was the first left-handed per-

Gordon Heath as Professor Higgins and Geraldine Prillerman as Eliza Doolittle, *Pygmalion*, 1944

son I knew and I watched him writing with the kind of awe one feels for a blind man who moves about with certainty wherever he happens to find himself.

Owen directed the varying talents of the student actors with exemplary patience and a great deal of encouragement and demonstration. He acted out bits for them to imitate, at the same time teaching them elements of style and explaining how gesture could focus emotion and illustrate words. The kids at Hampton thought I was playing myself in *Pyg* but Owen wrote me a memorandum afterward to say I was playing Leslie Howard. It must have looked different on me anyway, and why didn't he tell me before, instead of after, and direct me away from my impersonation? I ask myself this now, but then I seemed to have accepted the observation unblinkingly and refrained from pointing out that he had played Doolittle imitating, as nearly as he could, Wilfrid Lawson's ripe performance in the film.

During the summer of 1944 Owen went to Howard University where he staged a production of *Homecoming* (the first play in O'Neill's trilogy, *Mourning Becomes Electra*) on the steps of Douglas Hall, a Greek-mansion building with columns not unlike New England houses. He recognized in Sadie Browne, my friend from the NYA, a special emotional depth and persuaded her to forsake

Brooklyn long enough to play Christine, the great Alla Nazimova's role. He invited me to play Sadie's elderly husband and her lover. Owen played Seth, the hired man, with what he hoped was an accurate downeast accent. Owen thought my rehearsal performance as the aging husband was fine and flinty, but he observed that I had a tendency to project scorn for the character of Sadie's lover. He taught me another lesson exactly as Tyrone Guthrie taught Olivier when he was playing Sergius in Shaw's *Arms and the Man*. Olivier disliked the character of Sergius. Tyrone Guthrie, directing the piece, said "If you can't love Sergius, you'll never by able to play him" and Olivier set about loving Sergius. Directors make the point almost routinely now: you do not pass judgment on the character you are playing; you play him as he sees himself and you identify with him. I thought Brant was a dreary man and at first I couldn't make him come alive on stage.

~ BERTOLT BRECHT, THE German Marxist poet, playwright, and director, asked actors to play their attitude to their stage characters at the same time they played the character and to avoid "identifying."

Fortunately, I knew nothing of Brecht at the time of *Electra,* but later Brecht himself was staging *The Private Life of the Master Race* at the New School for Social Research in New York and he asked me to be a narrator. More exactly, he asked me to "act" a narrator! Brecht and his work were not yet known in America. His *Galileo,* which he put together with Charles Laughton, was not to surface until two years later in California.

Perhaps Brecht felt—like Hamish had—that blacks had all that "color and passion," but he was not asking for color or passion. This stubby little man reeking of cheap cigars looked, with his cereal-bowl haircut, as if he'd come to read the gas meter.

His heavily accented English was almost adequate but his idea of the actor's function in his plays was incomprehensible to me. This narrator was not to be a Sophoclean messenger or a radio announcer but the actor himself telling the story as himself, conveying at the same time his personal comment on the happenings. This much I thought I understood—but I didn't know how to do it. Brecht and I had a week together in which he hammered relentlessly at my preconceptions and let me attempt over and over again to strike the right note. I left Brecht to rehearse *Roots,* not much wiser than before about "alienation."

As a parting gift he presented me with a copy of his radio play, *The Trial of Lucullus.* Lucullus was a celebrated Roman general on trial after his death by the Judge of the Dead. Witnesses testify for and against him. Like Göring at Nuremberg, he speaks arrogantly for himself. The evidence is overwhelmingly against him.

Brecht was still evolving his theories—in his own language and for his own theater. He directed empirically, by trial and error, and not only hesitated to codify his theories but was also willing to accept what "worked." To translate this fluidity in terms that American actors could grasp was not yet feasible. He needed actors whose instinct and discrimination would give them the key to his intuitions—Laughton, for instance. When I saw his company in Paris and Berlin in the 1960s, I understood a lot more. Brecht didn't want his audiences to be "carried away" or to "identify" with the characters in his plays. He wanted them to be steadily reminded that they were in a *theater* watching a demonstration of a situation. Hitler was a clown, Mother Courage was a grasping fool, Coriolanus was a jack-in-the-box. Human nature (Brecht's included) being what it is, audiences seized upon whatever aspect of characters they could identify with and settled for that. Audiences are even harder to reform than actors. Shakespeare asked his audiences to piece out the play's imperfections with their imagination. Brecht tried to put the "imperfections" on stage without shadows so audiences could see what was going on every minute. The actors came on as circus or vaudeville performers. They entered, performed their acts, and went off, but the virtuosity of the "act" almost involved you, in spite of Brecht's intentions. The plays themselves were didactic. Climaxes occurred but nothing necessarily led up to or away from them. The plays were set in décors of rich textures and formal beauty. Costumes were *clothes,* taking on the shape of the wearers. Props were used and *looked* used—not just handled. Good and evil were not flatly opposed—they were part of each other. Nevertheless, the Brecht pieces are morality plays, sharing the austerity of that genre. (It would help to understand German, especially since we are assured that Brecht was a great poet and even extracted strength from what had become clichéd, linguistically speaking.)

The Berliner Ensemble productions of *The Caucasian Chalk Circle* and *Mother Courage* were *the* great occasions of my lifetime of theatergoing—strong and delicate, primitive and sophisticated, vibrating with color and light, like oriental ritual and symbolic theater, orchestrated for clarity and, what is more, annotated with place names and chapter headings between scenes. You saw what had happened and you knew what was going to happen next. Brecht did not claim to be an innovator but his vision of theater has begun to influence playwrights and directors *and* audiences everywhere in the world.

∾ BUT, AS I WAS saying—

Captain Adam Brant was my problem. It was too late to start loving him. I decided that he was really Rhett Butler, the intrepid blockade runner of *Gone with the Wind.* What was good enough for Clark Gable ought to be good enough for Owen! It was good enough for *People's Voice:*

Hamlet and his uncle,
the King (Owen Dodson)

Gordon Heath was personable and gallant as Brant. His first antagonistic scene with
Lavinia was swift-paced and climatic. His second characterization as Ezra, bearded
and gaunt like a pine tree, was full-bodied and tragic. When Ezra, made sensitive by
the constant presence of death, makes a final harshly wistful plea to his wife to pick
up the threads of their life, she blurts out the truth about her lover, causes Ezra's
collapse and poisons him under the pretext of giving him medicine. Heath towered
and crumpled in death with a magnificence matched only by the greedy triumphant
cry of Christine, free to seek her love at last.

The mood and the playing matched the material. New England emerged in Seth's
salty speech, the townsfolk's clipped acidities and Ezra's brittle flatness. (Anne
Harrington, *People's Voice*, August 15, 1944)*

I never told Owen I was cheating. Sadie was magnificent and the show was
impressive.

The following year Owen conceived a project for a music and drama festival
to be launched at Hampton in the summer of 1945. Gordon would sing a sheaf
of folk songs with guitar; the drama contingent would stage *Outward Bound,*
Pearl Primus would unleash herself and her fervent troupe in a dance program.
The music department decided to perform James Dorsey's folk choral symphony, "Jake and Sue." But the clou of the occasion would be Gordon Heath as
Hamlet against a decor of fifteen-foot screens, portraits of former kings of
Denmark conceived and painted by Charles Sebree. (Sebree much later wrote
in collaboration a Broadway vehicle for Eartha Kitt called *Mrs. Patterson.* The
play was an expansion of an anecdote about a little black southern girl who,
asked what she wanted to be when she grew up, answered, to the point, "a rich
white lady.") *Hamlet* was the culmination of the project. Owen imported most

---

* *People's Voice* was a Negro tabloid newspaper that used the format of *PM,* the New York daily.

of the leads. Marion Douglas, the grandchild of a renowned black singer-actress, Abbie Mitchell, was to play Ophelia. Marion was beautiful and vulnerable and had a disconcerting tendency to search out the sources of Ophelia's babbling in the mad scene. Owen said "Oh, how I hate thinking actors!" One knew what he meant. Marion's research made very heavy weather of a scene she had played instinctively, a performance wandering and fragmentary and heartbreaking. Owen spent the last days of rehearsal trying to make her forget all she had learned. Not quite—but Marion was still the best Ophelia I ever saw. Hank Scott, cast as Horatio, almost as beautiful as Marion, had to be weaned out of his (understandable) narcissism to make contact with his friend and fellow student, Hamlet. (Scott later went on the road as Brett in *Roots*.) Dorothy Ateca, the Queen, was genteel and bewildered by the forces swirling about her—a very acceptable if not compelling reading of the part. William Greaves, now a producer-director of documentary films, was a touching adolescent Laertes. Our Osric wore his costume as if it were drag and waved his hat as if it were a Restoration fan. Rosencrantz and Guildenstern never went to the same school as Hamlet but Austin Briggs-Hall was a shrewd and silly Polonius and a weary tortured Ghost (under the stage). I wore John Gielgud's costume with impertinent assurance. I had no model to follow or disagree with. I had seen Maurice Evans's *Hamlet* directed by Margaret Webster several times but I decided this time I was going to play Hamlet, not Maurice Evans. Owen's direction was two-thirds coaching and teaching as he went along. The last three days of rehearsal I spent learning the soliloquies, walking around on campus with Austin cueing me. In performance I seemed to make them the coinage of my brain (they were really the coinage of my memory) and they were much remarked upon. Shakespeare has packed so much drama into the work and the characters react so directly on each other that the spectator and the actors are carried along by the tensions created by the confrontations. We were hailed with extraordinary enthusiasm by the audience. This was before Joe Papp. A black *Hamlet* and the festival itself were unprecedented events. *Theatre Arts Monthly* reproduced a photograph of Marion and me as Ophelia and Hamlet.

Heath as Hamlet

Lastly, but hardly least, the Hamlet of Gordon Heath—this was a surprise, at least to this reviewer, knowing Mr. Heath to be a learned young man with a beautiful voice, a sing-song academic performance was expected . . . anything but! Here was a vibrant and an alive performance; a union of brain and muscle—an actor that used every part of his body to express what his intellect demands. It was all there from small sensitivities to mountainous lustful revenge. His range was remarkable, and as for his beautiful voice, Mr. Heath did not hesitate to sacrifice it to make some desired affects.—Walter Thompson Ash, *People's Voice,* 1945

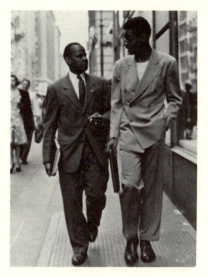

Owen Dodson and his
"secretary," 1945 or 1946

⌘ MY DEAR FRIEND and protégé, Tad Truesdale, a fixture at La Mama in
New York until his death in 1988, a dancer, singer, playwright, actor, and
director, too young to have seen Maurice Evans or Robeson, complained to me
that he had never seen a Shakespearean play on stage. I took him to the only
Shakespearean production then on view. It was Tony Richardson's idea of
Hamlet with Nicol Williamson in the title role. Nicol Williamson is an interesting cerebral actor, a specialist in contemporary neurosis. He is also an un-
prepossessing man with a discomforting hint of a Welsh howl in his speech, by
no means the glass of fashion and the mold of form. He held no hint of a "noble
mind" to be overthrown. He was parsonical, censorious, and rasping. The
production itself was lax and lifeless. I sat, uncomfortable through the first act,
excused myself and left, promising Tad I would pick him up at curtain time. I
went out in the street and was promptly sick in the gutter. I regretted my choice.
I restored myself with coffee, read a newspaper, and waited out the play's
passage. Tad emerged, eyes shining with excitement. I apologized for leaving,
only intimating how unhappy I was. Tad, walking a foot above the ground,
turned to me glowing and said "But what a wonderful play!" Ah yes—what a
wonderful play. I had forgotten.

⌘ OWEN UNDERTOOK A subsequent production of *Hamlet* after I left
America. In the title role was Earle Hyman, who went on to Broadway and
America's Stratford, alternating classic roles with contemporary pieces, black
and white. Owen very carefully avoided making Hamlet comparisons in my

presence, but Earle was taken under his wing more or less as my successor. I occasionally see Owen in Earle's performances (and in my own, too, if it comes to that).*

A Committee for Mass Education in Race Relations was formed, headquarters in New York, thirty-eighth floor, Rockefeller Center. The committee included Langston Hughes, Mrs. Paul Robeson, Charles Johnson of Fisk University, and Claude McKay, poet and novelist. Owen was the coordinator and he asked me to be his secretary. We worked together (with occasional clashes when I felt Owen was treating me as if I were still eleven years old), and I was useful. I knew pretty well how his mind worked and could, for instance, write business letters exactly in his allusive personal style. I could even write Owen Dodson poems. I caught the style rather than the substance. I rescued work he had consigned to the wastebasket but might have second thoughts about, and then rewrite with fresh inspiration. I used to recite his "Black Mother Praying" when I was invited to speak for this or that cause. I used to recite his poems waiting for street cars and subways. The committee planned to use films, theater, and radio to project an image of Negros as they lived, worked, and interacted in America. We put together a radio series, with Barbara Watson as producer, about the lives of "ordinary Negroes" called "I'm Your Next-door Neighbor." I wrote the first half-hour script about a nurse-and-intern romance. Owen wrote a script about a Negro comedian, loosely based on Bert Williams who built a successful vaudeville career on the black-face clown character he created. I put together a script for a "live" ways-and-means round table discussion about what we were trying to do in the "I'm Your Neighbor" series. Owen and the langorous Barbara** spoke at some length about how we wanted to improve the image of the lives of these "ordinary" colored people.

Owen submitted *Garden of Time,* his *Medea* play, to the American Negro Theatre and although a poetic "classic" play was not exactly their genre, they were willing to put the theater at Owen's disposal. Sebree did two sets, columns in a curved blue-sky backdrop for the Greek first act; panels from column to column making a dilapidated sinister interior of a ruined southern mansion, for the second act. I wrote new settings for the four songs in the piece that Orpheus (later "Blues-Boy") sings to Medea and sang them myself backstage in what was left of my boy soprano, to Bill Greaves miming with a guitar. The illusion was

---

* Owen staged a third *Hamlet* at Howard in 1964 [with St. Clair Christmas as Hamlet]. The idea seemed to me more obsessive than creative.

** Barbara Watson was the daughter of the first black Circuit Court Judge. She had been brought up in a very continental atmosphere with scores of European friends. She was meant to be "producer" of the series but was hardly ever around for conferences. We called her after her nonappearance for the first broadcast: "Barbara, where have you been?" Coolly, languidly, she said: "Oh, the job—Europe—packing, . . ." superbly unruffled and a credit to the State Department for whom she worked most of her professional life.

evidently sustained. "Greaves's" singing and Sebree's sets got the notices. Sadie Browne's Medea was admired but the play was summed up as wordy and slow. I was meant to be "assistant to the director" but what with playing Medea's brother in the first act, designing the poster, and singing the songs in both acts, I did very little "assisting." Owen's first venture in New York, mounted lovingly and carefully, was a discouraging failure. I think Owen expected to go on to Broadway and fame from there on out, but his kind of playwrighting was really for off-Broadway, if for anywhere, and off-Broadway had not yet been invented.* Owen's playwrighting formula, reworking classic plays in a black context, was never a tempting commercial proposition.

In 1945, critic Jean Nathan took a backhanded slap at the output of the American Negro Theatre, slating, among others, Owen's *Medea:* "a paraphrase of the legend, far beyond its author's competence, [which] amounted not only to heavy pretension, but to the kind of thing that the commercial theatre—say what you will against it, and that it is sometimes justifiably plenty—wisely would not touch." It was not a serious appraisal of Owen's possibilities as a poet or a playwright: it was a dismissal—arbitrary and destructive. Owen went on writing. We did not discuss the implications of Nathan's sledgehammer blows. Owen was not the first young playwright to suffer at Nathan's pen. Nathan was curiously carping, if not downright hostile, toward the more ambitious Negro efforts in the theater. In 1951 Owen brought over to Norway a troupe from Howard to play Ibsen's *Doll House* and Heyward's *Mamba's Daughters* at the invitation of Norway's Royal Theatre. He went back to America by way of Paris, where I was living by then, and we had a riotous reunion. He threw an impromptu birthday party for me at the pension where Lee and I lived. Lee was away filming on an island off the coast of Norway. Owen glowed as a member of my club audience. He was visibly enchanted by the atmosphere of l'Abbaye and he was proud of what I had accomplished. He told me about playing Ibsen in Ibsen's own country. The stage manager at the theater examined his ground plan saying "No, the chimney is on the other side and the table is on the left— not the right!" They had performed Ibsen and he belonged to them—ground plan and all. Owen told him he would be inviting chaos if his players had to play not only in an unfamiliar theater but also on a completely altered set. The stage manager—clearly against his better judgment—gave in and everything else was graciousness and accord. Royalty occupied the boxes and the critics didn't note the misplaced chimney.

---

* He tried to place his adaptation of *Peer Gynt,* called *Bayou Legend,* under Katherine Dunham's aegis. It was exactly her line of country. She thought so too, but only if she was directing it. Negotiations never ensued. Owen wanted recognition for his directorial talents but his play was performed as a college production—attracting only local attention. He had planned, he said, for me to play Peer (Reve in his version), but I was not even in America when it was performed.

Diary entry, September 1951/Paris:

Talk with O at some length about shortcomings of French theatre as I see it. We go to a Sunday matinée at the Comédie Française of *Antigone*. It turns out to be unbearably moving, hieratic and human, and, of course, exactly Owen's cup of tea. We weep for a full half hour over our after-theatre coffees. I do not go on about the "shortcomings" of the French theatre; simple amazement sits on Owen (me too!) Our coffees grow cold.

In 1962 Owen invited Lee and me to play Marlowe's *Dr Faustus* in his almost brand-new theater at Howard. I carried on a longish correspondence to establish first principles and logistics. Lee would play Mephistopheles and I would be Faustus and the theater would go all out with splendid costumes and a spectacular décor. Lee and I began to rehearse in Paris in our apartment; we learned the text and did a tentative "blocking." We were by this time tuned to each other as performers and rehearsals were our favorite indoor sport. Owen's bulletins broke off and questions were left unanswered. I was slightly apprehensive because it was so unlike the Owen I knew. We arrived in Washington and went to work. Owen had the cast on hand to watch us play a couple of scenes at performance pitch. He and the cast were open-mouthed with admiration for our interplay. Owen said our instinctive meshing was worthy of the Lunts and the kids were flabbergasted. Faustus is built on the conflict of the two protagonists but there are many small roles that add up to a large cast. Owen had directed a few scenes sketchily and was in the process of tightening and creating a continuity out of this very loosely constructed epic—a sprawling colorful clashing of the forces of good and evil wrestling for the possession of Faustus's soul. The swirling high jinks that Mephistopheles provides for Faustus's delectation (including a vision of Helen of Troy whose face "launched a thousand ships") were formless and unintegrated. Owen occupied himself with the required special effects but his notes for the actors were perfunctory and the students were panicky, waiting for forceful and detailed direction. He didn't direct Lee or me but we were entirely capable of creating our own patterns. I reverted very reluctantly to acting as "assistant to the director" as deprecatingly as I could without underlining Owen's inexplicable disinterest. Lee's mother, who had come from Seattle to be with us, made at my suggestion ingenious skullcaps covering the backs of necks of every member of the cast to disguise the modern looking short hair style that was blatantly anachronistic against medieval costumes. She also made Lee's impressive cowled robe. I suggested transitions, taught the cast the drinking song, and walked them through their "business" and positions as unobtrusively as I could. This "take-over" was entirely against my principles but I felt I had to save the play and Owen's face.

In the middle of the jubilant opening-night party Owen came to me blurrily tight and said slyly, "I know *you* directed the play. Don't think I don't know." I had no retort. I could only have said, "Why didn't you?" I suppose that marked a break, an almost imperceptible tear in the fabric of our close and passionate relationship. The Washington newspaper critics were approving and admiring—one observing that the rôles did not give the actors (Lee and me that is) "sufficient scope for their talents" (!). (Incomprehensible remark—maybe we made it look too easy?) Lee and I went back to Paris—Lee especially heartened that his hand had not lost its cunning. He was a splendid sardonic fallen angel.

Owen and I continued to correspond. He sent the programs of his subsequent productions and some of his new poems. Lee and I recorded a dozen of his poems and sent him the tape as a birthday present but a couple of his worried colleagues wrote that he was seldom entirely sober.

Owen stayed with us for a week in Paris on his way back from a 1968 holiday in W. H. Auden's Ischia house. He was in fine gleeful form but found a moment during a drinking bout to say again, "I know you directed *Faustus!*" I couldn't tell if he remembered it with chagrin or gratitude or rancor—probably all three.

I visited him in Washington in 1969 when America's youth was berserk and on a rampage. Owen's library and office in Howard were trashed. Students, especially blacks, wanted life to begin with them. History had falsified the past—they wanted it wiped out. Owen was sad and uncomprehending, as were hundreds of educators and archivists all over America. I read without his permission a draft of the article he was putting together for the local paper. It began "When Iphigenia walked the plains of Aulis. . . ." or some such and I lost my temper completely. For me Owen's mandarin education and his mandarin prose couldn't come to grips with the gritty reality. I wrote on his pad: "Owen, for Godsake, forget you ever read a Greek play. You are not a journalist and you haven't the equipment to report on or analyse this moment."

Owen was predictably furious with me, submitted his article, I think unaltered, and commanded me never to comment on his work again. I wrote him an apology which he accepted but the friendship was clearly hanging by a thread. When Owen came out of college he was seen as the natural successor to Countee Cullen—*the* Negro poet and brilliant playwright—but Jimmy Baldwin came along with his scorched earth prose and Derek Walcott's and Alice Walker's poems got national publicity and Lloyd Richards directed a hit play on Broadway. *Time* did a cover article about black writers that included a tribute to Owen and many honors came his way, but I don't think they matched his ambitions or his early promise and there was bitterness at the bottom of his cup.

Owen had a bad fall in the winter of 1975 and underwent a series of operations to restore mobility to his legs and relieve encroaching arthritis but he was permanently lamed and crippled. He worked, wrote, lectured, and drank. He began to make telephone calls in the middle of the night to read his new poems to old friends. I introduced him to Henry Lyman* who interviewed poets and had them read their poems on his regular radio program. Henry had known and admired Owen's poems before they met and he set up a session in New York. The interview and the poetry reading won the prize that season. I thought Owen overdramatized his own material with applied emotion unrelated to their content or message. Owen himself had become heavily oracular.

In 1978 I was invited to Denver to play Henri Christophe, the liberator and king of Haiti, in a powerful play by James Forsyth** called *Defiant Island*. Owen wrote to say he planned to come and asked if he could stay with me for at least two weeks. He had staged the play in Washington and was more than ordinarily curious about this production. I was delighted—it would be like old times. He arrived, crutches and all. I unpacked for him and insisted on his getting some rest before the theater. He came to the performance. I introduced him to the producer and my colleagues and improvised a tiny reception in my apartment with some cast members. He was a Grand Old Man of the Theater—witty and anecdotal in his absolute best form. He drank a bottle of Scotch during the evening and I had placed another at his elbow. When the guests left he sat on the bed and talked about the play and my performance. He pointed out the lacks in the direction and the other performances with his usual acuity and then he spent a quarter of an hour praising every element of my characterization. The reviews had been rhapsodic about me but Owen showered me with overwhelming praise until I was sweating with pleasure and exhaustion—the evening was a special kind of ordeal, of course. I kissed him, thanked him, and announced I was going to bed. He went into the living room, sat in an armchair, and finished off the second bottle of Scotch. Ten minutes later he launched into a mad drunken soliloquy, spewing out gobs of hatred, frustration, jealousy, and accusations against practically everyone he had ever known. All of his loves had failed him. The world had been ungrateful. I said, "Come to bed, Owen." He shouted from the living room, "Get out, get out!" He hadn't been making sense and there was no way to cope with his madness. He fell out of the chair onto the floor. I got up and tried to get him to bed but he was too heavy to move. I put a blanket over him and went to bed. A half hour later he got himself up and said, "I'm going. Please call me a taxi." It was three o'clock in the morning. He packed his suitcase and said, "Please call me a taxi." I said, "Where are you going?" "I'm going home!" I couldn't believe he knew what he was saying. I tried to persuade

---

* Henry Lyman: New England poet and producer of the radio series "Poems to a Listener," for National Public Radio.
** James Forsyth, Scots writer and playwright. His play, *Héloïse and Abélard*, was performed in New York in 1958.

him to rest, to sleep—at least to wait till a reasonable hour before he left. He sat up stony and unyielding. He was angry with me for leaving him on the floor. I was not exactly pleased with him but I didn't think he meant to go. I said, "I'll have to tell your sister what happened." I hoped that would make him think twice about leaving. He shouted at me, "You can't do that. Edith is sick." He was in a rage again but was determined to leave, and when the staff opened the theater I called a cab for him. I said, "Owen you have had extraordinary courage all your life—haven't you got enough courage to stop drinking?" He didn't react to that. So he went home. I was from then on a deadly enemy and he snubbed me in public. When my mother died in 1979 I sent him the announcement of the funeral which was to take place in the undertaker's chapel. He had always been fond of her. He called me on the phone. "Well don't let them put her in the ground like that," he said peremptorily, "sing or something." I had already planned to sing for my mother in the chapel. It was probably Owen's influence from way back. He was superb at celebrations, occasions, birthdays. He could always make an occasion special and give it a frame. He died in 1983. The gods had blessed him with great gifts and talents and early success, then capriciously robbed him of all he possessed. He had reason to think in terms of Greek tragedy. His last published work was the text for a book of photographs, *The Book of the Dead.*

Margaret Durand

Emlyn Williams, the Welsh playwright-actor (his one-man shows as Charles Dickens and Dylan Thomas toured America in the 1970s), wrote early in his playwriting career a touching, successful piece called *The Corn Is Green.* The play was about an eleven-year-old boy working in the Welsh mines and how he got an education, a scholarship, and a career. He owed it all to Miss Moffat, one of this schoolteachers in Wales who, scenting promise, pushed, scolded, taught, and prepared him for his Oxford scholarship. The teacher was not demonstratively affectionate but she obviously cared deeply about him as a person and a talent, and she remained a steadfast friend and adviser all of her lifetime. The boy was Emlyn himself. His autobiography* documents the course of this loving friendship and the propelling power of the teacher's support. Miss Moffat was created by Dame Sybil Thorndike on the London stage, by Ethel Barrymore on Broadway, by Katherine Hepburn on American TV, and by Cicely Tyson on the road (black teacher, white student body); Bette Davis played the part in the American movie and opened out of town in a stage production with the black actor Dorian Harewood as the protagonist. It didn't go to Broadway.

* Emlyn Williams, *George: Early Autobiography* (London: Hamish Hamilton, 1961).

I'm sure lots of colored boys owe a debt of gratitude to some one teacher along the way who encouraged, stimulated, and befriended them to the point that, for that moment at least, they did better than their best and had more hope for their future.

I was not as "underprivileged" as the miner boy, but I was very uncertain about where I belonged in this world. There were perhaps ten colored boys at the High School of Commerce and I had a fairly "high profile" as a member of the school orchestra. I was also a member of the public library at Sixty-eighth Street and I read at least four books a week. I had set out to read through the fiction section alphabetically by author and had gotten to AIKEN, Conrad, when I looked in, curious, at the collection of the school library. I was surprised to find it quite extensive, especially considering it was a "commercial" high school library. One of the librarians, a stocky, bobbed-haired woman with blue-green eyes and freckles and a hockey-player gait, came up to me behind the desk, twinkling, and said, "Well, Heath, we were wondering when you were going to come and see us." I didn't confess that I had always been slightly intimidated by her hatchet-faced colleague who seemed to be guarding the books like Alberich guarding the Nibelungen gold, suspicious of the authenticity of boys taking commercial courses who only read books under the pressure of the reading list. I had heard the boys talking about her—the "dragon-lady." But there was mischief in the corner of Margaret Durand's Irish eyes and she was frankly curious about me. "You read a lot. I see you almost always with library books under your arm. I saw you reading crossing the street a while back." I told her about my alphabetical project. She said, "That's *one* way, I suppose. You haven't yet gotten to AUSTEN, Jane, then. You should read her before you're much older." She made out a library card for me and noted that *Pride and Prejudice* was being taken out under HEATH, Gordon's name. "I hate to think of another year passing and you still not having read her." That was the beginning. I would pass by at the end of the school day and we would talk. Miss Savacol, the dragon-lady, would return books to their shelves, turn out some of the lights, and end her working day as meaningfully as she could manage. Miss Durand would settle in to ask me what I had done and seen in the interim. She was also passionate about the theater and I would talk about the Broadway scene with easy fluency as if I were a regular theatergoer myself. Actually I was a regular review reader. Miss Durand caught on when I reported on a play that had closed a week earlier as if I had seen it the night before. She grinned at me. "Heath, why do you pretend? Why don't you *go* to the theater?" Horribly embarrassed I confessed that I felt unwelcome in presenting myself at the theater box offices. They made excuses just short of refusing to sell me a ticket. "I have one seat in the second balcony." They were avoiding the chance that this black boy in the orchestra would be rubbing shoulders with white patrons resenting his proximity and capable of complaining to the management. Miss D said, "Oh, come, Heath, you can see and hear very well even in the second balcony and it's better than not seeing the play at all. Would you like me to buy a ticket for you? No—I don't suppose you would be comfortable surrounded by people resenting your presence—but the important thing is to see the plays—even from the second balcony. It's cheaper too." I squirmed all through this dialogue and was reminded of my father's refusal to sit next to a black person in the subway or streetcar. He didn't want it to be taken for granted that he was "with" that person. He would rather stand. At fourteen my sense of irony was very faint but I made a connection between the two situations. Miss Durand didn't draw parallels. She had come to America from the "Old Country" when "help wanted" signs displayed the rider, "No Irish need apply" from the length of America's east coast and inland too, but she did not wince nor cry aloud. American intolerance was an old story to her. "According to your method you wouldn't be getting to this for a while but you should read it soon. It's a Bible for the stagestruck, well, the Old Testament at least," she said, changing the subject abruptly and proffering a thick volume: DANE, Clemence, *Broome Stages*. I stayed up late and got up early, neglecting homework, wolfing meals to finish the book, triumphantly, in two days! *Broome Stages* is about (and I hope you know, already) seven generations of English Shakespearean actors as they lived and worked and acted always at the top of their profession and the top of their lungs; touring, barnstorming, quarreling, and competing, knowing no God but Shakespeare and no temple but the theater. Their tempestuous private lives were lived in public. I had loved AUSTEN, Jane, but I was ecstatic about the Broomes. "Is it a true history? Are they real?" Miss Durand grinned at me. "It's a novel, Heath. No one family were monarchs like that. Clemence Dane made it up. But she's a playwright. She wrote a play about the Brontës and just before you began your theatergoing (she twinkled) Dane had a play on Broadway about Chatterton, the poet who died young. Dreadful doggerel, most of it, but Judith Anderson made her reputation in it." Suddenly I remembered I had heard Owen intoning,

I've got a date with Death
Isn't that fun for me
No more sun for me
I've got a date with Death

—that was Clemence Dane.

"Heath, I think you might find your reading more profitable if you'd let each book lead you to investigate its magnetic field, if you see what I mean. The Broomes lived through the reigns of the Charleses, the Hanovers, Victoria; they lived through the Edwards and the Georges. They experienced at least two major wars. They speak of Sarah Siddons, Joshua Reynolds, Thomas Gains-borough. There are accounts of performances of *The Merchant of Venice, Othello, Midsummer Night's Dream.* There are a multitude of references that would repay looking into if you could bring yourself to interrupt your alphabetical progress now and then. Do you see what I mean?" Yes, I saw what she meant: instead of accumulating titles I might accumulate knowledge—and an additional load of priggishness—"a little learning is a dangerous thing," said Pope. But my high school adventure was reading and identifying sources and investigating back-grounds. Miss Durand was producing her own librarian education and tech-niques for my benefit. I didn't want to be a librarian but "shallow draughts intoxicated my brain." Miss Durand led me to Willa Cather and Thomas Wolfe, but, most of all, to the long line of British novelists who very seldom made the list of American "recommended reading" lists: Trollope, Fielding, Virginia Woolf, Kenneth Grahame, Kipling, and, for sheer fun, E. F. Benson and P. G. Wodehouse. One of the best was H. H. Munro who, under his pen name "Saki," wrote a bundle of short stories from the viewpoint of a permanent adolescent dissecting law, order, and morality, the tyranny of the State, and any number of overbearing aunts and other relatives. He revenged himself on doctrine held essential in his time with glee, giggles, and epigrams, and like thousands of English schoolboys, I imbibed the subversive mockery, the cruelty, and the constant of irreversible class distinctions that an unpredicted world war would fragment and all but destroy in the unforeseeable future. Saki would become as rabid a flag-waver as any other blue-blooded Tory. He was killed at the Front, never to know that Labour and the proletariat would preside over the dissolu-tion of the Empire. Coincidentally, Emlyn Williams wound up his acting career more or less impersonating Saki and toured reading his stories—they stood up very well. The BBC did a series dramatizing the stories with great success. Casual readers know—from anthologies at least—"Tobermory," the story of a cat who has been taught to speak, proves to have heard and seen human beings at their worst, and will not be condescended to. The book of Saki is full of quotable material. "She was a good cook as good cooks go and as good cooks go—she went!" *That* was Saki.

Miss Durand became "Peg" to me—my own Miss Moffat with whom I tired the sun, and probably herself, with talking. She opened all those doors to me, bypassing the literary peaks, the Henry James, the Dostoyevskys, the Miltons, the Thomas Manns. I went on to them on my own afterward. I "discovered" the works of Charles Morgan, the London drama critic, essayist, novelist, and playwright whose stately prose earned him a membership in the intellectual altitudes of the Académie Française. His *Sparkenbroke* was my idea of a death-less novel. Today I'm not sure why. The themes of single-mindedness and the struggle of literary genius to be true to itself gripped me—or was it because he was *Lord* Sparkenbroke? My other literary hero was *Lord* Peter Wimsey! Everybody loves a Lord!

But Peg was directly responsible for my immersion in the life of literature and my turning away from life as it is lived. She met my parents. She did finally take me to the theater (I had plucked up enough courage to go myself before that) and when I was in the hospital having my appendix out, she came to visit and we talked about the future. I was all for going to college and I was deeply shocked when she said "Oh, Heath, I don't think you should consider college. It won't be any real use to you." After luring me into this world of intellectual exercise, into the heart of academe itself, she had decided I had gone far enough and my formal education should go no further. I was too shaken to argue the point but the next day when my folks came to visit I told them about Peg's advice. They both said, "That's a white woman talking. She doesn't think you have the capacity to receive a full education because you're colored." I hadn't thought of her as "a white woman" and I didn't think she thought of me as "a colored boy." But I lay in bed trying to see and think clearly. When I got out I went to City College of New York and registered for the next semester. I brought my high school record. They said "you must get into our orchestra." I pointed out that I had to work and could only attend college at night. They said that at least half of the orchestra was night school students; perhaps it could all be arranged. It was "arranged" and I began a new sort of nightlife in 1936, but it didn't feel like a big step forward. Neither the discipline nor the teaching itself met my expectations and when Owen invited me to Hampton I left CCNY without a backward glance.

I made no attempt to renew contact with Miss Durand until 1945 after I had played *Hamlet*. I walked into the Commerce library. Miss Durand came out from behind the desk and twinkled at me, "Well, Heath, it's been a long time." Indeed: I had left home, fallen in love, given up the violin, left college, and come out of my teens. I was too shy to try to go backward and pick up the stitches with any sophistication. She closed up the library and we went out together. I blurted out what my parents had said about her attitude to my going to college. She said "Heath, you are an *actor*. You were an actor when you graduated from high school. College would only be an interruption in your progress and that is the only reason I advised against it. But you never allowed us to be real friends. You never asked me anything about my own life. You didn't even concern yourself with the hell I was going through with Savacol!" (Savacol had left and the library was now Peg's to administer.) Of course I didn't think all that was any of my business and I was always too shy to consider myself an intimate of Peg's. I didn't feel I had anything to offer her at the level of a real friendship and that had nothing to do with her being "white." She hugged me and said, "Let's go to the theater next week. Are you free?" We went to the

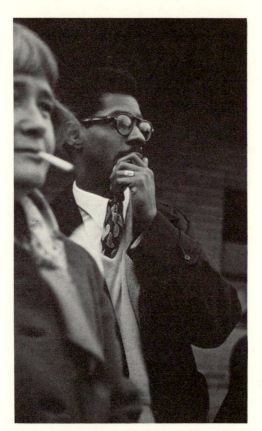

Margaret (Peggy) Durand and Gordon Heath at the airport in 1947. Heath was on his way to England and the British production of *Deep Are the Roots*.

theater and on from there. When I was appearing in *Roots* she went to the principal of Commerce and said, "You know, Heath is one of ours. You should ask him to speak to the assembly. He's a very articulate man and I think he would tell them many useful things." The principal sent me a formal invitation to address the assembly. I took as my text a passage from Proverbs: "Get wisdom. Get understanding. Forget it not. Wisdom is the principal thing, therefore get wisdom and with all thy getting, get understanding." I hope the speech was "useful." I was talking to myself as well. Peg and the principal were proud. The kids were animated and responsive. One of them asked me "Say, was you ever a comedian?" I kept it light and they laughed a lot. (Years later, Art Buchwald addressed the graduating class of the American College in Paris. He spent the time jabbing at the Nixon administration with his usual barbed wit. His audience was loudly appreciative. He ended up observing "You will ask what all that has to do with your graduating from this college. Well, when your friends ask you what you did on your graduation day you will tell them—you laughed.") [That made me cry then and I am crying as I write this, and dictate it, twenty years later.]

Peg came with my parents to see me off when I left for England. We corresponded over the years. I came back to New York in 1970 to play *Oedipus* at the Roundabout Theatre. She sat in the front row. My final exit was through the audience after being "blinded" but quite able to see under the make up. Peg had dissolved. Her lap was wet with tears—I saw clearly as I passed. For me it was the greatest moment of the run. I went back to Paris. Peg wrote she was going into a Catholic retreat in upstate New York. She was suffering from crippling arthritis. We continued to correspond but one day there was no answer to my letter.

Rosey Pool

Rosey Pool presented herself in my dressing room in Wyndham's Theatre in London in 1947 and claimed acquaintance with people I knew from America: Langston Hughes, W. E. B. DuBois, Muriel Smith, Vinette Carroll, and so on. "So on" was a swift tour of the horizon of the black British performers: Edric Connor, Aubrey Pankey, Elisabeth Welch. She dropped names with easy assurance and familiarity. She indicated that we ought to be friends and, after ten minutes, I agreed. We got to know each other in an association that lasted till her death in 1974.

Rosey was from Amsterdam. She had been one of Anne Frank's teachers. She was short and round (her dearest friends called her Roly, short for roly-poly), voluble, mischievous, and gregarious. She had escaped from a Nazi concentration camp during the war. She had taught her fellow prisoners Negro spirituals which she called "survival songs"—songs of faith, courage, and defiance: "Walk Together, Children," "Didn't My Lord Deliver Daniel," "By and By." She had established a correspondence with black American and Caribbean poets and writers. She understood the whole panorama of slavery in America—the efforts, the movements, the evolution of black and white relations. She could have been a professor of black studies in the 1940s, long before America decided it should know more about black history and achievement. I called her a curator of the Black World Museum. She owned or had read all the original writings about the black experience—Booker T. Washington to Chester Himes (some of whose works she translated into Dutch)—and she dealt in books in a collaboration with Paul Breman, also Dutch, who is still bringing his fine discrimination to bear in his antiquarian bookshop in London. Paul became a good friend and we have stayed in touch, meeting up at book fairs, channel crossings, and so on.

Rosey brought a bubbling vivacity and human warmth to her subject—anthropology and academics to one side. We went to the theater, concerts, poetry readings, dance recitals. She lived on Hampstead Heath, the highest part of London, pastoral and only slightly snob. Rosey was occupied, when we first

Rosey E. Pool

met, with welcoming her dear German friend, Isa, who had just arranged (painfully, I should think) to immigrate and establish residence in England. Isa was a doctor and became an X-ray specialist. She was a gaunt, Prussian lady, brusque and angular—tailored suits, short hair, and, in all matters, skeptical. She set herself up to contrast with Rosey. She was the vertical one against Rosey's spherical spontaneity—the Toklas to Rosey's literary Stein persona. The people who responded to Rosey's outgoing hospitality were narrowly observed by Isa and weighed against their pretensions. Rosey, being a flirt herself, was more easily seduced by charm and beauty. You had to prove yourself with Isa but she had her own little vanities and she was not armored from tip to toe, although she would have us believe she was. They were a great couple: European, trilingual, and free wheeling. Ro was an independent journalist/ critic for a Dutch newspaper and had useful contacts at the BBC and with the Dutch TV people. She set up a Negro poetry program with Muriel Smith and me for the BBC in 1950. Her newspaper asked her to do three interviews with Paris-based personalities: a French club owner, a French singer, and an American performer. She turned the project over to me, proposing to translate the whole thing into Dutch, submit it to her paper, and split the fees with me. It was typical of Rosey to take it for granted that I could produce that kind of journalism. She and the paper were pleased with the result. But she went much further. I had done a lead in a BBC TV drama called "For the Defense," playing a lawyer assigned to defend a white boy accused of starting a race riot. The idea of a black lawyer defending the boy appalls the boy's family and the boy himself is also hostile. The drama lies in the lawyer's tactics to convince the parents and the boy that he is on their side. (In London the boy was played by Vivian Matalon, who has since had a career as a director in America as well as in England.) The play was a great success. Rosey did a Dutch translation and sent it to Amsterdam TV. "Fine," they said, "but we have no one here to play the lawyer." Rosey got on the phone calling me in Paris from London: "Would you play it for us? I'll teach you the Dutch. You'll have to play it 'live' of course. I'll make a tape of the dialogue tonight"! It was a very expensive phone call. I laughed for five minutes to begin with. Then I said, "Yes. OK." We were both out of our minds. Isa told me afterward she had thought it a reckless gamble— but it turned out to be a triumph. I sailed through "Avocaat Pro Deo" with almost hysterical fright and impeccable (they said) Dutch.

Then Rosey wrote casually: "I'm putting together an anthology of poems by Negro writers who are not primarily poets. Do you have any hitherto un-published poems?" "Hitherto unpublished" summed up my poems exactly but I sent her three of the poems I had written to Lee in the 1940s. She used two of them in her anthology.* Argo Records in London made a twelve-inch LP from the collection and asked me to record, among others, my two poems.** Cleo Laine and Brock Peters were the other speakers—and I designed the record jacket as well. (I had designed the jacket for Rosey's book about Negro America, *Laughing to Keep from Crying****—the title taken from a Langston Hughes poem.) In 1958 Rosey and her London publisher, Erica Marx, asked me to stage an afternoon of black American poetry at the Royal Court Theatre in London (where John Osborne's plays were first put on). We got Cleo and Earle Hyman to perform. I chose the poems to make a panoramic collage of black life in America from slavery to Martin Luther King, choreographed the poems, and created a decor from my own blown-up woodcuts. The poems were predomi-nantly contentious battle hymns, not without humor and laced with irony. Fifteen hours of rehearsals—the poems committed to memory—a tour de force that introduced the British public to a body of literature they hardly knew existed, under the title "Black and Unknown Bards" from James Weldon John-son's proud poem:

O black and unknown bards of long ago,
How came your lips to touch the sacred fire?
How, in your darkness, did you come to know
The power and beauty of the minstrel's lyre?

* *Beyond the Blues.* Hand and Flower Press, 1962.
** *Beyond the Blues,* Argo Records, London.
*** *Lachem om niet te Huilen.* Lemniscaat. Rotterdam, 1968.

abbaye 3

gordon heath | sings spirituals

"Gordon Heath Sings Spirituals."
A 1961 record of spirituals,
"sung played and arranged by
Gordon Heath" (he also designed
the jacket). Lee Payant served as
musical adviser.

Rosey found ways to take Paris trips on expense accounts and I continued to work in London at intervals, so we'd always meet up to eat, drink, talk, plan. She and Isa were a vivacious audience at l'Abbaye and they loved my partner, Lee. When my mother came to France for a three-week holiday in 1954, I took her to London and she stayed with them for a week. They teased her gently, recognizing her timidity and unworldliness. Ro took her to one of Billy Graham's mammoth meetings. Mother was impressionable. Ro was Jewish. Lee's mother, also on holiday, considerably more experienced and open but exactly as naïve as mine, also stayed with them. Everybody loved everybody.

Ro set up a lecture tour for herself in America, speaking on university campuses about the world war, Negro spirituals, the concentration camps, and Anne Frank—kaleidoscopic, colorful, and minatory without pointing fingers or moralizing. She touched lightly on her past and equally lightly on her listeners' future and she herself was the embodiment of survival, cheerfulness, and hope. I had, of course, brought Owen and her together long before and he was around to help. She told the black students about themselves, their great African heritage, and their impressive creative contribution to America's culture.

I had known Ro for some fourteen years when, on a visit, I heard her singing with the radio. A revelation. She sang like a musician. I said, "I didn't know you sang, Rosey." She said, "I was the rehearsal pianist for the *Threepenny Opera* in Berlin. The Nazis broke the bones of my hands and I couldn't play any more." I was left with my mouth wide open. There wasn't a vestige of complaint or self-pity in the bald statement. I frequently tell that story to remind actors that the great personal tragedies are matter of fact in the recounting, and emotional display is out of place. The famous unuttered cry of Mother Courage when her dead son is brought to her for identification is witness.

Ro's last act as my Dutch impresario was to set up a half-hour TV show in a studio mock-up of l'Abbaye with Lee and me singing a typical session of ten or so songs to a live audience, half of whom had been to Paris and the club. It was not an exact replica and they couldn't capture the smoky intimacy of the real thing but it was a good try and Ro herself was in the frame for us to focus on. She booked me at the same time to do an Easter concert a few weeks later of Negro spirituals. I was beginning to feel like a Dutch expatriate in Paris! In the 1970s Rosey was stricken with pernicious anemia, directly traceable to her concentration camp deprivations. Modern medicine and Isa could not reverse the progress of the disease and Ro succumbed in a very short time. We saw her in London when she had just begun reporting daily to the hospital for treatment. When she died Isa made a strenuous effort to recover herself. She traveled and pursued her hobbies—book binding and collecting—but it was evident that she really didn't care and she outlived Ro by only a few years.

They were valuable people, lovely in their lives. They contributed an enormous amount to my European education, surrounding me with affection. Life is not the same without them.

Lee Payant

Three one-act plays rehearsing in the same building downtown were invited to be each other's audience for a semidress rehearsal. I don't remember the play I was acting in but the other two remain vivid in my memory. One of them featured an ominous installation: flashing lights, tape decks, illuminated name plates indicating major cities in the world—an underground top-secret bombing center, technologically the last word in atomic science, controlling thousands of missiles restively in space, targeting capital cities of both continents. We are to suppose that similar plants exist all over the world. A technical error occurs and the missiles start on their programmed way to exterminate city after city. Reprisals follow hard upon the first strike and one by one the cities are reduced to dust. The lights go out and so does the world—terrifying and prescient. But the third play, *Jerry, the Barber*, whose argument I remember not at all, had in the cast a young, dark-haired actor, hair and moustache streaked with white powder all as unconvincing as his angular impersonation of a settled middle-aged man—which he clearly was not. Afterward we all mingled. He took off his false moustache and combed out the powder. I said to myself: "That will do nicely for this evening." I walked over to him and said, "Didn't I meet you in a dance group uptown?"—a deliberately transparent ploy. He said, "No," visibly disconcerted and retreated to the farthest wall. Not playing the game—and from that moment a challenge. I reached for him again, "Can we have coffee together downstairs?" "Maybe tomorrow, I have to go home early tonight."

Lee Payant, 1949

Hardly a provocative dialogue and not really encouraging but my pride was now ahead of my desire and I intended to win the match although, perhaps, conceding this round. I was not accustomed to rejection. The next night he did have coffee downstairs with me. His name was Leroy Payant, commonly called "Lee." He didn't like "Leroy" as Americans usually pronounced it. It should be "Le*roy*" he insisted. His grandmother was French. He was from Seattle, discharged from the navy and intensely stagestruck. He knew me, had seen *Roots,* was impressed that I was interested in him but reluctant to get involved. I spread my peacock feathers, dropped names, invented productions I might use him in, suggested roles he might think in terms of in general, avoided any mention of *Jerry, the Barber,* and campaigned with what Dorothy Parker might have called "degenerate cunning." "Coffee downstairs" became a nightly ritual. He lived with a navy friend's older sister and brother-in-law in an apartment house downtown and worked as a secretary in the firm managed by the brother-in-law. When the navy friend came to the performance I saw that he was *the* friend—a reserved and serious Harvard graduate on the way to becoming a writer, slightly younger than Lee. He was not without humor and detachment and saw, I would think, exactly what I was up to—and I was certainly up to a great deal. I saw Lee every day, visited him, went to the theater with him, wrote letters to him, ate meals with him, and—classically—fell into the pit I was digging for him. I wrote three poems to him, sounding the depth of my involvement and a fourth implying resignation to whatever plane of friendship he decided upon. He fell ill—a version of the flu, but I think the result of his inner conflict: the loyalty and love for his friend and his increasing regard for and attraction to me. To say I chased him and chased him until he caught me might be a spectator observation, but I don't think Lee ever "plotted." He was open, gregarious, sincere, impressionable, devoted to his craft, and younger than youth. I went to see him on his sickbed—sunken cheeks, shadows under the eyes. I ached.

When he recovered he had made his decision. (We were to live and work together for thirty years in Paris—and I never called him anything else but Leroy!)

I had my *Hamlet* foils hung in memoriam on my bedroom wall. Lee and I would fence on my flat graveled roof—for fun and, I suppose, to remind ourselves that we were classical actors. Lee was studying with Tamara Daykahanova who presided over a no-frills acting course and was especially attentive to Lee's progress. She suggested that he audition for Margaret Webster who was putting together a company to tour *Hamlet* and *Macbeth* to the four corners of the states and English-speaking Canada. Lee and I carved out a scene from *Hamlet* with the King, Ophelia, and Laertes, leaving Ophelia invisible but allowing us to react to her madness. (Miss Webster said, when she came to Paris years later, she often wished *she* could have done it that way!) Miss Webster held her auditions in the Columbus Circle theater where she and Eva LeGallienne had made a gallant effort to establish a repertory theater with *Androcles, What Every Woman Knows, John Gabriel Borkman, Alice in Wonderland, Henry VIII*, and *Yellow Jack* before vanishing from the scene.

I have never seen so many would-be performers in one place. The auditions were wide open, extended to all comers. While Lee and I were biting our nails in the lobby in the midst of those almost-hysterical applicants, a girl came up to Miss Webster, open book in her hand: "Miss Webster, does Ophelia really *sing* this stuff?" A very harassed "Miss W" put her arm around the girl's shoulder, guided her to the door saying, almost lovingly, "My dear, you *can't* be serious about wanting a career in the theater!" Exit girl but enter Lee who Miss W cast then and there.

◆ From WMCA to Broadway

In 1945 WMCA, a decorous radio station just beginning to handle "commercials," advertised that it was holding open auditions for a Negro staff announcer. I don't know whose idea that was or how many people they auditioned for how long. They chose me. That made me the first black radio announcer in America. Jubilant parents, delighted friends, gratified and hopeful black performers were encouraged by the breakthrough. Some of them wrote me to say so. Newspaper columnists in the black and white press remarked approvingly upon WMCA's pioneering gesture.

I was less thrilled. I didn't feel that radio announcing was that high on the social scale or that that was where I wanted to be ultimately. I had had a long apprenticeship on NYA as an announcer by this time. I had played regularly on the Ave Maria Hour and in lots of the radio dramas, very seldom playing black parts. (In fact, very few scripts included black roles.) I recognized the importance of this job, racially speaking—the letters alone would have been convincing proof if any was needed. My father, who never thought acting would pay the rent, was reassured that I was now in a secure position with prestige thrown in for good measure. What is more, I was told unofficially but authoritatively that there were no runners-up from the auditions, which meant that there was no guarantee that if I left another black would be hired.

I didn't want to be an example or a symbol.

Working at WMCA was more fun than I anticipated, mostly because they were such nice, casual guys who treated me like a fellow announcer and took me for granted as such. They were impressed with my musical background and saw to it that I announced most of the classical music broadcasts. They were grateful not to have to grapple with Shostakovich, Debussy, Halévy, and Lehár in the same paragraph followed by footnotes that works were to be played

NATIONALLY FAMOUS DANCER, FIRST STARTED DANCING LESSONS WHILE ATTENDING HUNTER COLLEGE. IN THREE YEARS SHE DANCED HER WAY TO FAME. A COLLEGE GRADUATE, A CANDIDATE FOR A MASTERS DEGREE, A WELDER - CLERK-ATHLETE - TEACHER AND FINALLY A DANCER.

"THIS IS STATION WMCA"

GORDON HEATH THE FIRST NEGRO STAFF ANNOUNCER FOR A MAJOR NEW YORK RADIO STATION-WMCA. A NOTED ACTOR AND ASS'T DIRECTOR OF THE AMERICAN NEGRO THEATRE

"Interesting People," by Geo. L. Lee, *New York Amsterdam News* (October 27, 1945)

allegro maestoso and *vivace ma non troppo*. They were perfectly capable of handling all that, but they felt that it was really where I lived.

I was closest perhaps with Ernie Stone who had theatrical ambitions. When it emerged that we were born on the same day, same year, we celebrated by writing songs together. He wrote lyrics, I wrote tunes. We knew those songs would never make the Hit Parade but we had fun. My best friend at the station was Dr. Frank Kingdon, a political-philosophical commentator who had regular fifteen-minute spots to talk pungently about whatever was on his mind— very much in the vein of those lucid, liberal speakers at the Ethical Culture Society. I was a most devoted listener, both in and away from the studio. He might have been the one who persuaded WMCA it should have a Negro announcer but he didn't say so.

We were intensely conscious of *time* at the station. Ten seconds of "dead air" would provoke a crisis. The huge second hands of the omnipresent clocks were the silent sentinels and at least one eye was permanently swiveled in their direction. Even before WMCA became a "commercial" station, time meant a great deal of money. WMCA prided itself on its program discipline and split-second timing. One day a week we were, in turn, responsible for beginning the broadcasting day, cheerfully and fluently at seven in the morning! The engineers stood ready to launch recorded music to fill in, in case of announcer tardiness. It was the moment of truth for all of us night-lifers.

The owner of the station, Nathan Straus, conducted his affairs from the floor above, keeping in touch by means of memoranda that were usually irrelevant non sequiturs. He hardly ever seemed to know exactly what went on in a radio station. The announcers greeted his bulletins with glee and affection and couldn't wait to pass them on to the other departments. Years after I left, they were still quoting my contribution to the Nathan Straus lore:

I found myself going up in the elevator with Mr. S. He cleared his throat, "I hear you've got an important part in a Broadway play. I understand you're playing the part of a Negro!" That convulsed the entire staff.

I gave notice to WMCA after six months to go into rehearsal with *Deep Are the Roots*. They called it a "leave of absence" and Mr. S wrote me to say they would hold the job open for me. I never went back. My father thought it was very risky—giving up a job to do a play. I, of course, did not think of it that way.

I lived secretly, hugging grievances, chiefest of which was that Eddie was not Alex (who in the meantime had married). Eddie, on the other hand, mistrusted, my handling him (justifiably), recognized my posturing, scorned my hypocrisy for what it was, gave immediate expression to his own impulses, and drank much more than I thought was good for him. I was often the reason for his heavy drinking. He said he would like us to be alone on a desert island—just us—"no other people." "Other people" was the burden of his deep bitterness. I was not a "desert island" person and though I pretended otherwise, I was prey to many passing fancies. I loved the image of domesticity we presented to our world but in the long run it was too much like matrimony and I was up against Eddie's violent possessiveness. It was thrilling to be loved like that but agony was a by-product for both of us, especially because on most other levels we were a good couple. Eddie and I were born under the same sign. We were born a year and two days apart and I suppose were too much alike to live together harmoniously. We were both proud, jealous, and possessive. My discipline helped to smooth many of his rough edges. He learned a great deal about theater itself; he began to organize his talent and separate instinct from creation. I was "big brother" and sometimes resented because of it. When I was directing *The Little Foxes* and he was playing Cal, I nagged him to play it as it was played on Broadway. He resisted and found another vein of naiveté in Cal that suited him exactly. I learned not to attempt to insist on my own conception when it would do violence to the temperament and nature of the actor in question. The director must stretch his imagination to discover what the actor has in common with the role and proceed from that basis. You cannot or at least should not bully an actor into a performance. After *Foxes* Nathalie Donnet proposed an evening of one-act plays and scenes at the YMHA. I directed Tennessee Williams's *This Property Is Condemned* and a scene from Barrie's *The Old Lady Shows Her Medals*. Nathalie directed Eddie in a monologue from *Macbeth*. They both knew I would not have considered Eddie in the role—not even a monologue. In the event, he was impressive—brooding and haunted.

Eddie resented my condescension and I recognized that there was an underlying sense of competition in our relationship. In spite of the profound satisfactions of our life together there were always hostilities just under the surface. Eddie found employment in the WPA "work" program and was assigned to a street project in the middle of a rough winter. He wore two pairs of socks, two pairs of pants, heavy underwear, a wool shirt, a heavy sweater, a long overcoat, a battered felt hat, gloves, and mittens. He hated cold weather to begin with. "Don't bury me in the ground—let me burn!" I made a caricature of him dressed for work and wrote a parody of the "looking for a home" boll weevil to go with it. Although I conceived it all with much affection—even admiration—for his hardihood, he thought I was making fun of him, which was a reflection of the layers of mistrust that existed. I got exasperated with his menacing temper and one day we fought, literally, in that tiny apartment. It was not a bloody occasion but a centimeter of Eddie's earlobe was on the floor before we pulled ourselves together and laughed and cried at our idiocy. It did not mark the end of our relationship. It might even have cleared the air a bit, but Eddie was drafted shortly afterward and was shipped to Italy in an all-black troop. He wrote to me noncommittal letters, only sketchily describing his experiences and telling me not much about himself except to say he would probably marry Loretta when he got out. I pointed out that he was in no position to predict how he would be thinking when the war was over. He came back to the apartment: confined, restless, and ten pounds heavier. He came to *Roots* and saw through my performance—that is to say, he saw *me*. He, I knew, would not have cast me as Brett Charles. He was, nevertheless, pleased with my success. We mounted *Family Portrait* together and picked up our life more or less from the point it had been interrupted. Nothing had changed. I was still behaving like my father's son.

He would watch me go through a day as if I were perpetually performing for an audience. He said my actions were so stylized and controlled that I would end up eternally separated from reality—and that if I was endeavoring to make myself as unlike my father as possible—*that* wasn't working either. He would catch me being my father and call me "Cyril Heath"—a very discomforting but unmalicious tease.

When Lee came into my life, Eddie at first gave himself over to rage and revenge, although later he and Lee became friends to the extent that friendship was possible under the circumstances. I went to Paris in 1948 and Lee went on tour with Margaret Webster. Eddie looked up his father, worked in summer stock, and went out with Webster's second bus-and-truck tour in 1949.

I learned a lot from Eddie—although not about the holiness of the heart's affection, which he tried so desperately to teach me; not at that time anyway. His rare comic gifts, his instinctive timing, the directness with which his primary impulses animated his body, his openness and vulnerability—all these were object lessons in themselves.

> As things stand now, *Walls of Jericho* looks like it will be the first show to hit Broadway with Negro actors in the cast. Since the play was announced a month ago, it has been discovered by the producers Kermit Bloomgarden and George Heller that this title belongs to the late Rudolph Fisher who wrote a novel by that name some years ago. So the play title will be changed. Meanwhile, Elia Kazan begins directing it Aug. 13. It is written by Arnaud D'Usseau and James Gow, the same two writers who wrote *Tomorrow the World.* Evelyn Ellis and Gordon Heath have two of the three Negro parts, the third one, the role of an impish young house girl is still unassigned. I have read the script. Dealing with a young Negro lieutenant who returns to the south after being honorably discharged from the army, *Jericho,* according to the script the producers asked me to read, is magnificent adult and timely theatre which is not one of these down home tragedies. Our people will go all out for it. Paradoxically, it may be the other people who will squirm this time. But more about *Jericho* later. It is due on B'way about Sept. 24.—Abram Hill, columnist and director of the American Negro Theatre in Harlem, *New York Amsterdam News,* August 11, 1945.

I never knew (and never asked) how I came to be chosen out of the fifty or more aspirants for the role in *Roots:* the publicity surrounding my announcing job? My photograph in *Theatre Arts* as Hamlet? Lieutenant Charles was a far cry from Shakespeare and I was a far cry from being southern, tough, or militant. The producer and director must have been at least as wary as I. The other roles were filled by veterans of staggering competence and acres of professional experience. Evelyn Ellis, playing my mother, was the original Bess in *Porgy.* Charles Waldron, the southern senator, had had a long career in films and theater—Mr. Barrett of Wimpole Street himself. Lloyd Gough, the hard-bitten northern journalist, had been playing swaggering Irishmen for a decade, Helen Martin, the maid, had played a lead in Orson Welles's production of Richard Wright's *Native Son,* Carol Goodner had acted in London in John Gielgud's company—notably "Masha" in Chekhov's *The Three Sisters.* I was in the producer's office the day she was given a script. After reading ten pages she took off her hat, ran her hands through her hair, and said: "Something will have to be done about this—light blonde, I think." She was making out a grocery list, matter of fact, professional, intimidating—especially to an actor whose Broadway experience consisted of making forest sounds and speaking and singing gibberish (offstage). The other almost unknown lead was Barbara Bel Geddes (daughter of Norman Bel Geddes, the architect and stage designer) who bubbled and glowed and displayed a wide grin that fetched and carried for her.

The next publicity trumpeted the news that a play called *Deep Are the Roots*

In its October 15, 1945, issue, *Vogue* magazine did a feature on *Deep Are the Roots*. The article included a picture of James Gow and Arnaud D'Usseau, the authors, and Gordon Heath, the lead.

written by —— to be directed by —— with ——. That was us! new aphoristic title and all.

The lieutenant, Brett Charles, was brought up on a postbellum plantation where his mother is the housekeeper in a household comprising two sisters, their father, an unreconstructed senator, retired from politics but obviously KKK material. The older sister, Alice, is liberally enlightened by way of her conscience and the younger sister, Genevra, is open-minded by way of her youth and instinct. The maid, Honey, is spirited and light-minded.

Alice has busied herself with Brett's education, at least to the point of giving him a note allowing him access to the local library and treating him as one of the family as nearly as Poppa's strictures will allow. She has also arranged that Brett become principal of the local black school. Brett and Genevra can be said to have grown up together, but when, as children, they were observed playing scenes from *Othello,* they were gently but firmly wrenched apart—Brett's mother and Alice, for their separate reasons, in absolute agreement about the un-suitability of this recreation.

The play begins as Brett, military hero, is on his way home. Alice has her northern journalist fiancé as a houseguest and "Nevvy," defying her father, has gone to the station to meet Brett. (The senator has said to Nevvy "one does not go to the station to meet a colored man," Q.E.D.) Brett is warmly welcomed by Alice and her fiancé—the latter going so far as to shake hands with him! Brett is sharply aware that he is back in the South and that the simple warmth and acceptance he knew in Europe is not a feature of southern hospitality. He plays cool but goes to the public library without a note from "Miss Alice," frightens the librarian out of her negligible wits just by being there, and precipitates a scandal that is relayed to the family by the unrighteously indignant "Cousin Roy." Alice finds it all ridiculous but doesn't understand why Brett didn't ask her for a note. He explains that it is not becoming for a grown man to be treated like a barefoot pickaninny and though Alice has to concede the point, she is disquieted. The roots are very deep indeed. When Nevvy confesses that she is in love with Brett, Alice has a blinding rush of southern blood to the brain and abets her father in framing Brett for the theft of his gold watch. The senator intimidates the maid into testifying that she has found the watch in Brett's room. The sheriff and posse arrive, knock Brett unconscious, and haul him off to jail. Brett, released and ordered to get out of town, confronts Alice and defines and denounces her hypocrisy. In fact, the last moments of the play are a series of confrontations. Nevvy confronts Brett and asks him—on her knees—to marry her. Brett's mother confronts Alice to tell her a few home truths about white men and black women. Alice's fiancé tells her she has been untrue to her best self and victim of her instinctive racism. The senator confronts and defies them all, puts on his panama hat, pulls himself up by his cane, and goes out into the night to join his clan. Brett, though in love and loving, tells Nevvy he cannot marry her because he has pledged himself to work for his people and the South is his home. He cannot marry a white woman and function effectively as a militant black. The year, you will remember, was 1945.

And so, into rehearsal: Kazan—now "Gadge"* (short for "gadget," his Yale nickname) to all of us—short, stocky, ebullient, second-generation Greek, dynamic and demanding. Gadge took me over exactly where Strasberg had left off. The arm around the shoulder, the burrowing down into Brett's childhood through his war and all the nuances of life in the Big House, the persuasive analysis to extract what was in me to apply to Brett. He brought me newspaper clippings about the treatment of Negro troops abroad—their acceptance by their European hosts, their lionization in England, their fraternization with white girls, their integration into a new multiracial army, and the built-in resistance to equality in America and the fear that they would be something less than docile upon their return.

In a way, Gadge taught me what it meant to be black. He instructed me in "négritude" in the forties. He directed me with the same intensity with which

---

* He spells it "Gadg" in his autobiography but I never saw that spelling in any other publication and I cannot pronounce it in his version!

Lenny Bernstein conducted Dvořák—demanding and getting in return love and dogged application.

He dug beneath the melodrama and the polemics. He situated the characters, one by one, in their ways of life—their convictions, their instincts, their prejudices, their illusions—and set them down on stage to pursue their own purposes. When those purposes collided, the eruptions were volcanic. Slavery, the Civil War, Reconstruction, and the Second World War itself pointed and hardened all the hatreds and the guilt. The play's action was set in the now and we were all living, as well as working, in that context. Gadge's genius lay in collaborating with the actors to explore the inner life of the play's characters and ultimately to portray people rather than archetypes. It was a characteristic Group Theatre approach but Gadge's personal, individual intensity made it a love affair with seven actors, each of whom required different means of seduction.

The actors had been chosen for their "suitability" to the roles, of course, but no one was allowed to coast on personality, professionalism, or experience. Evelyn, for instance, was warned that, although she was the housekeeper, she was a responsible, dignified, authoritative figure—loyal but not subservient and entirely aware of the crosscurrents. She was not to exploit the easy, over-employed acting tricks, the cackling slyness of the black servant, the folkloric mammy.

Barbara and I, young and eager, reacted joyously to Gadge's probing invention. He said to me at the beginning: "I want you to take that guitar out of your dressing room and leave it home! I don't want soft influences around you. I want you *hard*." I worked for *hardness*. Two weeks after we opened he came backstage and said: "O.K., Gordon, it's hard enough." One of the actors asked me if I had noticed I was playing half the love scenes with my back to Barbara and suggested it was a Kazan mannerism. I was bold enough to ask him about it. "You've got a hard-on, that's why!" I was certain, even then, that it was an improvised reply—but it sufficed.

I don't think though that he managed to seduce the venerable Charles Waldron. The role of the southern senator was written with broad strokes that summed up an attitude but didn't create a person. Mr. W was never happy with the *Uncle Tom's Cabin* villain aspect of the role. He was an old, tired, bitter man playing an old, tired, bitter man and he felt the falsity of the dénouement invited disbelief. The authors rewrote but couldn't restructure—the senator was the fulcrum of the plot.

Kazan had a firsthand acquaintance with Broadway, having previously directed at least two of its sacred monsters: Tallulah Bankhead, perhaps more monster, and Helen Hayes, more sacred, but both VIP's in the Broadway parade.

Roots was clearly his meat—all those larger-than-life situations, all those out-sized passions hinged to a profound social and political commitment in the tradition of the Group Theatre, the Stanislavsky Method and the fermenting off-Broadway theater of protest. Gadge's gift for keeping a tension pulsing underneath the text and the action clothed and unified the whole.

Rehearsals gathered momentum and intensity. My script was crosshatched with notations recording Gadge's injunctions—not where I was meant to be on stage but the intentions and motivations that colored each delivery and the silences during which decisions were made. Gadge said: "In life you are always thinking, choosing, but you are always doing it at the same time you're moving, reacting, speaking. Those silences are rehearsal tools. They will be narrowed down to a half a second by the time you are playing the role. You don't *stop* to think—you go on thinking no matter what." (Brando, amusingly enough, frequently seems to stop to think, but then he is usually playing a character who thinks slowly!) My script, by the way, consisted of "sides"—pages containing only my lines and the cues that preceded them—a discipline that helped one avoid anticipating what one was going to meet or provoke from line to line. Of course, repeated rehearsal filled in the blank spaces but the habit of flexibility and spontaneity had been established.

In general Gadge directed the actors individually and privately. I wished I could eavesdrop—there was surely much to be learned, especially Gadge's repositioning in relation to each actor. He was an actor himself—in fact it was he who brought the news of Lefty's death when the union was waiting for Lefty* long before Godot was in question. But Gadge never acted out a line or a scene during our rehearsals—not that I saw, anyway. My fellow actors encouraged without criticizing. Carol took me by the shoulder at one point saying: "This is your scene. You must take over." Then she taught me to "upstage" her. Upstaging consists of getting your fellow actor in a position slightly in front and to one side of you so you can speak, look, play directly to the house in the most advantageous position. Tales are told of actors upstaging each other until they both end up at the back wall! Movie actors do something like it to dominate in camera shots. A movie kiss, for instance, is a matter for debate. Two profiles? Whose nose is closest to the camera? A shot as the leading lady looks over her lover's inexpressive back? Or do we do a matching shot to give him his advantage? Timid beginners find themselves overshadowed, blocked, diminished, but Carol unselfishly took me in hand and taught me how to "take stage."

Gadge came to me the week before we opened: "Gordon, don't forget you're the star of this play—it is about you, and you must come on as an important

* *Waiting for Lefty,* by Clifford Odets, was a Group Theatre production (1942) about a taxi drivers' strike during the Depression.

presence—*the* important presence, in fact." How about *that* as a snow job?! I thought then and I still think that the play is about a southern gentlewoman who has always thought of herself as an active liberal without prejudices and is finally revealed to herself as instinctively racist. Carol placed herself as a proud, competent character actress who would, ideally, not be recognized from one role to another as the same person. She sank herself into the part and gave a beautiful, detailed, and honest performance but she didn't think of herself as the star and her first-act dress was drab and Barbara Bel Geddes emerged as the star of this particular piece. (During the run Carol became rancorous and difficult, partly because the reviews acclaimed Barbara and took Carol for granted—but I am ahead of my narrative). Much was rewritten; much was redirected. Gadge and the authors worked in close collaboration. The producers worried—and quite possibly prayed. In any case, Kermit Bloomgarden lost a lot of weight before opening night. His property was highly combustible, controversial, ground-breaking material and it was expensive. He felt he had purchased the finest ingredients available but he could not vouch for the eating thereof.

We were to open in Princeton, New Jersey. We learned that the hotel would not accept the three blacks with the rest of the company. Panic, dismay, and fury. The management begged us not to make an issue of it. The play and its message were more important—not only to them but to us, they argued. We agreed and to everyone's credit, not a word of this ironic Jim Crow got to the press—at anytime—so far as I know. By the afternoon of dress rehearsal the set was not quite ready. We rehearsed, tensely, two- and three-person key scenes on the stairs and in the lobby of the theater.

Opening night performance in Princeton was smooth, assured, and—certainly as far as the blacks were concerned—determined. We'll show 'em! The house was warm and intent. On to Philadelphia, where Edmund Lowe and June Havoc were opening across the street in a whodunit. We wowed them in Philly. Gadge called a rehearsal the day of opening night at the Fulton in New York (later the Helen Hayes, since torn down). We played in front of a Broadway first-night audience that was with us from the first-act clash to the last-act reconciliation. The house roared, applauded, and stamped. Not my mother and father—they were too busy weeping with pride. It was before this irritating perfunctory present moment of standing ovations but there was on the other hand not much reaching for hats and coats. They were discussing the play in the aisles!

The critics were, for the most part, rapturous. They hailed the play as the first serious contribution to the 1945 season, pointed out that the plotting was awkward, the climax forced, the direction sometimes slow but powerful and the whole—riveting! Stark Young, a scion of the South, writing in the *New Republic,* did not feel the accents, the atmosphere, or the locutions were at all southern. He exempted Barbara, implying that she had found the authentic rhythm. (I think that Gadge has a kind of insensitivity to speech flavors—Method practitioners tend to bypass such problems—but that is material for a whole chapter.) Young did not, of course, accept the character of the senator. It was crudely drawn. He should have been a gentleman first and a gentlemanly racist afterward. One knew what he meant.

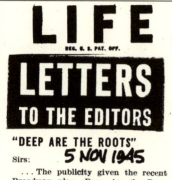

LIFE
REG. U. S. PAT. OFF.
LETTERS
TO THE EDITORS

"DEEP ARE THE ROOTS"

Sirs: **5 NOV 1945**

... The publicity given the recent Broadway play, *Deep Are the Roots* (LIFE, Oct. 15), is most repugnant to every Southerner. *Deep Are the Roots* has two very patent untruths upon which its plot is based: 1) No self-respecting Southern girl of a good family as Genevra Langdon is supposed to come from would ever fall in love with a Negro even if he whipped the Germans and the Japs singlehanded, and 2) reactionary Senator Langdon, as you dub him, would have been joined by as many good Southerners as could have congregated around him to help ride the Negro Brett Charles out of town on a pole. ...

W. DIXON DOSSETT
Beulah, Miss.

Sirs:

... Please accept my grateful commendation on the yeoman service LIFE magazine is performing for the cause of democracy in this country. Ever mindful of the tremendous influence you wield in shaping public opinion, you have zealously attempted to portray the news in accordance with democratic tenets in a free society.

... We are especially pleased with your reporting of the current Broadway drama, *Deep Are the Roots*. We feel that the dissemination of news concerning such a play will play an extremely beneficial role in facilitating the rehabilitation and readjustment of returning Negro veterans into community patterns, meanwhile pointing out and emphasizing the variance between professed democratic ideals and actual practice.

JULIUS W. ROBERTSON
Washington, D. C.

My own notices were good enough but one or two of them spoke of the "simple dignity" of my playing. An irritating formula. What about the burning determination, the stored-up resentment, the hardening resolve? "Simple dignity" meant I was stiff and Abram Hill said so in the *Amsterdam News* after seeing the play in Princeton. He did add: "but knowing the way this actor works I am sure he will loosen up by the time the play reaches Broadway." Well, maybe. Gadge was warmly complimentary about the performance and since he gave me no notes I supposed he meant what he said. He had warned the cast not to try to use what they read in reviews to alter their performance. The same went for gratuitous spectator advice. He had given me goals to reach all through rehearsals and though he was no longer there I continued to reach for those goals and perform for him all through the run—and I never brought my guitar back to the dressing room!

The run began and Kermit Bloomgarden got back his lost weight and his investors' money (after forty-five performances). Opening night my pal from WMCA Dr. Frank Kingdon, took

Deep Are the Roots drew various responses from its audiences.

me and my parents for supper at Café Society Uptown. Management, staff, and clients applauded when we entered—a heady, never-to-be-forgotten moment. It was only the beginning. The Negro and the white press referred to me always as "the star of *Deep Are the Roots*" (*and* Barbara *and* Carol *and* Evelyn) and every protest group asked me to appear in their support—from the Urban League to the NAACP. I didn't necessarily have to speak—my presence would suffice. I have a newspaper photograph of me looking over Dashiell Hammett's shoulder as he signs an anti-Bilbo petition.* Owen wrote "freedom rallies" performed in Madison Square Garden. I narrated, and at the climax Adam Clayton Powell, Baptist minister and eventually a New York congressman, unleashed his oratorical evangelism that roused the rabble to support, contribute, proselytize, and scream themselves hoarse about that new world a-coming.

Lillian Smith's *Strange Fruit* opened on Broadway the same season. It was another white-and-black play with Jane White and Mel Ferrer, but it suffered from being second on line. Robert Ardrey's *Jeb* the next year, with the estimable Ossie Davis, was equally strong in atmosphere, but it lacked the slick MGM sheen of *Roots,* and it disappeared after thirty-nine performances. *Strange Fruit* lasted long enough for Lillian Smith to propose a party, saying, "I don't see why our casts can't be friends," which was evidence of her good will but slightly unrealistic. Broadway had room for only one black-and-white protest play at a time. *Strange Fruit* played fifty-two performances. Mel Ferrer eventually married Audrey Hepburn and Jane and I played together with mutual admiration in *Peer Gynt* as the Troll King and his daughter and in an ANT [American Negro Theatre] play about the clash between Lincoln and his charismatic Civil War general McClellan, who was as arrogant as Gen. Douglas MacArthur in Japan. Jane played Mrs. Lincoln with tight-lipped precision and we had long; solemn discussions about the possibilities of playing non-Negro roles. Jane was especially disadvantaged, being too light skinned to be your next-door Negro and not sufficiently fine featured to pass as a white. Much later, when the theater operated in an entirely changed, desegregated context, Jane played Shakespeare and Strindberg and many etceteras, including the musical *Once Upon a Mattress*. Canada Lee, in the audience of *The Washington Years* (D.C. not George) was reported to have observed: "What's-his-name looks just like McClellan!" "What's-his-name" was me, and Canada's neat put-down might have enlightened Miss Lillian Smith a bit about being "friends" in the theater!

The party took place. Miss Smith was stately and gracious but she needn't have bothered. The notable party was the one we gave ourselves. Evelyn sang,

* Theodore Bilbo was a reactionary southern senator; Dashiell Hammett, author of *The Thin Man* and numerous other detective stories, served a six-month jail term for contempt of Congress just before the McCarthy period.

Gordon sang; Helen Martin regaled us all with a series of vignettes from *Roots* with impressions of everyone in the cast. Satirical, hilarious, deeply cruel because deeply accurate. (Fortunately, we didn't play the next day.) Helen caught Carol's highhandedness, Barbara's impulsive innocence, Lloyd's "aw shucks" Gary-Cooper casualness, Evelyn's motherly swooping, my solemnity— a gallery of caricatures mounted like pinned butterflies. We laughed, wet-eyed—admiring, but not of ourselves. Helen, who didn't know him, was my father to the life. I learned a great deal from her impersonation but I needed more than the one day—we all did—to recover my amour propre. "Simple dignity" indeed!

Mr. Waldron left us and Eddie Jerome gave us a paid-up Mafia-chief sena-tor—and to hell with magnolia blossoms and mint juleps! On the other hand, Barbara's replacement was actually from Alabama—like Tallulah. Frances Wal-ler made four syllables of Br-e-e-tt and Stark Young might have been mollified.

I missed—or almost missed—an entrance one night. *The* entrance when the sheriff and his posse lurk downstairs to arrest Brett. Howard and Alice stand transfixed, the senator gloats, and for that moment no one on stage breathes as Brett comes down. Well, they held their breaths this night for an interminable twenty seconds while the stage manager shrieked my name to the upstairs dressing room. The on-stage suspense was way beyond anything Gadge had created. During the post mortems—the curtain down, the tension lifted—Lloyd said to Carol, "What were you doing in that wait?" "Praying, Lloyd, what else?!" I had done the unforgivable, but they all forgave me. I also came in the theater after the half-hour call often enough to be warned that they would put on my understudy if I did it again. One rainy night I started out late, couldn't get a taxi, arrived five minutes after the half hour. Jimmy Edwards, my understudy, was tying Brett's uniform tie in my dressing room. I watched the performance from out front. All things considered, he and the play made a solid impression. I felt he had more thrust than I and was closer to Brett's inner rage than I ever would be. Brett was a very good role with built-in sympathy and the experience should have rid me of conceit but I was more resentful than chastened. I had asked the management in the ninth month of the run if they would put Jimmy on for a matinée performance so I could see Laurence Olivier's *Oedipus*. The Old Vic from London was in town and that was the only chance I would have. Nothing doing. They wouldn't allow it. I held that against them—forever after.

Carol was disgruntled and spitting fire backstage and in dressing rooms. She gave a performance one night that was obviously so out of control we were terrified she would fall into the orchestra pit. She said all the words in the right places but she held on to the furniture and us and reached a state of exaggerated animation and irresponsibility painful to watch and impossible to play to. I was devastated. I had never seen a performer in this condition and I loved her. Cool, capable, and controlled Carol was maudlin and sentimental and the play went down the drain that night. Carol came out of the show and was replaced by her understudy and soon after, Barbara O'Neill (Mrs. O'Hara in *Gone with the Wind*) was playing Alice. Her playing was smooth and professional, but I thought more aware of camera angles than subtexts.

I went to see Carol in a Broadway revue a month or so later. She was competent and adequate but she was not really a revue artist and it was, on the whole, a sad occasion. I visited her at home where she was irrationally bitter about *Roots* but told me that the death two months after we opened of Robert Benchley, her great and good friend and drinking buddy, was a blow from which she had not recovered. I had no idea how much of the situation *that* explained but she didn't enlarge upon it and she was, with me at least, the same warm, spontaneous pal as she always had been.

Kermit Bloomgarden gave us to understand that *Roots* had been bought by Tennents Ltd in London but it had not been decided who was going to go with it. Nothing was certain. (Nothing ever is.) I went on with a project dear to my heart: a play about the mother and brothers of Jesus called *Family Portrait* by Lenore Coffee and William Joyce Cowen. I had always seen the Ethical Culture Society auditorium as a theater and that wooden frieze as the backdrop for a play—and here was the play. It looked in on the family at the time Jesus was preaching up and down the land having left his three brothers shorthanded in their carpentry shop where he was acknowledged to be the best carpenter of all. His brothers are furious about his defection and the oldest—bigoted, snobbish James—is outraged about the company Jesus keeps, thieves, whores, fishermen, and the unwashed poor. Mary is inclined to accept, without understanding, whatever Jesus has decided to do to fulfill his own destiny. The brothers persuade her to come with them to Capernaum to try to convince Jesus to come back home and give up his ridiculous evangelism. She goes with them reluctantly but stays at an inn nearby when they go to confront Jesus who is preaching on the shore. Mary, weary and unquiet, begins a conversation with a young man at the inn. She asks him shyly if he knows Jesus. The young man is aglow with enthusiasm and says he himself is a loyal and admiring disciple. "I would die for him," he says. Mary is very touched and heartened and when the brothers return, having been snubbed in public by Jesus, she presents her new friend saying he had been telling her he was a good friend and a follower of Jesus. She turns to the young man to present him to her sons and apologizes saying "I'm sorry, I don't know your name." He smiles with friendliness, "Judas, Judas Iscariot." That is the end of the first act. Jesus never appears. I didn't see the play when it was done on Broadway with Judith Anderson as Mary but I read it and the notices. I did it with an all-black cast including Eddie as the youngest brother, Austin Briggs-Hall as James, and as Mary, a marvelous,

Gordon Heath directed and acted in *Family Portrait* in 1947. He is shown here in his role as Judas, with Osceola Archer, who played the part of Mary.

mature actress who should have had a resounding career in the theater. She had the luminosity of Duse and a sweet stillness that one glimpsed in Fay Bainter and Pauline Lord. Her name was Osceola Archer and she was colored. She taught acting at the American Negro Theatre and she had a simple elegance in life that she transferred to this peasant housewife and mother, Mary. I was awed and proud that she consented to take the role and be directed by me. There were moments during the rehearsal when she became preachy and "poetic"—one of the traps of the play, which was colloquially written but had biblical echoes in spite of itself. I sat beside her under the unwinking gaze of the ten-foot shepherds and told her what I had heard. She said "I know what you mean." I said "If I say quietly to you 'Osceola' just 'Osceola,' to tell you 'it' is happening, would that help?" "Yes, Gordon, I will listen for you—and myself." I was more than ever her devoted slave. I called her name perhaps three times in the ensuing week of rehearsals and never after that. For me she had become Mary. Eddie and my friend and colleague Elwood Peterson (we worked together in Paris later on) put together a choir and they sang spirituals behind that green curtain to link the scenes. I played Judas and Nathalie Donnet played Mary Magdalene. Eddie's company filled the rest of the roles. I thought it was worthy of the bas-relief and my beloved auditorium.

Before I got to London I had seen most of what Broadway had to offer: Katherine Cornell's *Candida* and *Cleopatra* I thought sumptuous; Helen Hayes's Viola I thought thin, although Maurice Evans was a full-bodied Malvolio; Tallulah Bankhead was incisive and sulphurous in *Skin of Our Teeth* and *The Little Foxes*. But soaring above them all by virtue of genius, there was Laurette Taylor, more like life than life itself in *Outward Bound* and *The Glass Menagerie*—hers was a seamless technique that looked like an absence of technique. Two miraculous creations—her cockney slavey and her southern mother—the greatest ever—as my theater generation will testify at boring length because they were indescribable and you had to have *been* there!

Oklahoma! had just begun to foreshadow Broadway's developing gift for combining excellence and efficiency in all the departments of musical comedy.

On the masculine side, there were splendid supporting character actors but only one undoubted genius—and that was Orson Welles—director, actor from theater to radio to film and back, enlarging possibilities from one medium to the other, so multifaced and multifaceted you couldn't see where he began or ended. He was multitudes and he had not reached twenty-five! There was flair and gusto and headlong theatricality in all of his work. Burgess Meredith might be the Hamlet of the future but Orson was the Belasco, the Barnum, and the Barrymore (for John B had slid off his throne, leaving his crown behind for Orson to seize—like Bolingbroke from *Richard II*).

Black theater, as represented by the American Negro Theatre in Harlem, had latched on to a play about a Polish hooker adapted by Philip Yordan to supplant *Anna Karenina* and *Anna Christie* with *Anna Lucasta*—less mournful than the latter, more skittish than the former. The black *Anna Lucasta,* admired for its ensemble playing and the farce, audience-pleasing ingredients ran and ran, using up during its three-year Broadway tenancy a score of replacements including Sadie Browne. Critics once again discovered the possibilities of Negro performers in non-Negro roles—although even before it reached Broadway it had been "blackened" and "un-Polished" (to perpetuate two bad puns at once). The characters were hardly written in depth to begin with but the critics said it proved blacks could play human beings without reference to color—a lazy summary. What blacks had done was to bring their color to save a soap opera on stage long before Bill Cosby did the same for television.

So Hilda Simms was proclaimed a star and Fred O'Neal and Frank Silvera displayed their very great actor-cunning. Earle Hyman played the country boy without insisting on his classical background. Canada Lee replaced an actor for a short time. Finally I felt as if I were the only colored actor I knew who *didn't* play in *Anna.*

Finian's Rainbow was a much more solid achievement—a merry and bitter satire of southern bigotry wrapped up in Irish whimsy. This unlikely combination was put together with such professional savvy (as *Variety* would say) that it really worked on Broadway. I note these two productions partly because they both came to London while *Roots* was running and they give me an excuse to retell a story that was making the rounds at the time.

The early forties were an era of conspicuous "liberals" making conspicuously liberal gestures. One of these gestures consisted of giving interracial parties— especially among theater people. Yip Harburg, who wrote the book and lyrics for *Finian* was among the do-gooders. (*Finian* attested to that.) The story was a passionate argument overheard between Yip and a fellow d-g-er about who would be responsible for what at the next proposed party.

Yip said "We'll have it at my place." "No," said the other guy, "It was at your place last time."

"Then I'll bring the liquor." "No," said the other, "I've got a full cellar."

Yip: "Do you need my car to pick up people?" "No, sweetie—I live at Forty-fifth and Seventh—they're all coming from their theaters. No sweat."

Yip, outdone, was subsiding but had a last-minute inspiration: "OK. Your place, your liquor; I'll bring the Negro!" Apocryphal? Perhaps—but token Negroes were worth their weight in symbolism.

The Federal Theatre did plays about that third of a nation President Roosevelt said needed looking after: workers, the poor, and the exploited. The Negro Unit of the Federal Theatre Project did plays about black heroes: the liberators of Haiti, John Henry, Harriet Tubman. The FTP mounted a dramatization of Sinclair Lewis's *It Can't Happen Here* about the hidden mechanisms of American-style fascism that *could* indeed happen here. It was launched in fifteen American cities simultaneously. Today's headlines were tomorrow's documentary plays—the silent minority was making itself heard.

In the 1920s, the Moscow Art Theatre had visited America and theater was never the same. How did the troupe contrive to put life into every corner of the theater and leave no doubt that the actions were the people they played? The Group Theatre in New York followed a discipline based on Constantin Stanislavsky's delving into what actors did and how they came to do it—how they prepared themselves to create by means of subterranean, even subconscious, digging into their psyches and drawing on their life experience. Lee Strasberg, Harold Clurman, Elia Kazan, and Robert Lewis did their own delving, using Stanislavsky's writings as a guidebook. *An Actor Prepares* was not a "how-to" textbook but an analysis of what Stanislavsky had seen happening between conception and performance. *My Life in Art* was a narrative of Stanislavsky's own progress as he developed his theories pragmatically with his actors and himself in the Moscow Art Theatre. From his written works, directors distilled a "method" that contained their version of Stanislavsky's insights; exercises designed to explore the disciplines that would lead to Truth on the stage and discard acting clichés and stereotypes. A new vocabulary came into being: "sense memory," "beats," "intentions," "objectives." Directors made pilgrimages to Moscow to observe Stanislavsky at work and sit in on lectures and conversations. Everything S contributed to rehearsals at the MAT was faithfully written down as it transpired. *Stanislavsky Directs* completed a published trilogy. The American adaptations tended to be doctrinaire and many versions claimed to be definitive. There were scoffers and unbelievers and hostility to the idea that acting could be examined and taught according to a set of principles. Instinct and talent and experience of the stage itself would do nicely, thank you. S did not claim that his method would produce actors—he wanted to place the tools to work with in their hands, or at least within conscious reach. Lee Strasberg installed himself as the resident guru in America and administered the Actors' Studio—the Stanislavsky school. Method actors began to feel that their profession was something between an art and a science bordering on a religion. Stanislavsky wanted to make his discoveries available. Strasberg wanted to make them exclusive. In a touching mimicry of the Master, he conducted his classes with a recording machine at his side activated only by his voice, like a burglar-proof electronic vault. His ex cathedra pronouncements were on tape as Stanislavsky's had been put to paper. Stanislavsky Directs: Strasberg Teaches. As it happened the context of American theater in the 1930s was not hospitable to the Stanislavsky itinerary. The lessons of the Method couldn't be applied like a Band-Aid or a tire patch. They required dedication from a group working from the same base and slow intimate growth. Actors and directors had to learn that new language. Actors emerging from Method discipline had a new look and a new sound and a new unmistakable authority. Communication on stage was immeasurably deepened. But it could only be achieved under repertory conditions. Stanislavsky worked it out within the subsidized frame of the Moscow Art Theatre for which we had no equivalent and no basis for continuity. The

Group went into production in 1931 with, among others, a resident play-wright, Clifford Odets, who wrote plays to the company's measure with the throb of Jewish family life and European sensibilities (the MAT had, of course, Anton Chekhov). The Group actors individually and as an ensemble were a revelation to the public and the critics but most of all to their contemporaries. They were the Word made flesh and theater practitioners all over America had to recognize their significance. The Group was identified (inaccurately) with leftist political trends, lost Franchot Tone and Odets to Hollywood, could never operate on a sound financial basis, and in 1941 it gave up, but actors, directors and teachers sowed grain like Johnny Appleseed in all the regions where theater existed—even on Broadway. Strasberg dug himself in and ran the Actors' Studio with an iron hand until he died. I left all this ferment behind when I went to Europe.

I was invited to direct a production of Lillian Hellman's *Little Foxes* (back in the Deep South—O Lord, how long?) at the YMHA with an interesting cast including Barbara Baxley, then a tempestuous ingenue, challenging Nathalie Donnet, the drama director at the Y, who came down hard on the villainy in the role of Regina Giddens. Eddie played Cal, the house servant, mischievously, and Phil Pruneau played Leo, the adult delinquent, with a flair of his own that owed little to Dan Duryea's slimy—and one would have thought—definitive portrayal. I couldn't vouch for Stark Young's acceptance—it was the Young Men's Hebrew Association after all—but I was proud of it and melancholy not to be present for the opening night. I was still Brett Charles eight performances a week. The cast and I wept together and exchanged loving messages in the afternoon. My fatherless children came through triumphantly on opening night—I was told. I'm afraid the role of Birdie, poor, victimized Birdie, will inevitably walk off with the play. Our Birdie, Peggy Cartwright (Patricia Collinge, tremulous and vulnerable in the original version) pulled out unforgettable moments one after the other and broke hearts night after night—mine first.

Nathalie had the inspiration to propose *Death Takes a Holiday* with me in the title role. I had not, of course, seen the 1929 Theatre Guild version with Philip Merivale, but the film intrigued me and Fredric March's panache seemed dead right (unintentional pun). Death manifests himself as a White Russian prince, obsessively curious to learn why men fear him. Translated from the Italian, it retains a European atmosphere in spite of (or perhaps because of) the stilted English of the translation.

Adopting a monocle and decked out in military uniform and impressive medals, I found myself swept away by the metaphysical intimations of this *Redbook* romance. Death, a guest at an Italian count's villa, surrounded by titled but trivial ladies and high-ranking military, is a magnet to them all. The ladies flirt, the men pay court, but Death remains a perturbing enigma. Who he is is

A "decadent lady" and Death. Gordon Heath played the title role as a White Russian prince in *Death Takes a Holiday* (1948).

left unanswered until the lovely Grazia, virginal daughter of the count, already half in love with easeful death, knows him, sees him for what he is and, of course, falls in love. He is inhabited by an emotion hitherto unknown to him and concludes that the existence of love makes mankind fear Death—et voilà! His holiday ending (no one has been able to die and the world is fearful and demoralized) His Highness wraps his cloak around Grazia and they leave the horror-stricken eminences to ponder the imponderables of love, life, and death.

The story has the irresistible simplicity of a legend: *Sleeping Beauty, Beauty and the Beast,* and that innumerable caravan of tales in which Death (or the devil) takes on a human shape to teach humanity a lesson. In this version Death is the pupil, but in the end, imperious and ruthless as we know him to be. Beckett it is not—but given the fin de siècle ambience and a certain European elegance adhering to titles and aristocrats, it is a haunting piece and our audiences thrilled and shivered.

Nathalie disciplined the melodrama, Jock, our designer, provided a romantic Italian terrace, and the wardrobe mistress came up with some lovely decadent gowns for some lovely decadent ladies. I made another appearance as

Death in Allentown, Pennsylvania, in 1948. Overheard in the lobby as one lady inspected the photos: "I didn't know Death was colored!" Jack Lemmon was the juvenile lead in this summer stock production (following *John Loves Mary*).

I reveled in the role of Prince Sirki. Playing Brett was living and working in a straitjacket. All of my baroque tendencies had to be suppressed and discarded. Brett was simple and single-minded, unquestionably masculine, hammered out to fine steel (like Siegfried's sword) by his war experiences. I was none of those things. Peter Hall* reports that John Gielgud said, "I'm happiest on stage when I can swing my cloak." That's me. Not so much a swinging cloak, perhaps, as an ambivalent, complex, maimed figure cloaked in ambiguity, fated with hubris, and courting disaster and destiny. (When I had to leave *Oedipus* at the Roundabout Theatre I suggested Earle Hyman as my replacement. He watched the performance and said to me afterward, "You play on three levels at once. I couldn't do that!")

Sirki was a part I could *taste*. I had little acquaintance with death but Owen was on intimate terms with His Majesty. Father, mother, and brother, had been struck down and his lifelong involvement with old grim death had undoubtedly affected me.

* Peter Hall, former director of London's National Theatre.

∽ *Deep Are the Roots—London*

A HALF HOUR OUT from LaGuardia Airport one of the propellers of our Douglas DC6 stopped functioning. We had three others to go on with but it was not reassuring—not even to the professionals evidently, for we turned around and came back. Helen Martin and Evelyn Ellis sat and planned a bon voyage party with streamers saying, "Gal, ain't you gone yet?" A Spanish woman asked expectantly, "Where are we?" We were, in fact, installed in the airport snack bar and fed Swedish hors d'oeuvres. Twenty minutes later the all-clear sounded and we clambered back in, with four propellers whirling like mad. The air hostess said, "A nut was loose. No one we know," a remark she must have saved up from previous mishaps. It went quite over the Spanish passenger's head.

We were off! We were on our way! Two anticlimactic touch-downs at Labrador and Newfoundland and then the sky, ocean and clouds and monotony until the coast of Ireland slid into view and we came down at what we were told was Shannon. The Spanish woman said it looked just like the snack bar at LaGuardia, which of course was exactly what we were all thinking. But before we could take a vote on it we were whisked away into the streaky dawn on our last lap. The captain announced "Heathrow" but we knew that was British understatement and that he was too modest to say "London" right out.

We came down in gray daylight staggering into His Majesty's Customs. The immigration boys were starchily well mannered and, since our working papers were in fine British order, passed us through without so much as a raised eyebrow. Pat, our stage manager, was at the gate to meet, drive, and shepherd us to our Bloomsbury hotel. Bloomsbury! Ah, we were going to be put down in the middle of literary history, if not to see Lytton Strachey and Virginia Woolf plain, at least to view the blue-and-white plaques commemorating their appearance and disappearance. The hotel itself was a drab bed-and-breakfast affair boasting a pale, overworked slavey and a high-colored landlady we overheard complain-

Gordon Heath's father and mother and his friend Margaret (Peggy) Durand saw him off at the airport as he left for London and the British production of *Deep Are the Roots*, May 4, 1947.

ing about harboring "theatricals" in her lodgings. Helen, always on the qui vive for evidences of prejudice and patronage, was a trifle startled to be faced with an intolerance pointed in this unexpected direction.

We went out in the streets, looking so hard that our eyes ached—chimney pots against the sky, streets that *curved,* tiny parks interrupting clusters of low-slung buildings, the neatness and regularity and the gaping spaces where bombs and fires had gouged out crevasses that had only just been filled in and leveled off and were now awaiting rebuilding. Helen appraised the women's clothes, conceding almost nothing to rationing. She eyed the males with rather more tolerance, withholding final judgments. An occasional hum of appreciation escaped her but obviously more data would be required. Everything— shops, hotels, restaurants, automobiles—seemed smaller than life. One could see such a lot of sky! My head was full of imprecise images: Dickens jostling Maugham (well, side by side, let's say), Wodehouse and Shaw and perhaps less appropriately, but inevitably, Shakespeare. We came to our first bridge and could see the Abbey and the Houses of Parliament on the horizon. The impression of dilapidation fell away and I felt the weight and glory of all those centuries of British pomp, circumstance, and power plays. I was hooked!

The bed of the "bed-and-breakfast" was adequate, slippery counterpane to

Gordon Heath and Betsy Drake
in the London production of
Deep Are the Roots were featured
on the cover of *Theatre World*
(September 1947).

one side (where it usually was), but the fried tomatoes and watery eggs were outdone in horror by the concoction presented as "coffee." British institutional cooking matched its reputation during that honeymoon—and I might add, forever after. Rationing had very little to do with it. Cooking was a distasteful duty like national service.

We foregathered at the theater—the Globe—where we would rehearse in someone else's décor until our own was built, painted, and installed at our theater—Wyndham's, just off of Leicester Square and considered a lucky, prestigious showplace. We met our fellow actors. There was Patrick Barr, whose amiable blink and soft smile of sweet reasonableness did not for a moment suggest the blunt ruggedness of Lloyd Gough. When Gadge had proposed that Lloyd bring a flower from the garden for Alice the morning after, Lloyd squared his already square shoulders, flicked his nose with his thumb, raised both eyebrows, and said: "Gadge, can you see me doing such a thing?" Gadge couldn't and Lloyd didn't but Patrick, though utterly masculine, might have. Allan Jeayes, who played the senator, occupied a senior-citizen position in the English theater exactly as our Charles Waldron did. The Nevvie (Genevra) was a bright-eyed, short-haired blonde, imported, like us, from the United States—gawky, impulsive, appealing, and almost too pretty. Her name was Betsy Drake. (She entered history at a subsequent moment, but to that, later). Our new director, Peter Cotes, presented his, and our, leading lady, Joan Miller. Joan seemed to us more European than English but she was shy and sympathetic and we were charmed. "We," Helen, Evelyn, and I, were very possessive about "our" play. Gadge had made us into a family and *Roots* was our progeny.

The most dazzling of our new acquaintances was Hugh "Binkie" Beaumont, the producer. In this English theater world Binkie was all of the Shubert brothers put together. Urbane and shrewd, he was powerfully at the head of Tennents, his near-monopoly theater kingdom. He was slim, dapper, pale, with smooth corn-colored hair, a large generous mouth, a silky voice with a cutting edge, and he smoked cigarettes in a holder and exuded fastidiousness. He introduced us to everyone, gave us his blessing, and left us to get on with it. We did not get on with it. Peter was a bright young director with ideas, but not bright enough or perhaps too stubborn to accept the fact that Binkie had seen the play in New York and wanted it reproduced—not redirected. He didn't want ideas. What was good enough for Kazan and a New York public for fourteen months was quite good enough for him. Even so, if Peter had shown any signs of understanding the folklore of the post–Civil War scene in Dixie or if he had acknowledged that we knew more about it then he did, all might have been well. As it was, a record amount of hostility was built up between the New York contingent and the director from the first day.

At the end of the week Binkie appeared on our borrowed set, lit a cigarette, adjusted it in his holder, and said: "My dears, we are going to do without Peter. I'm afraid none of you—none of us—sees eye to eye with him about the play and Joan, whom we all liked, decided she didn't want to do it if Peter left. Now I want you to meet Daphne Rye, who will take your direction and put this play on as I intended it to be. I count on your memories to reconstruct what happened in New York." This time he did not add "God bless you." Daphne was Tennents' casting director. She knew everyone and about everyone. Plump, platinum-haired, an alert pair of eyes hidden behind tinted glasses, a wicked and devastating tongue with perspicacity and intuition to match—she was a formidable figure. She introduced us to our new leading lady, Faith Brook— Faith of the Roman-matron profile handed down from her Dad, Clive, the original Sherlock Holmes from the British cinema in the patrician du Maurier tradition: evening clothes, immovable upper lip, brooding eyes, always referred to as "the distinguished actor, Clive Brook." Faith brought that distinction up to date, playing Alice with a hauteur that made her last-act comeuppance infinitely touching. There was a vulnerability that was as much a part of Faith as Alice and I was hooked once more.* Daphne counted on us for details of the

---

* Faith was vulnerable, but by no means defenseless. Halfway through rehearsals Daphne reported with a certain amount of glee: "Faith says she admires you and your performance enormously but

reconstruction. Evelyn, who had become *Eve*-lyn in England and who was giving an impeccable performance, off-stage, of exquisite frailty and helplessness, was indeed helpless when asked about moves, motivations, and rhythms. "I was at the French windows when Alice came on." Helen countered scathingly: "No, Eve-lyn, you were at the armchair and you crossed to the door upstage." Daphne caught on quickly. Helen had watched and listened and stored away images of the stage's traffic like a squirrel gathering nuts against the winter. I was almost as useless as Evelyn. My preoccupation in New York was me, and building the character of Brett took all my concentration. Daphne set about putting the play together from Helen's blueprint and those fixed points Kazan had nailed into place—namely the three of us. It says a great deal for Daphne's tact and ingenuity that we began to function as an ensemble. The give-and-take of mutual discoveries, the building of relationships, and the exploration of the tensions were secondary considerations in this prefixed commercial product. We were re-creating in this context—a blow to creativity.

The American experience was not part of British actors' repertoire.* Their accents and inflections, their tendency to understate, their obliquity were all at odds with the cut-and-thrust of modern American melodrama. Nevertheless Daphne sewed several fine seams and Binkie announced himself to be well pleased when we set out on our pre-London tour, taking in Brighton, Leicester, Edinburgh, Glasgow, and Llandudnow. Audiences were impressed and baffled. The play's reflection of America's neurotic racial attitudes, from the well meaning but self-deceiving to the rabid and obsessed, came over to them as a Margaret Mead study of tribal superstitions—not exactly what they expected to see in the theater. The critics admired the acting and the direction and piously hoped it was all sensational fiction. Brighton, out of season, was charming vistas. Edinburgh was imposing and craggy, with that castle fulfilling all our preconceptions of the genre. I was in "digs" facing "Arthur's Seat" in a wee cottage. My wee landlady had a wee dog, and a wee pussy, and in her parlor, a wee golliwog. I felt very strongly about Golly in his white ruffled shirt and tailored blue trousers. My bags packed and on the doorstep after the week's stay, my wee landlady came downstairs with Golly in her arms, held him out to me and said, "You'll take good care of him" with that Scottish intonation that made it a commission. Golly, with his hair straightened and a red tailcoat, still sits opposite my bed and has been along on most of my travels. Glasgow was lively

that you are upstaging her all the time!" I could only plead guilty but I hadn't realized how deeply Carol Goodner's lessons had lodged; I vowed to mend my ways.

* The cross-fertilization that has resulted at this moment in swift, hard-hitting productions like the National Theatre's *The Front Page* (1986) was not yet under way. But my own dear Faith has recently finished playing in Clare Booth's *The Women* on the West End (1987); a presentation slated almost unanimously by the critics for the uncertainty of the accents and the slackness of the rhythms.

and like a city—especially on Saturday night! Llandudnow ("not truly Wales," they said) was not in season either but I didn't think I would come to care.

In businesslike Leicester I took my precious sweet-ration coupons to buy chocolate and was gently admonished: "Oh no, love, no chocolate before Moonday." "Not before Moonday?" I echoed involuntarily—which may have been a reaction to the piquancy of hearing very pretty colored shop people in Edinburgh speaking with broad Scottish burrs. Echoes? In the Leicester theater during the morning run-through we kept hearing bits of dialogue bouncing back from the far walls. Binkie installed himself against the proscenium, cigarette holder at the ready, and addressed the theater manager on the subject. That worthy announced that the microphones were always on in his theater. Binkie said icily: "This play is for London, *not* Leicester. I want those microphones turned off *now* or we withdraw the play." The mikes were disconnected on the instant. Vivat Tennents!

So, by difficult stages, we got back to London, which was now more like "home" than ever. Our slightly dowdy set was erected on Wyndham's stage and we faced a London first-night congregation. The tautness of the New York version was diminished by the too well-bred acting but the situation and the interracial love story were strong enough to hold and affect the audience even if it was as the reviews put it, "a problem with which Britain has little or no concern." Our first night was triumphant and, as we held hands and bowed, the orchestra played "God save . . ." ("too soon" said the *Daily Mail*), and we looked forward to the future.

The gala opening-night party at Binkie's Sussex place was casual but posh. Noël Coward and I were the only nontuxedoed males, which immediately created a bond and a friendship. Evelyn wore black-and-white satin and silver foxes. Faith wore a gown low in the front and lower in the back and made a stunning spectacle worthy of the occasion. We drank champagne and beamed at each other.

ꙮ At Home Abroad

July 1947

for Dad especially:

dear Dad:

sorry I haven't written that promised letter. you would enjoy so much of London for so many reasons. the cultivated speech. the cricket in Hyde Park. the houses of Parliament, Big Ben tolling the hour. the miraculously untouched stretches of heavy trees and green fields and precise children with exquisite manners. the quiet accounts of a tennis match on BBC. the flag that goes up when the King is in residence at Buckingham Palace. the way clerks and salespeople say "thank you" when they serve you. the movie houses in which you can smoke and the theatres where you can do the same. Edinburgh would have been your cup of tea too with the mountains and the castles and riot of flowers and I know you would like the English countryside with the ivy-colored cottages and the heavily timbered roofs and ceilings—and the pubs in the city with the bitter beer and the jabbing wit of the cockneys. you would like the gentility of the street car conductors and the pride the policemen take in directing you in detail to your destination. it would be nice to know you were able to stand in Charing Cross Road and watch a new set of people queing up to buy tickets to "Deep Are the Roots." stalls, not the orchestra, gallery, not balcony and programs are sixpence and tea is a shilling at intermission, pardon—interval. you might be shocked at the tarts on Picadilly who step in front of you and say "I fancy you, boy" but you could not help but be fascinated. you would sit all evening in the old churchyards and read your *Times* (five pages, not twenty-five!) and promptly at four-thirty you'd have a pot of tea with jam and scones and perhaps a sweet. one and six and thruppence for the girl. (sweet 9d extra). you would find too many potatoes and too few stringbeans on the menu and no rice at all but you could probably handle your knife and fork in approved style (knife in the right; fork in the left and never put down your knife or change hands) and you might sing "God Save The King" in the theatre instead of "My Country 'Tis of Thee." I think you would feel in many ways

121

that you belonged here, as I do somewhere deep in the British part of my bones. you would be sad that it is such an unhappy struggling country, swallowing so much of its pomp and pride at once and on short rations spiritually and materially, but you would feel the core was still hard and invulnerable and the people indestructible. you would love it.

I miss you both. goodnight and tomorrow tells the tale.

Love from Brett in London.

(day of dress rehearsal)

THE FOREGOING WAS, of course, a love letter, and I was, indeed, loving London. I had seen the Old Vic company in New York in *Henry IV* parts one and two with Ralph Richardson as a witty and dropsical Falstaff and Olivier as a fiery Hotspur and a shriveled, beady-eyed octogenarian Shallow, looking as if a mild breeze would blow him away or that he would crumble any minute like those unfortunate ageless inhabitants of Shangri-La (*Lost Horizons*) exiling themselves and ending up as a handful of dust. I also heard a radio version of their *Peer Gynt,* with Maggie Leighton, as the "Green-clad woman," emitting the most lascivious gurgles I had ever heard. The nobles spoke nobly, the "common people"—soldiers, servants, rustics, peasants—all performed with a suppleness and interaction stemming from the long labors of repertory theater and hundreds of years of devotion to their genius playwright.

The first performance I saw in London was the Vic's *Richard II* with Alec Guinness playing a dandified and detached Richard, in a decor that seemed to be all stilts and staircases. Ralph Richardson intoning John of Gaunt, more weary of the text than of life. George Rose came on as the Lord Marshal and galvanized the proceedings with a clarion delivery that made us know he was heralding a moment of immense importance and urgency, like a prize-fight announcer trumpeting the imminent clash of behemoths. With seventeen lines in this minor role he lifted the play on to epic dimensions. Harry Andrews took it from there as Bolingbroke, the king's savage antagonist. The whole bloody business got under way and you knew that Richard was doomed. Maggie Leighton as Richard's queen swayed pathetically like a sapling in a high wind, suffered and was widowed, making her effect with only the two short scenes allotted her. I had a letter introducing me to the character actress in the company but I went impulsively to Miss Leighton's dressing room to introduce myself and say how moved I was. I caught George before he got out and we went on with a friendship begun when the Vic was in New York. George was welcoming and avuncular. He introduced me to a fellow Vic member, a stocky sharp-eyed Scotsman, Ewan Roberts, who decided on the spot I would need looking after. He invited me to a "meal" at his place which was a room in the Hollands' house. The Hollands were Norman and Thora and the five-and-a-half year-old dark-haired, rosy-cheeked Roger. Norman worked in an office but wrote one-act and full-length plays in his spare time (and probably on his boss's time as well). Ewan was skeptical of Norman's staying power and Norman was not convinced of Ewan's future in the theater—so they were even. Thora had the most lyrical voice in all Kensington, lovely long hair to match, and was, besides, that rare object, a fine cook. They were to become my "family" in London. I got my mother to send foodstuffs from America. So many staples were unobtainable in postwar London. It was worth it just to behold Thora's joy at the sight of a pineapple for instance. Norman, big and bluff and given to pawky North Country humor, regarded my clothes with the same rapture that Thora reserved for rice and jello. "May I try on your overcoat?" It fit him very well actually. I saw him acting in Priestley's *When We Are Married* in a local rep company production and very funny he was, too. He was always matter-of-fact with Roger whom he treated as a grown-up. An ex-boxer, he would box with Roger as if he were six-feet-two (Norman's height) and when Roger complained he was bruised during the sparring Norman would say "pooh, pooh" and insist he was "hardening him up." I was trying to "harden up" Norman about playwrighting—his and the exercises I had observed between servings of tea in the London theaters themselves. Tea, very weak, was also being served on stage after stage—that and class distinctions and serene snobbery. Exposed as I had been to Odets, Williams, Miller, and the slashing accusations of WPA productions at home, I was impatient with these homogenized, parochial offerings, so well made, well spoken, and finite. I talked about Tennessee Williams piercing through protective layers of the neurotically disabled, the victimized, the insulted, and the injured in an envelope of poetry and compassion. Norman felt Tennessee's prose was purple and self-indulgent. But fifteen years ago he admitted graciously that Tennessee's plays were legitimate and eloquent endeavors. I had retreated from my earlier convictions, finding Tennessee's late plays feeble and repetitive so we met each other halfway so to speak. They are still my "London family." Norman has written 120 plays, published seventy-six, won fifteen play-writing awards, had ten plays adapted for television, etc., etc. I tried vainly to persuade a producer to do in Paris in French his full-length play about Oscar Wilde in prison. It was much better than the one they chose to do. Ewan remained a stalwart member of the Old Vic, understudied and played for Sir Ralph Richardson, married a literary agent, had two children, and went into a hit play on the West End as a Scottish butler. I think Ewan and Norman ended up admiring each other without reservations. Roger is a hardy plant as tall as me and his father and a marketing director of the Newspaper society. Thora and Norman are proud grandparents living in Wimbledon.

I continued to devour London theater in great gulps. The freemasonry of the profession and the publicity surrounding *Roots* gave me easy entrée to "back stage" and, stage-struck and star-struck as I was, I walked into dressing rooms without presenting credentials. Noël (as far as England was concerned there was only one Noël—dieresis included—in the United Kingdom) invited me to see him in his own bitchy comedy, *Present Laughter.* He was mischievous and witty—wittier than the play—and adored by the public. I went around to the stage door. His valet stood outside his dressing room and as I approached said, "Mr Heath?" which was typical of Noël's thoughtfulness and friendliness. We talked. I said the proper things about his playing and the play. He said he was writing a serious play about an England invaded and occupied by a foreign power. "Ah," I said, "When William Came."* He looked at me delightedly. "You're the first person to make that reference." I doubted that—but I was, perhaps, the first *American* to do so. "It's going to be called *Peace in Our Time* (derived from Neville Chamberlain's summing up of his abortive Munich conference with Herr Hitler.) *Peace in Our Time* proved to be a messy and mawkish piece and I didn't go back to see Noël afterward. As the popular song had it: "And if you can't say anything real nice, it's better not to talk at all, take my advice."

James Bridie, the Scots playwright, had provided a vehicle, *Doctor Angelus,* for the sinister Alistair Sim, who played an insane doctor embarked on murdering his family and patients, aided unwittingly by his young assistant. When the murders are traced to our hitherto plausible doctor, he goes shriekingly mad and his thunderstruck assistant can only testify, "but he was so good to me!" George Cole, Sim's protégé, was not your ordinary handsome juvenile. He managed to convince you that his naïveté was not idiocy but went along with his loyalty and belief in his chief's integrity. He was in his own way a bit off-center and quirky. I admired this handling of a tricky part and went back to introduce myself. George went on to be a valuable member of the acting fraternity. His performance as the over-mothered son obsessed with kite-flying in Maugham's filmed short story, *The Kite,* displayed his special talent for playing stubborn eccentrics.

I went backstage to meet Flora Robson, *Dame* Flora Robson, that is, who had just finished filming *Saratoga Trunk* in which she played Ingrid Bergman's octoroon nanny. She assured me, quite unnecessarily, that she "liked" colored people, which reminds me: English people in social situations, frequently, if shyly, asked me: "What do you prefer to be called: Negro, colored, or what?" Since they—many of them—had called us "niggers" among themselves over a long period (commercial advertisements proclaimed the availability of goods in green, black, or nigger-brown) and we at home had agitated to have Negro printed with a capital "N" but also called ourselves, in and out of print,

---

* *When William Came* is a short novel of H. H. Munro (Saki)—on the same idea.

"colored," one could understand and be amused by their confusion. I usually answered "O, eyether [sic] will do."

In Somerset Maugham's comedy *Jane,* Jane was no "plain Jane" but the superbly equipped and sparkling Yvonne Arnaud whose French accent had endeared her to the British public to the greater glory of Tennents Ltd. Like Noël she carried the play on her shrugging shoulders. Somewhere late in the first act the juvenile, Simon Lack, came on; a vision in white polo shirt and shorts, swinging a tennis racket and (really) asking, "Tennis anyone?" As James Elroy Fletcher observed on one of his Persian quatrains: "The sun has risen twice today." He got dressed in succeeding acts, by which time I had my breath back and was more or less resolved to go backstage and introduce myself. I was a head taller than he already and he remained seated in his dressing room. I said, "hello, I'm Gordon Heath," he said, "I know." There was a long silence: I don't know which of us was the more disconcerted. I allowed as how I had enjoyed the performance. He thanked me and I left. Years later he came in to my Paris club (l'Abbaye) with Coral Browne, an actress and a wicked and knowing lady. They sat at my side and introduced themselves. I gasped. "Simon Lack! Do you remember I came to your dressing room?" "Oh, yes," he said and they both collapsed in hopeless laughter. This is the Coral Browne who (reportedly) faced with the apparition of a giant phallus wheeled on stage as a jolly afterpiece to John Gielgud's and Seneca's *Oedipus* (Peter Brook, director) turned to her companion reassuringly: "It's no one we know, dear."

The English theater phenomenon that intrigued me most was the spate of intimate revues—a form that America had blown up to elaborate starry dimensions: Earl Carroll's *Vanities,* Ziegfeld's series of "Follies," smart, slick, and expensively dressed. Vaudeville in America was fading. "Intimate" revues were not commercial propositions. Cabaret in the big cities sometimes adopted a revue format but the cover charge was high and the patrons were rich, rowdy, and raucous. In London, revues were theater diversions, mounted cheaply and loyally attended in modest-sized theaters. The revues featured performers who could sing, act, and—more or less—dance. They were a succession of mildly satirical sketches interspersed with songs and casual dance numbers requiring no great virtuosity. The whole was conceived as popular entertainment, disarming, occasionally mocking, and fond of "in" jokes about well-known figures in the English theater. To an American eye the revues were slightly amateur but unpretentiously charming. A "late night" theater established in 1936 called "The Players Ridgeway's Late Joys" marked out a special territory for itself—a re-creation of a Victorian music hall with a master of ceremonies—the "chairman"—in full, frilled-shirt evening dress who, rapping with his gavel, proposed a toast "to the Queen, God bless her," but the queen in question was Victoria. The patrons sat drinking, cheering, and joining in the choruses printed on the song sheet given out at the entrance. The "chairman" introduced each act with a patter that regular customers could and did often recite along with him: "and now, Ladies and Gentlemen, who but your own, your own, ever adorable . . ." and so on—all Victorian and Edwardian numbers in costume, performed "accompanied at the pianoforte" with authentic brio and relish for the heavy-handed, melodramatic, sentimental, and comic favorites of long, long ago. There was a core of permanent performers, and stars of the revue and legitimate stage did "turns" as guest artists. Nostalgia and good fellowship were the order of the night. "Dear old pals, jolly old pals, give me the friendship of dear old pals," the song sheet ended up. That was the note sounded and adhered to for the entire evening. Gemütlichkeit and unchallenged ancestor worship. "The church clock still stood at ten to three."

∾ London Particular, 1947

BESIDES NEW FRIENDS, London contributed new sights, sounds, and idiosyncracies.

The toy trains of the Underground and its succinct maps and finely designed posters; its giant escalators plunging deep into the earth and up again.

The double-decker buses and the proud pillar mail boxes and telephone kiosks all painted a brilliant fire-engine red.

The left-handed traffic, the patient queuing at bus stops. The smooth incurious politeness of the man on the street and the lively familiarity of the jocular bus conductors. The upright dignity and spaciousness of the taxi cabs and the encyclopedic knowledge of the cab drivers.

The massed vegetables and fruits of Covent Garden market that should have made traffic impossible, and, of course, the flower sellers—ah, there, Eliza Doolittle! The zebra (zebbra, that is) crossings and the curving and straight avenues that somewhere along the line would converge into a "circus"—a wheel with spokes.

The *London Times* whose front page then was entirely given over to "Personals": births, marriages, and deaths—sober and symmetrical. The newsstands, with their boldly hand-lettered placards compressing the day's headlines: *Fulham Train Tragedy, East Anglia Victory,* and the muckraking Sunday paper, *News of the World,* dealing almost exclusively in titillating scandals, authentic and invented.

The pavement artists' creations in pastel and chalk, with an upturned hat at the side to receive contributions and an underlined legend in white chalk, "All my own work."—Well, of course, whose else's would it be?"

The mores of theater: there were queues for "pit stall" seats (the cheapest) and "buskers"—sidewalk entertainers who sang, fiddled, accordioned, fluted, and orated. At least one who treated the standees to chunks of Shakespeare, floridly delivered with good enough accent and discretion. Tea on trays could be ordered for intermission even before you took your seat. Most theaters had minuscule bars that were immediately jammed when the curtain came down at intermission. You had to persist and it required more than ordinary dexterity to get close enough to the bar to place your order and consume your drink before the buzzer warned you back to your seat. London revealed itself as a theatergoing population.

The barrel organs still caroled in the City—"The Last Rose of Summer" and airs from *Oklahoma.*

The Chelsea old-age pensioners stumped along in their silver-buttoned uniforms. The guardsmen paced heavily in their stiff oatmeal-colored uniforms. The school-boys wore their school caps and school shorts with their striped school scarves demurely draped or flying in the wind.

They City gentlemen still wore bowlers and carried furled umbrellas.

The war had shaken up lots of conformities but from what I could see and sense (and hope), England had not changed that much. True, Labour was in, but so were the king and queen, if the flag flying from Buckingham Palace was to be believed. Big Ben still tolled the hour and Mrs. Wallis Simpson ("that trash," according to my father) had been exorcised and the national anthem was played after every theater performance—the players and the audience stand-ing—as for the Hallelujah Chorus. It was even played after the last film showing in cinemas—a gesture held over from wartime, now perfunctory and otiose. The Empire was spinning "down the ringing grooves of change" but you had to put your ear to the ground to hear, especially if, like me, you were a new arrival in a newfound land.

I used to go to Hermione Gingold's revue at the tiny Ambassadors Theatre, the third in a series, called *Sweetest and Lowest.* Her wild leering humor and her sheer camping outrageousness made me laugh long and loud. I went backstage. She drawled insinuatingly: "My spies told me you were out front but I would have known anyway. Feel free to come anytime. Since the GIs went home no one has laughed like you!" She made it sound like an invitation to an orgy. Her stage (and dressing room) presence was wicked and piratical. In my favorite sketch she came out as one of those elderly frumpish lecturers to women's clubs in a rat-nest wig, drooping necklaces, and a floor-length shapeless ball gown that had seen much better days. "Today," she would enunciate piercingly, "I am going to talk to you about Indiaaaa. It is a *Large* problem," she would continue, making a helpless gesture with both hands outlining almost but not quite a globe, "and Mr. Kipling, Mr. Kipling was a constant visitor to our house. He gave my aunt a jolly Indian scarf with which she afterwards hanged herself. *Up* she went!" she screamed gleefully. The lecture was a misguided tour: "Shali-mar—renowned for the pale hands of the local women." "India's salvation," our lecturer informs us, holding tight to her teeth, "will be music. Native music inspired by the West—when the midnight Choo Choo leaves for Chittagong." She was the den mother to a small troupe of seven(?). Christopher Hewett (who you know in the United States as Belvedere on TV) was scout master willing to be equally outrageous in his turn. Hewett lived next door to Gingy and looked after me and Gingy like a watchful relative. I would visit Gingy with my guitar and warm myself in her tiny flat—Sunday brunch with Grieg's "Holberg Suite" on the phonograph—falling in love en route with the first dog in my life—her black poodle called "Poo" whose intelligence and spirit always amazed me. Gingy was not particularly witty in life. She was, like most professional comics I knew, slightly melancholic, but her inflections were unexpected and droll. She didn't intend to be the life of the party at home. (Peter Ustinov complained to me just before a TV talk show, "They always suppose that I'm going to be devastatingly funny. What a bore!") Gingy was from the "legitimate" theater and had played Shakespeare, Strindberg, and Shaw before establishing herself as a revue personality. She was still a handsome woman with fine legs that she didn't hesitate to display at some moment or other in the show. She toyed with the idea of doing O'Neill's *All God's Chillun* with me. Christopher Hewett reminded her ungently of her age and wouldn't let her take the idea any further. I didn't think the man's role was for me either, but I appreciated the thought. (Paul Robeson had played it with Flora Robson in London in 1924.) In 1950 Gingy played with Hermione Baddely in *Fallen Angels*. The two Hermiones took outrageous liberties with Noël's play—"camped it up" in fact. Noël was livid, but it was a *great* success. Ever since the GIs in London had taken Gingy to their hearts she was convinced she should perform in America. She came and never left. She appeared in films, TV, revue, and theater: *Gigi, Bell, Book and Candle, A Little Night Music*. She was a TV personality—purring but sharp. When asked on a talk show what she thought of Elsa Maxwell, that elephantine international party-giver—"Oh" she hazarded, "What can you say about Elsa—just another pretty face!"

Christopher also came to America. I saw him as Captain Hook in Sandy Duncan's *Peter Pan*—doing the lot. I went back to see him with one permanently raised eyebrow. He addressed my eyebrow defensively, "I played it exactly like Sir Gerald du Maurier. I researched the part!" That's as may be but his revue technique was very much in evidence. In the New York production of *Hadrian VII* he was in a procession of bishops coming down the theater aisle. He was only local color at that point but he and his robes sashayed as if he were going to be crowned at Westminster Abbey. He *was* devastatingly funny and you couldn't look at anything else in the procession. His English experience made him a valuable theater person and he acted and directed in America with very few pauses in between.

George Rose, with his solid body of experience in supporting roles, was much admired and continuously employed in America. I saw him in *Pirates of Penzance* playing a fey Modern Major General and giving Katherine Hepburn in *Coco* more expert support than she and the show deserved.

Gingy came to the dress rehearsal of my touring *Othello*. I saw her afterward. "You were lovely, dear Gordon. Poo threw up at the interval but he's all right now." So she escaped into kidding. Actors do that to each other. They prefer mercy to justice but they are also scornful of gush—most of them.

How much real misogyny formed the gallery of female grotesques Gingy put on the stage I had no way of knowing. She was not fathomable—certainly not by me—only friendly and encouraging. She had a grown son and presumably had had a husband. I never heard her speak of either. The son was a director in the theater, Stephen Joseph, a passionate advocate of open and in the round staging.

When Gingy was playing the role of Mme Arnfeldt in New York, I was urged to call her by my dear friend Hugh Wheeler, who had written the book for *A Little Night Music* and was staying in Noël's New York flat just above Gingy's. He was fond of Gingy who was said to be "difficult." Hugh said she was entirely professional during rehearsals and the run but was really not well. She sounded fine if weary on the telephone. She left us not long after.

Hugh had written the book for the revised *Candide* (1974), and *Sweeney Todd* (1978), and his first play, *Big Fish, Little Fish* (1961), directed by John Gielgud, was much admired. By the 1980s, Hugh was increasingly somber about his work and the theater. He had switched careers and gone on to theater and cinema after producing a string of popular "whodunits" under the name of Patrick Quentin and written one novel. He looked like a Princeton under-graduate—crew-cut, perpetually apprehensive, low-keyed, and sensitive to atmospheres, more English than American, brooding and witty, with a throw-away humor like Max Beerbohm but casual and unaffected. He circulated easily among the most active and celebrated artists, Noël Coward particularly, but also Liza Minelli, Alan Bates, Shirley MacLaine, and the like, and he adjusted to a variety of egos—I think by staying on the sidelines and avoiding confrontations. He was a recurring theme in my life. Every year or so we would find ourselves in the same country at the same time and we would try to unravel the immediate past over a meal or a drink. He was usually on his way to somewhere else: to Jamaica, to Ischia, to London, to Paris, to New York, to Massachusetts (where he actually lived). He would tease me about what he called my "stupid nobility" on the stage and the professional notoriety I attracted while he toiled and plodded along with much more worthy (and better paying although he didn't say so) activities all hidden under a bushel of anonymity. That was less true after his succès d'estime with *Big Fish, Little Fish* and his follow-up play, *Look We've Come Through*. He boasted he was at least on the map what with two Broadway commercial failures. After *Sweeney Todd* he had no real complaint but he did feel the work he was doing with Hal Prince was deserving of a better audience reception and that mediocrity had been elevated to high places. I saw him last in New York at holiday time, 1980. We went by taxi to look for a Christmas card that wouldn't be too sickly. The taxi would wait, Hugh would go through the store, becoming increasingly discouraged, outraged by the ugliness of the cheap cards and the cheapness of the expensive ones, reminding me at each shop that he had to catch a train. "I will not, repeat, *not* settle for a Hallmark card!" With rising hysteria he mislaid his glasses, lost track of his gloves, panicked and rushed his taxi off to Grand Central in the middle of jammed-up traffic. Actually he *did* miss his train. He wrote to me on his Christmas card (bought in Massachusetts) accusing me of foulest treachery in letting it happen. Hugh was little, and early in life he played helpless and tentative. Later in life the habit of helplessness was installed. I warned him it would be so. He was scrupulous about his professional commitments and loyal in his friendships and I think shrewd about money. In his last days he was an invalid, or at least forbidden to travel. We talked on the telephone. I was in Massachusetts but absolutely as far from his place as one could be in the same state and I couldn't get to see him. To hear him—at least—he was exactly as always. He died in 1987.

᭧ MY "TEMPESTUOUS INGENUE" from *Foxes,* Barbara Baxley, suggested to Bob Nichols, studying on the GI Bill at the Royal Academy of Dramatic Art, that he look me up. Bob, little and chunky, with a Disney squirrel grin and an urchin liveliness, was violently stagestruck and fun. I nicknamed him "Pudge" and took him around to meet la Gingold and her circle, with whom he gained instant acceptance. He was twenty-three, going on seventeen, with a naïveté quite masking a determination to excel and succeed. He looked forward to playing classic roles, supporting ones, that is, in Restoration and Elizabethan plays. He would be a character actor certainly and probably a comic one. He was like a puppy attacking fringe and shoelace with an indiscriminate intentness.

Bob and his fellow Americans at RADA were dissatisfied with the creaking curriculum and outspoken about its inappropriateness to living theater. It was gratifying to be able to reproduce with Stratfordian rotundity the opening lines of *Henry V:* "O for a muse of fire that would ascend the brightest heaven of invention," but the fire faded and the invention lagged behind after the superfluity of repetition and the students were left with a lot of mouth resonance and little else. What, exactly, had that to do with acting? They were beginning to feel like artifacts in a museum: "Please do not handle the objects on display." We talked about what was going on in America and how RADA could be persuaded to move into the second half of the twentieth century.

Dolores Gray, acclaimed star of *Annie Get Your Gun,* as American as blueberry pie, was enrolled in RADA while she was still demonstrating how Annie got her gun seven times a week at the Coliseum. She, too, was not entirely convinced of the validity of RADA instruction. The Americans put on a production of *The Little Foxes* with different students playing the leads in each act. Dolores, of course, played Regina. They were intent on demonstrating what they were *not* learning at RADA. RADA eventually overhauled its administration; John Fernald* was appointed principal and instituted certain reforms and combated the indifference of the incumbent staff of instructors.

Bob Nichols proved to be a real theater person. Like Bottom in *The Dream* he was ready and eager to play a roaring lion or a sucking dove. He was taken to the bosom of the Players, their captive American, tossing off those music hall and vaudeville favorites, "The Man on the Flying Trapeze" and "The Bowery" as to the manner born. Christopher Hewett found a tiny flat in Hans Place for him around the corner from Harrod's and Bob invited me to share it with him. *Roots* closed and we spent a pastoral autumn, eating Yorkshire pudding and flan, straightening bus queues, watching the leaves change colo[u]r in Hans Place and the cyclorama of the traffic at high and low tides of the Thames—and, of course, going to the theater.

Bob got film work in Germany and pursued his career relentlessly. He married Jennifer, daughter of the distinguished actor Alan Napier, and went back to America, became a father, and worked in the theater wherever there was work to be found. I saw him playing Ben in a summer stock production of *Foxes*. At the moment Ben sees his way clear to outmaneuvering his sister and brother, Bob leaped in the air, clicking his heels together in great high glee. Ben was not likely to express himself so exuberantly, but it was the essence of Bob, the vaudevillian. I saw him holding his own in Boston against a wayward Mickey Rooney in *A Funny Thing Happened on the Way to the Forum*. He had just finished playing Captain Andy on Decca's new and notable full-length recording of Jerome Kern's *Showboat,* is starring with Mitzi Gaynor in the National Company of *Anything Goes,* and has written three plays. I had dinner with Jennifer and Bob recently in Paris. The seventeen-year-old Bob still peeps out from behind the very serious and hard-working family and theater man. The grin and the ebullience are intact.

So I moved about in London, gathering friends unto me that I seemed to have always known. Denis de Marney to whom I was sent by Tennents to have publicity photos taken was one. Manic Denis who had the soul of a performer and comfortable Bill lived in a frenzy they shared with neurotic dachshunds, a magnificent collated record collected, and a grand piano. There were also those

---

* John Fernald is president of the Oxford University Dramatic Society, professional director in the West End, director of the Liverpool Playhouse, principal of RADA for ten years, and professor of dramatic art at Oakland University in the United States.

torn and ambitious boys at the Old Vic, George Rose, Harry Andrews, Ewan Roberts; those rollicking people at the Players—Johnny Heawood, fiendishly witty at almost everyone's expense, upholstered Hattie Jacques, billowing and bawdy, Maurice Browning, crippled from an early bout of polio but feverishly active as a composer, actor, and compère at the Players.

Tennents assigned me a dresser who kept my uniform pressed and held my trousers for me to put my legs through. I had one change—shirt and pants from pristine to ragged and torn and a bandage to tie around my head to lend verisimilitude to my jail escape offstage—twenty minutes into the third act. A dresser was superfluous but David found ways to make himself indispensable. This chestnut-haired, freckled cockney was a walking black market, a repository of theater gossip, an Artful Dodger who worked in the post office by day and placed himself wholeheartedly at my service in the evenings.

He knew where to get clothing coupons, American cigarettes, and French pastry and he hovered when I received visitors in the dressing room. He had lively opinions of everybody but was careful to take his cue from me before pointing any remarks. After four months he accepted an offer to work full time for John Mills (now *Sir* John). He packed up, weeping, "I hope your mother won't hold it against me!" He knew I had described him in letters home. He came back to see me shortly afterward. He said he liked *Mr.* Mills very much. The last time I saw him he had enrolled in the Canadian Navy and showed off his uniform, which went very well with chestnut hair. Meanwhile, back on the plantation, *Roots* had transferred to the Criterion Theatre in Picadilly Circus, which was a tempting site for casual theater-goers, but it really wasn't a Saturday-night-treat kind of play. *Punch* advised its readers to "throw their lorgnettes in the Thames" and see the play. Betsy Drake was considered a charmer in the best American style: "We should like to see her as Rosalind or Beatrice." My photo was on the cover of their three theater magazines: "Will he inherit the mantle of Robeson?" John Van Druten's *Voice of the Turtle* arrived on the West End after a hats-in-the-air run in New York with our very own Margaret Sullavan only to be dismissed by the critics as a trivial affair unworthy of their attention—especially compared with the high seriousness of, for instance, *Roots*. Betsy was restless and dissatisfied. We on the outside couldn't think why. The kingdom was united to grovel and follow wherever her star danced. Tennents released her however, and on her way home she met (and married) Cary Grant. Binkie giggled: "How *about* our Betsy! Well played, Madame."

Turtle didn't make it, but *Roots* played for six months which was honorable but not the landslide success we all expected. We did one last performance at Cambridge and were applauded to the echo—without mikes—in the theater.

⌒ The Othello Syndrome

Paul Robeson

THE FIRST OTHELLO I saw on a Broadway stage was Paul Robeson (1942).* It was the biggest hit of the season. Owen and I could only get standing room. The critics had been cheering, the public was enthralled. It was a historic event in the theater: a black man—all six foot three of him—playing this major Shakespearean role triumphantly and polarizing the pro- and anti-Negro sentiment. Othello caresses his white wife in the first act, slaps her in the second, and murders her at the end; not a motion picture—these are real people! We were unbearably excited. The curtain went up (they *had* curtains in those days) and after that expository scene preparing for Othello's advent, a majestic, robed figure made his entrance—noble, proud, commanding. He spoke and the thunder rolled. The harlequin Iago capered around him throwing his monumental solidity in relief. We stood rapt. "Put up your bright swords, for the dew will rust 'em." Othello was taking charge. On to the Venetian Senate where he counters the accusation that he has used witchcraft to seduce Desdemona. "Rude am I in my speech," he begins—lying in his teeth—and then delivers a poetic, polished, and circumstantial brief, recounting the details of his courtship—courting the Senate simultaneously. He wins the case and Desdemona hands down—besides, the Venetian state needs him to crush the Turkish enemy in Cyprus.

By this time we had heard almost all the notes in this Othello's scale. We began to anticipate the repetitive melody. The bass section threatened to overwhelm speech, the sonority fogged the careful diction. No matter. The first scenes need little more than presence and Paul had a plenitude. Once in Cyprus

---

* Since Othello as a role had come to represent the height of a black actor's ambition—the seal on his life's work—I began to "collect" performances and accounts of same.

the acting begins and Owen and I, independently of each other, started to fidget. Since we were standing, the fidgets took the form of walking about in crippled circles, trying not to disturb our fellow standees. We emerged crestfallen at the intermission. "What will they say when a *real* Othello comes along?" we asked each other plaintively. Margaret Webster, the English director who had piloted Maurice Evans to Broadway stardom with *Richard II, Hamlet,* and *Falstaff,* later queried in print: "Is it possible to have a great Othello without having a good one?"—a very moot question. Paul was a great-souled man but he had not yet a technique to project the shades of madness and obsession that possessed the Moor. He was hamstrung and muscle-bound. "Roar" he did, but it was a hollow sound. It did not convey the tortured brain or the heart's pain. Stark Young, sympathetic to the effort, wrote that he had not the "instinct and phrasing" for wearing the costumes. The monumental became stolidity. His body did not cooperate with the tremors, the collapse, the twisted rage the words indicated. We were sick at heart; what disloyalty not to admire the man and the impact of his breakthrough and what arrogance to disagree with the critics and the public.

Canada Lee

Canada Lee was furious—jealous, of course, but also genuinely disappointed by Robeson's failure to plumb the depths. Canada began to study the role and the next year played it in the theater of the New School for Social Research. He didn't have the stature for the part and in a mistaken effort to "humanize" the material, he domesticated and colloquialized it. This great guy, Othello, see, misled by his best friend, betrayed by his white wife, and seeking vengeance on a white world—a soap-opera plot with diction and postures to match. He couldn't fall from a giddy height—he never attained that height. This was not Broadway and the critics didn't report on it—which was just as well. Canada kept on trying and played Othello again in 1948 in New York State, but the basic lacks remained basically lacking.

Robert Earl Jones

My next skirmish with the play came about when Robert Earl Jones (James's father) asked me to direct him in the title role. He was an exuberant, big, booming good fellow with stevedore-muscle strength. He wanted to do the play because he wanted to do the part. Why not? It was to be done on a shoestring. We couldn't afford sets or costumes. Never mind—we'll do it in "modern dress": telephones and cigarettes and a lot of anachronistic props and business. Opening night in New Jersey, 1947, I made a silly speech to the audience about the play being the thing, existing and effective, undependent on costume or period. Owen was beside himself with disdain for my hypocrisy and feebleness. I didn't examine or treat the play as a modern restatement that would comment on and counterpoint the language. "Modernity" was an unintegrated gimmick. I should have said "we haven't any money and we have not attempted to make a virtue of necessity." I spent most of my time and concentration trying to direct Robert Earl. I didn't know enough and neither did he. He had nothing like the training needed to come to grips with the verse or the characterization. Being big, black, and imposing was not enough. The only gain to me personally was a clear demonstration of my shortcomings and the performance Lee gave as Cassio (in spite of his fury at my refusal to cast him as Iago). Cassio, a weak man but a strong part, took the honors this time. Lee was, in the recurring critics' phrase, "a talent to be watched" and Othello was a role to be avoided and a play to approach with prayer and fasting.

Austin Briggs-Hall

The most moving and passionate Othello I ever saw was in an incomplete version in a workshop performance in the forties with an actor in full charge of the raging tempest Othello becomes. The actor's name was Austin Briggs-Hall. He was small and black and West Indian—an actor who investigated his roles from the inside out, experimentally piling detail upon detail but finally winnowing the lot and presenting the whole complex man, eloquently noble, authoritative, murderous, and suicidal. Austin was Polonius* to my Hamlet, a role he was born to play, being disputatious in life and a vehement debater with an untiring tongue—very West Indian, in fact. We played Algy and Jack in a Harlem production of *The Importance of Being Earnest.* We played in a potted version of *Crime and Punishment.* He was an extraordinary Raskolnikov, neurotic and haunted, knocking at the gates of Hell, demanding entrance. In *Death Takes a Holiday* he played an army major trying to fathom the mysteries of existence, far from his ordinary line of speculation. This bluff military man wrestling with the verities he had never before considered—like Richard Bennett's major in Orson Welles's film, *The Magnificent Ambersons,* trying to elucidate the significance of death and beyond. Austin penetrated to the core of this inarticulate but vulnerable major, breathing in his rhythm and speaking from his brain. We understood the man and appreciated the actor. Austin and I played together for the last time as father and son in *Hamlet* (he was my father's

---

* Austin always said delightedly: "Only *you* would have cast me as Polonius." Amusing partly because *Owen* had cast him, but anyone in the theater who knew Polonius would have thought of Austin forthwith!

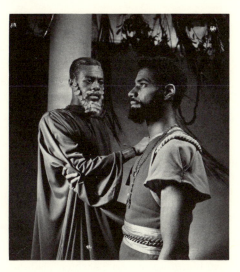

Austin Briggs-Hall and Gordon Heath as father and son in the American Negro Theatre's production of Owen Dodson's *Garden of Time* (1945).

ghost as well as Polonius). Earlier that same year he had played my father in Owen's *Garden of Time* at the American Negro Theatre, of which he was a founding member. He toured with Margaret Webster's second bus-and-truck tour playing Lucius in *Julius Caesar* and Biandello in *The Taming of the Shrew*. He came to see me whenever I played in New York—keen and critical—but for reasons unknown to me, he and the theater parted company. He said, however, if I ever put a troupe together in the United States he would want to be part of it. He died in 1988, sincerely mourned, and he has been greatly missed. I thought he was the best black classical actor of my generation.

Walter Huston

Walter Huston, John's father, played Othello for the Theatre Guild just before my theater-going time. Robert Edmond Jones, the great theater designer, wrapped the show in yards of Renaissance richness. Brian Aherne (Iago) stepped out of a Veronese painting. But even in the atmospheric Valente photographs, Huston looks like a Spanish pirate. A good, even very good actor, but the critics rejected his conception as fatally lacking in the poetry that keeps Othello from being just another ignoble savage.

John Neville/Richard Burton

In 1956 at the Old Vic in London, John Neville and Richard Burton alternated as Iago and Othello (as had Edwin Booth and Henry Irving in the 1880s). Both of them stopped off at Iago and never arrived at Othello.

Errol John

Errol John, with whom I had worked in the television *Cry, the Beloved Country,* was British, lightweight but dark-skinned. He had a go at Othello in 1956 and was slaughtered by the critics. He had, they said, neither the voice nor the weight to carry the part. He won the Observer prize as a playwright with *Moon on a Rainbow Shawl.* I hope its production was consoling and compensatory.

William Marshall

William Marshall, American, with the required height, breadth, and blackness, played Othello at the Dublin Gate Theatre in 1962 with Orson Welles's old pals, Micheál MacLiammóir and Hilton Edwards. I didn't see it but William assured me he was a good Othello. Harold Hobson, the London *Sunday Times* critic, gave him a warm notice—which made us a trifle suspicious. Hobson was a legend in the profession for his occasionally bizarre appraisals of performances. One of our dear English friends, the actor Robert Flemyng, said wistfully, "Gielgud, whom I idolize, before he brought me to New York in *The Importance of Being Earnest,* said, 'Robert, my dear, the trouble is you have no style!' I long for praise from Ken Tynan who has never, in my stage lifetime, given me a good notice. Hobson gives me very good notices to which I pay no attention at all, damn it!" (Some actors don't give a damn about what the critics say. I wish I were one of their number.) But William played Othello on the West Coast to quite good notices on the whole.

Sir John Gielgud

Sir John was going to get it in the neck himself. He dared Othello at Stratford-on-Avon (1961) under Franco Zeffirelli's direction. Opening night his beard came off during the second act, but evidently the entire performance was catastrophic and that detail was only symbolic. It was too easy to say, from the distant perspective of London, that he had miscast himself—a tenor in a baritone role—but I was curious nonetheless. There must have been wonders by the way. Val Gielgud, his brother, was producing me at the BBC in a TV piece at the time. He said, "John doesn't want you to see him. He's too embarrassed by his own performance!" I stayed in London. Afterward, Sir John picked himself up, dusted himself off, and went about the business of being a great actor—just as always. To fail as Othello is no disgrace. Along with Hamlet and Macbeth, it is a role that almost never satisfies everybody. These three are targets in a shooting gallery—and *Lear* has so often been pronounced "unplayable" that no one expects it to be played.

Orson Welles

Orson produced and played Othello on the West End in 1951—a reverberant and empty performance on stage. His film* was inventive and alive but his financial difficulties led him to cut corners and too much of the text. His own playing was heavy and inconsequent; glorious settings and magnificently conceived passages but thin characterizations and faulty dubbing.

Ralph Richardson

In 1938 Laurence Olivier played Iago to Ralph Richardson's Othello at the Old Vic. Olivier, with Tyrone Guthrie directing, attempted to motivate Iago from the premise that Iago was in love with Othello. At a rehearsal Richard responded to Olivier's voluptuous kiss on the mouth with a "There, there now; dear boy; *good* boy," and would have none of it. I don't know what Olivier substituted for the "love theme" but the production seems not to have succeeded and Richardson was obviously wrong as Othello.

Godfrey Tearle

I saw in 1948 Sir Godfrey Tearle's Edwardian Othello—authoritatively spoken, dignified, and slightly dull and old-fashioned—no collapse, no fit, frenzy quite absent. A prime minister mindful of his constituency.

Comédie Francaise

In Paris at the Comédie Française everyone was miscast—especially the translator. Shakespearian productions in France are generally an obstacle race. The language is never as allusive and wide-ranging as the original. The puns are leveled out (not necessarily a bad thing). French is specific, not suggestive, and the breath-taking Shakespearean mixture of the homely and the sublimely poetic vanishes, leaving bleached bones on the shore. The histories, being more didactic, fare better, but it is an uneasy matter at best. The Othello in this production pointed to Mecca—interesting but unconvincing. The production itself was absurd.

Raoul Julia

I saw other productions in New York in the eighties. Raoul Julia at Joe Papp's theater in Central Park couldn't begin to cope with Richard Dreyfuss (of film

---

* Micheál MacLiammóir's book, *Put Money in Thy Purse* (London: Methuen, Ltd., 1960) is a hilarious account of Welles shooting the film in Venice and Morocco.

fame) as Iago. Not a clue had the latter, just generalized venom and unhinged monologues. Julia presented an outline of Othello that was never filled in. The production was perfunctory and forgettable.

James Earl Jones

Then there was the Winter Garden production (1982). Iago and Roderigo sat at a bistro table just opposite Desdemona's father's second-story window and discussed Desdemona's marriage at an outdoor-voice level. Othello trundled in and rumbled on. I waited to see what Desdemona would be like and then left quietly. I admired James enormously in *The Great White Hope* (and lately in *Fences*) but I wouldn't say he had then the equipment for leading "classic" roles. He worked too hard and too painfully to speak "well" for one thing.

Earle Hyman

Earle, an old comrade, played it at the Roundabout Theatre in 1978. I found his performance incomprehensible. I never knew what he was getting at. He had played it more or less successfully at Stratford-on-the-Housatonic and at Antioch in the fifties. Perhaps he was trying to avoid reproducing his earlier performances but this one was bafflingly eccentric. The *Statesman* and *Nation* reviewed Ralph Richardson's 1952 Stratford season saying, "Sir Ralph cannot possibly know what he is doing." That's what I felt about Earle this time around. Sir Ralph was perhaps the most unpredictable of the great English actors—unpredictable and often other-worldly. That Stratford season seems to have been particularly aberrant. His Falstaff, his Peer Gynt, his Cyrano, and his appearances in Pinter plays were extraordinary theater events.

෴ From almost the first moment I landed in England, journalists, critics, and colleagues speculated openly about when—not if—I was going to play the Moor. I saw the photos, read the notices Robeson had garnered in 1930 when Peggy Ashcroft was his Desdemona at Stratford-on-Avon. The photos were disconcerting, the costumes were disfiguring, and he looked like an overgrown schoolboy. Still, he had the presence and that voice and the Isles had never seen anything like it. He was a legend and *Show Boat* with "Old Man River" and his social success, especially with women, all propelled him to spectacular fame.

I was not that keen to play Othello. It was too expected and I would surely suffer by comparison with my predecessor. I played—predictably—*The Emperor Jones* on radio and TV, Canada's old role in *Cry, the Beloved Country* for the BBC TV and fared well enough critically. Inevitably the British Arts Council pro-

Playbill for the 1950
British tour of *Othello*

posed *Othello:* a five-month (record-breaking) tour through the Midlands, North England, Scotland, and Wales. It was to be directed by Kenneth Tynan, one of the Oxford *wunderkinder*—skin and bones, lank light hair, and a distressing speech defect that twisted his face and didn't allow his words to keep pace with his surging ideas. Before rehearsals ended we were all reflecting in some way or other his disability—not mockingly but admiringly and subjugated to his imagination and iconoclasm. Othello in Venice would be dressed in the Queen Anne period—mostly because Ken hated tights: black satin breeches, buckled shoes, black and silver turban, frilled and billowing shirts, and a handsome, rust-red, long suede waistcoat. Bianca, the whore, would be a waif; Emilia, Iago's wife, would be a placid, buxom, brown-skin lady, the "Willow Song" would be set to the melody of Tchaikovsky's "Italian Caprice," and the ribbon of incidental music would be an on-and-off-stage guitarist. The murder of Desdemona was conceived as a ritual execution—Othello carrying out a sentence of death like a Japanese samurai with a scimitar poised in his open hands (but never used!). He strangled Desdemona with the fatal handkerchief she claims to have lost and he commits suicide cutting his throat—from which gushed blood, shocking the groundlings, from the Northern industrialists to the dour Scots and the even dourer Welsh, look you. My Desdemona was a stocky blonde, adoring but unfazed and able to put up a good fight. Many in our audience were seeing the play for the first time and they didn't know how it would come out. Desdemona slugged in the in-fighting—she might even win! Valerie White's Desdemona inflamed Othello's jealousy with perfect self-possession, as if she couldn't believe he could be so stupid. But the jewel of the production was Julian Somers—the best Iago I've ever seen. Raw, crude, a common soldier, jealous of being overlooked in company promotion, hating Othello for being black and in authority and preferred by the state of Venice and Desdemona. Cynical and obscene but presenting a hail-fellow well-met, grousing sergeant. This Iago was a superb stage manager—all things to all men, but especially to his general who valued his unpolished "honesty" and had reason to appreciate his acumen—as I had reason to appreciate Julian's tact as an actor in all our scenes together. We had fine notices from local newspapers all through the tour—even after Valerie—great chum like Carol Goodner—gave a couple of bumpy performances and left us a few weeks before the run ended. Perhaps the tour was too grueling—that record-breaking five-month stretch. I had only enough energy to carry me through the long, late and early bus trips, nightly performances and relaxation in the company of a charming British faun, Martin, playing an unlikely Cypriot native (whom I had not met in an uptown dance group either). I didn't join the youngish company in their enthusiastic sight-seeing—exploring the Wordsworth lakes and climbing in the lowering Welsh and Scottish mountainsides, inspecting the Cardiff castle—all those three-star tourist attractions. I was often reminded that I was the oldest member of this lovable crowd.

Ken Tynan was extremely articulate in spite of his stutter. He knew what he wanted from the actors but he was very seldom able to help them carry out his quicksilver direction. I don't think he had an inclusive vision of the play. He had prejudices and inspirations and we had to justify them on stage. The play began with a glimpse of Othello's wedding reception—in a doorway, light streaming from the interior—Desdemona chatting with guests, including Cassio and Emilia. Othello was more elegant than anyone in Venice, including the Doge. He had to be: you cannot be "monumental" in satin breeches, silk stockings, and buckled pumps when you are six-feet tall, slim, and looking much younger than your thirty-two years. So I opted to play a hypercivilized general—a nonpareil of Venetian nobility—polished and deadly. I got back into Moroccan robes in Cyprus, thankfully—but I carried out the ritual murder in a loincloth! The Cypriots were hostile and violent in their occupied country—not easy to delineate with six extras! The portable set, trellises, awnings, a bench, and a bed, provided what a reviewer called "symbolic touches." Even Shrewsbury in North England, living near enough to Stratford-on-Avon to be just a little snobbish about an itinerant troupe infringing on its patent, admired the production and the playing, tut-tutting about the innovations, but held from beginning to end. I walked about in the village streets in my voluminous duffel coat and black beard on market day. The population, carefully, did not stare, but a little boy, about five years old, pulled on his mother's skirt, "Mummy, look at the black man!" She was too polite to turn around. He persisted, "Mummy, *look* at the black man!" She didn't and wouldn't and he had the spectacle all to himself. It wasn't an unfriendly atmosphere—they just were not gapers. Ken went on to become England's most brilliant theater critic since Bernard Shaw and literary adviser to Olivier at the new National Theatre. He had a large share in choosing the NT's repertoire and put pressure of Sir Laurence to play Othello. Ken was disliked almost as much as he was admired. Drama critics are not out to curry favor and he all but destroyed not a few mummers in passing. Olivier prized him as a gadfly and an intellectual stimulant.

He didn't intimidate us and was never cutting or cruel (unless you want to point to his choice of period and costume for our production), not to our faces, at least. He nicknamed me "General Camp" ("I had been happy if the general camp, pioners and all, had tasted her sweet body"—Act 3, scene 3) but not publicly. He'd come up to see the show on some of our play dates and, exactly like Daphne Rye during *Roots,* would ask first, "Who's sleeping with whom?"

Our resident guitarist, Juli, a little cockney lad with dirt under his fingernails and a passion for jazz, would play enthusiastically for our improvised parties on the road. Once he was playing a Bach prelude, immersed in it, though we were his rapt audience. He came to the end, looked up at us and said casually, "Segovia stumbles a bit in that passage." We were appropriately speechless. Juli grew up to be Julian Bream, England's most celebrated lutenist and guitarist who plays on records and in concerts to appropriately speechless audiences.

I played *Othello* on BBC TV in 1955—practically over Mr. Robert Adams's dead body. Mr A had been *the* Negro actor in the British Isles on the strength of several films and a number of supporting roles on stage. He was also a barrister and my London agent said he had managed to issue a challenge on the floor of the House of Parliament to my being employed and cast as Othello when, he asserted, there were actors, British subjects, with adequate talent to do as much or more. The authorities consulted the BBC casting director who assured them that they had auditioned the black actors, including Mr A, in the U.K. and none of them came near to their requirements—either G. Heath or no one. Mr Adams's claim was disallowed. I knew the West Indian and African actors in England and their hostility to the phenomenon of foreign actors imported for the big roles in all the media. The fact is that most of them were, at the time, insufficiently trained and spoke English with their own accents and lacked discipline and organization. They also felt themselves victims of a certain kind of "racial" prejudice. I had played not only Brutus Jones in *Emperor Jones* (who was—at least, American), but a South African in *Cry, the Beloved Country,* a West Indian in the play *The Man on the Stairs,* an African barrister in the film *Saphire,* and so on. Equity rules placed me as an "International Star," which meant that I could only play leading and featured roles whenever and wherever. Now here was the plum classic role of the decade and they were not even in the running. They were, understandably bitter. Times have changed since and directors in England have been using native black actors much more imaginatively. The actors themselves are better trained, more flexible, less insular, and more militant. As the nonwhite population increases, filmmakers are forced to reflect their existence in contemporary life and their uneasy or triumphant integration.

My TV *Othello* was directed by Tony Richardson who said with *his* slight stutter, just before the first reading with the assembled cast, "You must remember that Othello is v-v-very jealous and D-d-Desdemona is entirely innocent." (I wrote it down!) We were grateful for this insight. A slightly bemused Rosemary Harris was my Desdemona and Paul Rogers, the Iago. Paul ate grapes and spat out the seeds more or less at the camera (you could tell he was the villain). The BBC boasted it was the best TV Shakespeare to date and sent it to Moscow. I don't know what they thought of it there. They had a showing for me and my mother in London (1973). I found my performance "cabin'd, crib'd and confined" by the chalk marks on the studio floor. As the *Statesman* and *Nation* reported, "We could not quite believe that Mr Heath would hurt a fly," but the rest of the notice wasn't bad (and my mother loved it!). I got loads of fan mail and collected on the rerun (but not from the Soviets!).

I saw a rock musical in London called *Catch My Soul* ("Perdition catch my soul but I do love thee"—also Act 3, scene 3) with a rangy Texan singing Iago and a black rock star, Lonnie Satin, singing Othello (music far from Verdi, in which Othello is a tenor). There was no need to analyze Iago's motives—he just hated niggers. The transposition to the south of America made a lurid and vulgar spectacle—book by William Shakespeare. The next year, 1972, a Paris production of *Catch* was proposed and I was asked if I was interested. I was. I thought—mistakenly—I could play and sing a classic Othello in this frame. A British director came over to handle it. What was left of the text, in French, was close enough to the original, but we had to use hand mikes for the song (also in French). That in itself turned off the public and the critics. But I bore the brunt of the criticisms. As one they wrote scathingly of the show and me in particular. One critic said, "This performance proves that "they" (blacks, that is) "don't all have natural talent—and I'm not talking about the captivating Miss Nancy Holloway!" (black singer-actress who played the strumpet, Bianca). Insult to injury. Only Tom Quinn Curtiss in the *International Herald Tribune,* although objecting to the mikes, allowed that I was better than adequate. When critics

Gordon Heath in the 1955 BBC production of *Othello*

are all but unanimously damning I am inclined to conclude they are right; besides my friends did not entirely disagree with the critics. The show closed in a week. I had a long, slow, painful convalescence.

Tommaso Salvini

Salvini, the Italian actor, seems to have transfixed English audiences in his time—long before mine—with Edwin Booth's Iago.

Frederick Valk

In 1946, the Czech Frederick Valk earned Tynan's most admiring adjectives—although the poetry could not have been intact, the passion was overwhelming.

There was a certain confusion in the attitude of critics and observers. They held that it was the verse and the speech that produced the greatest effect and summed up the performance of Shakespeare. When Olivier challenged that conviction and deliberately chose to speak lines as he felt them and make his own emphases, they said he was mangling the verse. When he came of age theatrically, his authority and genius carried the day and they had to acknowledge the utter rightness of his interpretations. Neither Valk nor Salvini could speak "beautiful" Royal Academy iambics but their passion and identification with the character lifted the English out of their seats. *Othello* is *about* passion and Othello is an exotic presence—and to hell with pear-shaped vowels!

Sir Laurence Olivier

Sir Laurence, steeling himself for the ordeal, blacked himself up all over, worked on his voice production to add a few bass baritone notes, and put on stage several kinds of Negro—carefully studied and mimed with his usual uncanny skill. His first appearance: coal-black, red-lipped, fuzzy short-haired wig, dressed in a white wraparound robe, sniffing at the reddest rose this side of Picardy (probably from Desdemona's wedding bouquet—if I know Ken Tynan), and all this with a swaying, arrogant calypso walk—a picturesque and beautiful apparition. (Joan Plowright, his wife, said to me wistfully, "It's very disappointing when he washes it all off at night!")

Most of us black actors attempting Othello play it with the lofty diction that Shakespeare seems to demand. (G. B. Shaw said the secret is in the music of the poetry.) We work to find the rhythm and the poetry on its own level. We are frequently inhibited as a result. We resist "black" intonations and "black" comportment. We are really out to play "white" Othellos! Sir Laurence turned all that on its head and played him as a contemporary black, letting the poetry fall where it might. He chose, I thought, the wrong kind of Negro(es) to impersonate and his rightly celebrated "technique" showed through the burnt cork. I admired the virtuosity but felt nothing for the man. He took hair-raising chances, growling, purring, screaming, whimpering, chanting the verse, playing Lear and Caliban with all the stops pulled out. He was dangerous and regal and touchy and vain and unlikable (so is Othello on the whole) but one watched the wheels turning and never became involved. Frank Finlay's Iago was never allowed to be the mainspring of the action and Maggie Smith's Desdemona was a trifle nasal and hostessy, but wonderfully touching at the end. John Dexter's production was packed with juicy details and the tale unfolded excitingly, but we did not weep. Mine is a minority opinion but not a unique one.

Ira Aldridge

I cannot omit the black American actor, Ira Aldridge (1807–1867), the grand-daddy of us all. He played Othello in England, Europe, and Russia. He played Lear in the Russian provinces (the rest of the cast spoke Russian!)—a curious phenomenon altogether. His photographs reveal a short, almost squat man, bearing a slight resemblance to Canada Lee. One wonders how good an actor he really was. The style of classic acting in that period was florid and oratorical. He seems to have been daringly naturalistic. His blackness had novelty and he evidently handled his career and his publicity shrewdly. He married a white woman and lived and died in Europe. What would we have thought of him? He was compared to—at least referred to—as "the black Roscius." Roscius was the most famous and prosperous Roman actor to his day (B.C.), which seems to me to go a long way back to make a comparison, but he belongs to legend (Aldridge, I mean) and who can say where legend and performance meet!

Footnote without asterisk: Afterthoughts—

There they are—these, our players, seeking to storm the heavens, put on the spot, fragmentarily and unfairly.

Othello misses greatness by being fatalistic.

What he loves belongs to him—Iago as well as Desdemona—as God loved Adam because he created him.

Othello is certain what he thinks is right because it is what he thinks.

There he is, poor man (and poor actor!) set down in a melodramatic, improbable farrago, all around, but beneath, him.

"It is better as it is" he says when Iago wants to threaten Desdemona's father. "I have done the State" [of Venice] some service and they know it" in his last speech; how lofty can we be? (de Gaulle? Napoleon?)

Shakespeare created (albeit with some condescension) a Racinian figure who, like Shylock, climbs out of his surroundings, who cannot be the "hero" but is the "leading man," by enormous lengths, to be sure.

Black reaction to Eugene O'Neill's *Emperor Jones* is regret that he made Jones a debased Henri Christophe, the emperor of Haiti, whose actual history is virile and noble. Sometimes I think Shakespeare debased Othello in the same way (even though Othello had no real existence) and that is one of the reasons so many people are left unsatisfied even as they succumb to the ingenuity of the plot and the poetry, but Othello is "made of sterner stuff!"

"Moor" in Shakespeare means "black" and he with all his theatrical cunning and instinct saw it working as black against white, color-wise, that is, and then he wrote beyond himself—or the character went beyond him.

The Anglo-Saxon, Gallic, Latin, and evolved African temperaments are alien to this Moorish, disdainful, in-born hubris. The performance should be in Allah's hands—pointing to Mecca is not a bad starting point. Ken Tynan had me holding a scimitar but it was a belated gesture—it should have been the heart of the matter.

Othello, in its way, is as "unplayable" as *Lear.* But these are "but wild and whirling words." Verdi said the last one: *Othello* was probably always an opera.

∾ Paris, One Way

A POUTER-PIGEON BOSTONIAN with a Bourbon profile and legitimate social pretensions and slightly less valid artistic and political ones had attached herself to me around 1948. I attached myself to her in return and imprudently let Marge into my life.

She was a woman to be reckoned with: a great cook, a great driver (she had driven an ambulance in World War II), endowed with appreciative and hearty laughter, cursed with frequent migraines, and possessed by an inherited sense of responsibility to culture and causes. In most ways, a typical public-spirited Boston woman right out of the pages of Henry James: complex and driven, fueled by her ego; possessive; jealous; and domineering. If I had thought "Henry James" to begin with, I might have been more on my guard.

She invited me for weekends at her house in Harvard, Massachusetts. We talked of writers and artists, played records of Sacha Guitry and Yvonne Printemps and French operettas. Photographs of the façade of Chartres Cathedral were pinned to her walls.

She knew of Owen and met Eddie, Lee, and Beryl. Beryl was invited to her downtown New York apartment—a piece of transplanted Shaker New England. Beryl inspected it all, expressionless until she opened one of the books. She gurgled happily (referring to the notation of the date and place of acquisition written carefully inside the back cover of the book), "Oh, you do the same thing as Gordon!" Not a fortunate remark; it should have been "Gordon does the same thing as you," at least. My lady began knitting Beryl's name into her long scarf.

She gave Eddie a job working as household help and employed Lee to handle some of her affairs and accounts. She did her best to embroil us all even further—Pandora as Lady Bountiful—but we joined forces finally against her.

Our literary conversations came to rest with the introduction of the name

Thomas Wolfe, dead at thirty-eight. She admitted with covert pride that she was a character in one of the novels. She was not treated tenderly in Tom's account. They were in Paris, she and Tom, seeing a great deal of each other, for Tom was, in his tortured way, in love with her Boston companion. She sighed, "If only I could have reached Tom. I might have rescued him before his fate overtook him. So few people realized that he would have gone on to great heights if death had not intervened." (Most people considered that Tom was written out and almost as many, without malice, hoped so.) "I want to do a book about him. I want to put the record straight, explain Tom a little and prove as nearly as I can how much the world of literature lost when Tom died." I was touched: *Look Homeward, Angel* had been our adolescent vade mecum, the bible of teenage rebellion. Like James Dean in his time, the book offered a symbol of growing-up turmoil and hostility to parental authority, or the lack of it. The rest of his work rambled, insistent that his experience must be recorded in conscientious detail because it happened to *him*. Long-winded autobiography that only his *passion* for life gave a kind of life.

"My dear, only you could help me realize my dream. I couldn't do it without your help." I confess that my real regard and affection for the lady was joined to the possibility of exploiting her as well. I encouraged her to follow up her dream and off we went to the Houghton Library at Harvard University to rifle the Wolfe collection. Wolfe's letters to his love, to his New York mistress, Aline Bernstein,* the designer, and to his publisher, Maxwell Perkins, had already been incorporated into his fiction. It was clear that Tom wrote compulsively and endlessly and Max and Edward Aswell at Scribner's and Harper's rearranged and put together the compilation between covers so they could be called "novels." Tom confessed that he wrote too much and without discrimination and owed everything to Max's organizing genius. It was not going to be easy to extract my lady's thesis from this material but "with my help" perhaps we could put up a good show. "My dear, I can't do this here. I will only feel close to Tom in France. That's where I knew him," she wept nostalgically and reached out to me. I held her hard, masculine perfidy rampant. I had waited for this moment. "Could you undertake this exhausting task with me. Come as my secretary, my colleague, whatever. . . ." (She had said to the woman in charge at the library, "I will be bringing my *colored* secretary to work with me." She couldn't understand why I was furious.)

I am your friend; I am your secretary. If it is important to you that I am your Negro friend or your Negro secretary then I am not your man. If it is important to your friends that I am a Negro friend and to your business associates that I am a Negro

---

* Aline Bernstein, celebrated theater designer for the Theatre Guild, also wrote a book telling *her* side of the story.

secretary then I am not theirs, either. When you imply it is important by pointing it out yourself you are placing yourself on the level of those who think it is important, distinctive, necessary to be told, a special circumstance. When you say "he is a Negro" they hear "*but* he is a Negro" or "in spite of the fact that he is a Negro." If they felt as you do, there would be no need for you to specialize; if they do not, they are not my friends and I have no desire to meet them. In other words you are apologizing either for my being a Negro, or saying in compensation, "I dont know how you feel, but I'm proud to be his friend". If you introduced me and spoke of me simply as your friend you would already have said you are proud by implication. I can see no other reason. (Letter to Marge, 1948)

"Oh my dear, I wouldn't hurt you for the world. Please forgive me." (Tears and supplication and a vicious migraine.)

The same year she put ten thousand dollars into Huddie Ledbetter's* career. Huddie was singing work songs and blues in the downtown clubs. He would do his engagement and then, lured by the promise of unstinted gin, would sing for anyone anywhere as long as the gin lasted. Certainly he was being exploited and her offer to back him was intended as security for Martha, his wife, whom she genuinely loved. Besides cherishing the idea of being Lady Bountiful, she wanted to prove Huddie was an extraordinary and unique guitarist. She consulted with musicians to solicit their authority and support for her claim. She proposed to put Huddie in a tuxedo—no more gaudy woolen shirts and jeans. He was going to be a concert artist. I don't know what I thought of all this nonsense. Maybe Huddie *was* the Segovia-Django Reinhardt of the folk guitar. Marge's ego was so far in front of her that it obscured her real motives even from herself. Huddie had a lot of ego in his cosmos too and I don't think he liked white people much. He liked women and liquor.

She asked me to stage-manage his gigs. "Huddie," I said, "C'mon, Huddie, let's get out. Leave them wanting more." He stood open-mouthed, then he chuckled, then he laughed. "Man," he said, "You are really something!" but he came away with me.

The next weeks were dedicated to organizing our emigration: lawyers for Ledbetter, inventory, packing, soliciting advice from anyone who could be cornered, boat reservations, wires ahead for housing in Paris, and all that.

She had a black (light-skinned) houseboy, Clifton, who handled her and her household with detachment and cynicism and only occasional hysteria. He was efficient, thorough, and indispensable and he would go with us. The migraines confined her to bed for days at a time. Perrier, which she called "buzzy water"

---

* Huddie Ledbetter, known as "Leadbelly," was serving a term in a southern chain gang for having killed a man in a fight. According to the legend, he was released after singing for the governor of the state. John Lomax, the folksong collector, interested himself in presenting Ledbetter as a public performer.

("buzzy" for short), sympathy, and pills, and all her paper work brought to the bed. She read in bed, holding her books to the height of her eyes, resting very lightly on her elbows—strong wrists, aristocratic hands. She sought to live with grace. She was deeply conscious of her ancestry and mindful of the judgments of posterity. She was not rich but she had money. She would not, of course, touch capital. She paid me as a secretary, but not extravagantly. She did not offer to subsidize my career, although, as it turned out, I would have been a more profitable investment than Ledbetter. No matter. I wanted to get back to Europe and she needed help with her Thomas Wolfe project. We were booked to sail on a classless ship of the Holland-American Line. And that, dear children, is how I got to Paris! The preparation for the trip was tedious. It was not that she refused to delegate authority—she delegated it right and left. To Lee, Eddie, Clifton, her lawyers, and me, to say nothing of all those innocent bystanders she buttonholed en route. She double-checked at every juncture, contradicted herself, and dithered right and left playing her delegates off against each other with an ingenuity worthy of a better cause. She was, I realized, even then, terrified by the implications of what she had undertaken. My support was equivocal. Her motives were mixed and at odds with each other. Leaving America was a wrenching experience. She was apprehensive that the press would interest itself in her movements and she boarded the ship like a fugitive from justice, scurrying to her stateroom to protect her anonymity, and asking us to stay out of sight and avoid the "reporters." But long before the ship pulled out she wrapped tulle around her throat for courage, muttering: "Well, if I must, I must" and went on deck. (Lee wrote me afterward that she had focussed on a woman in the onshore crowd and waggled a hand at her. The woman blinked, looked at her, baffled.) Marge thanked Clifton for fending off the "reporters." Lee wrote there was indeed a reporter who said: "Wasn't that Gordon Heath on the ship?" (I never told Marge.) Her pretensions were insufferable and we were off to a bad start. I was ill-tempered and withdrawn for the entire voyage. She held court all over the ship and tried to tease me into a better mood but had to settle for Clifton as her companion. He was insouciant, intending to enjoy every moment. Marge as a spectacle amused him enormously.

We reached Paris by way of half-rebuilt Rotterdam. We were installed in separate rooms in a small hotel in the Latin Quarter opposite a family restaurant whose proprietor was an old acquaintance of Marge's. Mme Bohy tagged napkin rings for us after our first meal together. The food was of course a joyous experience. The prices were modest and the atmosphere was warm and welcoming. I relaxed—not much, but a little. Marge was reluctant to begin working. She gingered up a sluggish bureaucracy and got a 1948 Ford (promptly named "la Fille" like its Harvard predecessor) in two days. She proposed to tour the Normandy coast which she had known well as an ambulance driver. We stayed in the first-class hotels with first-class cuisines but the beaches were still stark shambles. We doubled back by way of Chartres. There were angels in the air and the cathedral itself with its stone-saints façade and the winsome battered clock cherub didn't prepare one for the femininity of the whole and the crystalline transparency of the stained glass. The windows were only half reinstalled, having been removed during the war and stored away, a feat almost as breathtaking in the imagination as conceiving them in the first place. We came back to Paris refreshed and realigned as partners. Marge tried to arrange her memories and her perspectives from the past. Exhausting—especially because she was frantically rearranging and fitting pieces together to make them support her theory.

So here I was, back in Europe, across the channel from the land of heart's desire—thanks, really to Thomas Wolfe, apostle of rebellion. I didn't permit myself to form attitudes about France. Marge had reverted to her prewar self: France was her kingdom, Paris her fief, and the French so malleable, so responsive to her authority, her command of the language, and her understanding of their lucidity and logic—such dears, all of them. I went with her to Rumpelmayers to buy those wonderful disques d'or, thin circles of chocolate with gold flecks. At the cashier's desk she professed to remember the manager, the cashier, and most of the help from ten years before. "But of course you remember me. I used to come with my little boy"—her hand indicated his height—"he loved the disques d'or." They all hastened to assure her that she and her little boy were alive in their memory and always had been. It was clear to an onlooker that they didn't know her from Clara Barton but they went along charmingly with the gag. "Mais, bien sûr, Madame—et comment va l'adorable petit," etc. As we stepped back out on the Rue Royale she touched the corners of her eyes, moist with not-quite-shed tears, saying "You see, they *do* remember— bless their hearts."

(I had no intention of falling heir to Marge's nostalgic illusions and impressions. In five months Lee would be arriving—experiencing France could wait until then!)

We marked time and welcomed diversions: Josephine Baker in "her" night-club dressed by Patou, using the pillars that rose to the ceiling as props and décor, moving sinuously between them, clutching them as if they were her dance partners. False eyelashes like fans—the birdlike voice we knew from records was huskier, lower, and fuller, more like a singer than a denizen of a rain forest, but she herself was assured, sleek, and glamorous. The opening night appearance of the Dunham dancers saw Josephine in a box sparkling with diamonds like a glass chandelier. The Garde Républicaine in red and white uniforms and silver helmets with horse-tail plumes lined the entrance of the Théâtre de Paris as if it were a royal wedding or—at least—a visit from a foreign ambassador. The dancers took it all as their just due and returned elegance for elegance. Not since Diaghilev's Russian Ballet ravished Paris thirty years before had a dance spectacle so completely captured "le tout Paris."

But finally Marge had to cope with getting a book written. She went to bed and nested there. She talked, she reminisced, she glorified her "progress" like Elizabeth I being assured of her subjects' loyalty. I spliced, pasted together, rewound, and began to write the book myself. "My dear, you know I can't write. That's why I needed you." She couldn't tell the truth either. She needed a fiction editor to handle the material. It became clear that the situation with Tom in Paris was based on his closeness to a former Harvard classmate with whom Marge was in love, even though she knew he was homosexual. She hinted that Tom was subconsciously drawn to him also but professed to love her traveling companion to protect himself. She found Tom provincial, gauche, prejudiced, unable to profit from his European pilgrimages, and unable to appreciate her sophisticated taste and maturity, but she was jealous of him all the same and furious about his portrait of her in the book as a devious and destructive woman. She speculated about the "ambiguous" relations of Maxwell Perkins and Tom. She implied that she understood Tom much better than he could ever understand her and he was, generally speaking, beneath her notice and concern. So—her whole superstructure was a fraud: Tom was a hick, confused about life, Europe, and himself, while she, the gifted woman of the world, tried vainly to befriend and enlighten. He took up with that "undistinguished" (her word) Jewish theater designer in New York and he died before he could learn to appreciate Marge. The implications of her version trickled very slowly into my consciousness. Marge was a much more interesting and complex subject for a book than Tom. Her "authenticities," as I wrote to Lee, suspended my judgments—to say nothing of my own camouflaged motives and my responsibility to the project. I knew she was a liar, egotistical and possessive, and my correspondence with Eddie and Lee uncovered a lot more lies and misrepresentations in her dealings with all of us. I began to feel exactly like Tom in Paris, victimized and threatened, enmeshed in the webs she spun to isolate me from all that I held dear. Lee continued to warn that she would destroy me or that I would destroy myself, and my determination to see the book through was the most destructive element of all. All my instincts agreed with him, but I had promises to keep and secret guilt to quell.

Moune de Rivel, the lovely Guadeloupian singer who had appeared in New York at Café Society Uptown and once graced the cover of *Life* magazine, knew Marge as a patron of the arts. It was she who said simply, "What are you doing with that old woman? You're an artist—you should be performing. Come and sing with me in my club." I took my guitar and joined her three or four evenings a week, singing in French and English, evidently well matched with Moune whose tiny club, four blocks away from our hotel, prospered. She had come back from the States relieved to be in Paris. It was her home—if not her birthplace—and the French were her people. She sang to a small guitar Antilles folk songs and songs by contemporary composers who wrote material for popular singers firmly in the tradition of Reynaldo Hahn, Satie, Poulenc, and Debussy. The lyrics were purest poetry. Montand, Juliette Gréco, Piaf sang the dramatic, charged ones. Georges Brassens, Jacques Brel, and Charles Trenet performed their own. The songs were basically cabaret material reaching a wide public by way of those notable singers who "plugged" them—as we would say in Tin Pan Alley terms. Moune introduced me to this world.

Marge was jealous but careful to acknowledge that what I did with my evenings was my affair—but it was the thin edge of the wedge and she knew it.

We were absurd as lovers. She said, "You don't know much about women, do you?" I knew as much as I wanted to about her. Our "collaboration" was a joke—a parody.

She accused Lee of being careless in handling her affairs in New York. She accused Eddie of being indiscreet. I reminded her that both accusations were based on her own lying testimony. Lee had done exactly what she had asked him to do. She, herself, had given Eddie—not me, as she claimed—the key to come and go as he liked and we had already rebutted her with the facts. She provoked, time after time, these torturous confrontations during which she managed to ignore the truth. With the thin smile she reserved for such occasions, she flicked darts at me. I erupted out of this Strindbergian miasma and denounced her treachery and double-dealing. She retreated into a blanket apology and acknowledgment, piteously claiming that her doctor had told her she had only a short time to live and she was not entirely responsible for her behavior. "Forgive me, my dear, you can't know what a comfort you have been!" and she turned her face to the wall. I wrote to Lee who had access to the doctor through mutual friends. The doctor said: "There's nothing wrong with her except those migraine headaches and they are as much psychosomatic as real." I went mad on the spot and started to strangle her theatrically enough, with my bare hands. Her strong wrists and my returning sanity halted me in the middle of the act. But our "collaboration," needless to say, ended at that moment. She made out a check for that month's salary and though I stayed on in the same hotel I never saw her again. I did see Clifton from time to time and he told me she had sent for her son and Ledbetter. So life, if not business, was going to go on—as usual. I attended the concert she staged for Huddie in Paris months later. There was so much pretension surrounding the presentation that the French public was irritated and unimpressed. I was with Art Buchwald who was then contributing items to *Variety*. "Who is this Ledbetter?" he asked me on the way. I replied, a trifle disconcerted that he had never even heard of Huddie:

"He's probably the most authentic of contemporary folksingers." "Authentic—what's that?" I never knew if Art was pulling my leg, but I went on, "He is such a folk *person* that whatever he sings comes out as a folk song. He is the real article." We didn't see each other after the concert and I didn't go back to see Huddie. The concert was depressing. The French didn't really dig Huddie. They were inclined to like him as a personality but the irony and mockery of his songs about the ways of black and white American mores, the undertones and the legend didn't penetrate, the frame was wrong.* (Even in America, Huddie was a cult figure rather than a national celebrity.)

Marge's effort to present Huddie as a polished artist and a guitar virtuoso was a mistake. "Mr. Ledbetter" should have been "Leadbelly." As an impresario she was a failure and Huddie's European career never got off of the ground. One of the French producers she approached came to me and asked if I would do a concert for him. Ledbetter was "assez sympathique," he said, but Marge had demanded outrageous fees for Huddie and she was "pas gentille." The French public had, for the most part, reacted like Art Buchwald after the fact—"authentic—what's that?" Marge, being informed of the offer to me, said, "Gordon Heath! He knows nothing about anything!" I did the concert nevertheless.

Lee had come over and joined me in the hotel. We came upon Huddie standing disconsolately just in front. I introduced Lee and asked Huddie how things were going. He said, "Man, I can't take this. She's got me prisoner here. I don't go any place. I can't get a woman and I can hardly get a drink. I want to go home!" I invited him to my club (then Jacob's Ladder) and he spent the evening with us. "Nice little place you got here—fills up quick!"

Marge bought herself a place on the other side of Paris and Huddie went back to the United States.

After his death, Huddie's song, "Irene," became a hit and it was recorded in a less earthy version by a number of soloists and groups, pushing it high on the list of best-sellers. Martha, I was informed, was entitled to a percentage of the royalties.

Marge hired a series of secretaries and helpers to put the Tom Wolfe book in shape.

At the Café Flore, in mild September, tables sprawled lazily out from under the awning and French boys in low-waisted slacks and French girls in short, impractical but stimulating skirts, appraised passers-by with a frankness approaching insolence. Tall black Americans were rare birds and, by definition,

* For instance:
All you colored folks, Come listen here to me:
Don't buy yourself no home in Washington, D.C.
Lord, it's a bourgeois town!"

Jean Berdin and Gordon Heath at a café in Paris

jazzmen. I made my first French friend: Jean ("Jawn," that is), nineteen, in blue jeans (jeens) and white shirt before they were fashionable, was irrepressible and impatient to demonstrate his command of the American language. He did, actually, speak very good American although not quite good enough to support his claim (made in front of but not *to* me) to hail from South Dakota. He was being allowed to sit in as drummer in a small band that played in the Club St. Germain des Prés around the corner.

Raymond Fol was an intimate of the Duke and Strayhorn and authoritative purveyor of American jazz (but then, what other jazz was there?). Well there was Raymond and his brother, Hubert, Django Reinhardt, the superb Gypsy guitarist, who, like Jean, didn't read music; there was the Hot Club of France and Claude Luter, clarinetist whose playing was as strictly from New Orleans as he could arrive at, installed in a "cave"* on the other side of the boulevard in the building that housed the legendary theater, the Vieux Colombier. And there was Hugues Panassié, rushing into print and debate with the music establishment about the legitimacy of jazz itself, attacking the classically proud and insular snobs and conservatives. On the other hand, the young French swingers claimed that Negro spirituals and jazz were America's only contribution to world culture. When Panassié's handbook, *Le Jazz Hot,* appeared, they felt it had analyzed and documented the supremacy of jazz forever after. Jean's apprenticeship brought him into first-name contact with all that peripatetic vanguard of greats: Miles, Duke, Bird—there was glory enough in that all by itself. Jean arrived in the world a trifle late. His parents were already in their forties and had produced two girls. They needed a boy. Grandfather had founded a thriving company handling pressed iron and other metals. Jean's father was now director and Jean would inherit and carry on in the best bourgeois tradition. That was taken for granted by everyone, Jean included. Mme Berdin was a nurse during the war, having been educated to be a doctor (extraordinary for a French woman at the time). M. Berdin was gassed and a hospital patient, *her* patient, when they met and their courtship was carried on by correspondence when he was discharged from the hospital. There was poetry in their union and a steadfastness in their marriage. There was lots of love left over for Jean and they didn't clamp down on what they recognized to be his passionate hobby—music. He was probably spoiled by those three women in his life. He was stubborn and petulant, and, of course, extremely lovable, but he was spending too much time in Bohemia to the detriment of his school work. He was packed off to school in Rouen to make up for his failed exams and to separate him from the distraction of Paris nightlife. Marge was disarmed by his brash vivacity and invited him to see the Dunham dance spectacle with us. At the intermission he pulled out his exercise book and said to Marge, "I'm glad you're here. You can help me with this!" (his English assignment for the next week). She did, too. Rouen was the boondocks for Jean. I made the trip to Rouen (some sixty miles west of Paris) to visit him. He was

---

* A cave was a basement-cellar space usually with stone vaulting and/or beamed ceilings like old-time dungeons (which sometimes they had been).

stunned by the idea of anyone coming to Rouen of his own free will and was touched and grateful. Nothing could reconcile him to Rouen. He didn't even admire the notable cathedral Monet had painted often and lovingly.

He invited me to his apartment to meet his family. His father had bristling black eyebrows which supplied him with varying degrees of sternness. His plump mother had dimples *and* freckles and a coronet of white-blond hair and outgoing friendliness and fluency. It is very unusual to be invited to a Frenchman's home on such short acquaintance but Jean belonged to a much more open generation and had accustomed his folks to the comings and goings of his free-wheeling black American musician friends. His mother was obviously intrigued, eager to connect and learn about these other-planet beings. There was no question of balancing teacups on our knees and making polite conversation. She was interested in people and wanted to know what they did and thought. My French was, like Jean's "American," not quite up to "fluency." I felt I was being introduced to France. It wasn't that Mme B was "typical" of anything at all. The apartment itself was a comfortable combination of unostentatious but tasteful fittings, molded ceiling, a glass chandelier, Louis XVI chairs, paintings reflecting very personal taste. She made me feel entirely at home.

My London agent sent word that the Richard Wright/Paul Green theatrical adaptation of Wright's novel, *Native Son,* had been translated and that a Paris production was in the offing and would I get in touch with Richard (who lived almost next door to us in the Latin Quarter) and have a look at the script. Richard seemed to be all for it and I hijacked Jean on his Paris weekends to coach me through the text. He had already translated "Go, Tell Aunt Rhody," a Burl Ives folksong, into acceptable French and it was part of my repertoire that amused my nightclub audiences sufficiently to justify its inclusion. We were very excited by our preparation for the role. "Bigger" Thomas was played by Canada Lee on Broadway—a ghetto product composed of rage and frustration. I personally thought Canada was too old for the part but his own repressed violence suited very well and he and Orson Welles's production, sensationally raw and driven home by Canada's strength, was (sensationally) successful. I was not born to play "Bigger" but maybe the French wouldn't know the difference; it would be a black man in a black part. I told Jean I'd take him to dinner at the Tour d'Argent on opening night. Nothing whatever came of the project. *Native Son* was never put onto a French stage. I *did* take Jean to dinner at the Tour as a kind of wry and low bow to Richard who had been asked to play "Bigger" in a film to be shot in South America! Since Richard closely resembled Ralph Bunch, our United Nations representative, a smooth and urbane gentleman who was not even black but light brown, it was absurd on the face of it, but Richard went off to do it and though I am assured a film was made, it never surfaced. Richard came back to Paris unabashed but uncommunicative.

Gordon Heath and Babe Wallace make up for their parts as American singers in the 1950 Paris production of *La Demoiselle de Petite Vertu*, by Marcel Achard.

Our friendship—Jean's and mine—could not be summed up as a romantic attachment. He adopted me as a brother, or an uncle, but I was his property like a member of his family. He wrote me poignant letters from Rouen as if I were all he had left in life to cherish in a vein of sentimentality I would not have expected from a worldly French boy—even one in the middle of a protracted adolescence; besides which, I had been introduced to a golden-eyed Persian boy who was studying art and whose father had a Persian rug shop on the Boulevard Haussmann that he managed with his two sons. I was not introduced to his family. Hayemi did not get along with his older brother, he would explain between long Persian sighs for punctuation. Hayemi loved Golly, straightened his curls, made him a tailcoat with trousers to match, and painted him as Manet's "Drummer Boy."

Hayemi lived in a Paris suburb but spent most of his time in Paris. He invited me to a right bank "cocktail" (the French covering word for informal social gatherings.) Lots of theater people I couldn't identify yet, but most of all and immediately identifiable, was Arletty, the film actress (*Children of Paradise*). I thought her as alluring, mysterious, and glamorous as Garbo. She was wearing a close-fitting cap of yellow ostrich feathers—the legend was intact. Even as I stared, Jean appeared on the scene, instantly furious that I had not come with him. Both of the children squared off—I didn't know what the correct etiquette would be in such a situation. It looked like sabers at dawn but Hayemi told Jean he was one too many and Jean, with very bad grace, accepted the fait accompli. Hayemi, no bigger and not much older than Jean, was entirely in charge. Their jealousy and possessiveness were beside the point. Lee, ending his tour and practically en route to France, was the reality. They knew the significance of his arrival on the scene and I was both tender and ruthless. Jean demanded attention. Hayemi was philosophic and comparatively experienced and willing to live within the moment.

Jean finally caught up with his education but went prematurely into his ailing father's business. I don't know if the jazz world lost a valuable addition to its ranks when he was absorbed into the business world but he put all that behind him. He came to my seventieth birthday celebration in 1988 and enlivened the occasion wittily and nostalgically.

The day came in May 1949 when I accompanied Hayemi to the St. Lazare station, where he took the train to his suburb. At the very moment Hayemi went through the barrier, Lee walked through, entering Paris. They passed each other. I called Hayemi back. He caught his breath, said: "Mais c'est formidable. Formidable!" and he shook hands with Lee as with an old friend. He remained an old friend to both of us all our life together and his affection for me has remained constant over the years.

∾ Music Hall in Paris

IN 1958 WE WENT to the Folies-Bergère like good Americans, lured by Jo Baker as mistress of ceremonies. She shimmied and shimmered. She wore a clinging black gown and danced a variation of a tango with a slinky but sturdy partner who lifted her and draped her around himself in the best ballroom dancing tradition—elegant and detached. She changed into some ruffles by Balmain—a simple country girl who warned you not to touch her tomatoes but threw favors out to her guests from time to time. We were all her guests—that was what was most striking. She gathered up us thousand souls and hugged us to her as closely as those volumes of mousseline would permit. She was glamorous and folksy. The stage was her living room and she wanted you to be as comfortable as she was. She went to great lengths to teach us the words and melody of the refrain, allowed us to sing it once and then shifted on to another song like tout de suite. She reached down to the hem of her floor-length creation and began to lift it with excruciating and provocative languor to the ankle, her sequin studded heels sending out light rays, the skirt mounting, the breath held—we were going to witness a zapateado of shattering violence. Her body and ours tensed for the display—then she let go of the hem, the skirt swirled around her and that was it! A tease, that Josephine. She often gave us the settings without the event but the effrontery and the impishness were enough to carry the day. Her "look at me" was irresistible and both the cynical and the hypnotized shouted the house down.

But her apotheosis quite literally was her appearance at the Folies three years later—another Farewell Appearance as Mary, Queen of Scots, crowned, wearing an enveloping white, six-foot-wide crinoline gown and a fifteen-foot train, held and maneuvered by uniformed attendants as she came down that Folies stair-case, majestically unhurried. At the bottom she turned away from the audience, a black veil hid the now beheaded queen. She went back up the stairs, the train following in her wake, the lights dimmed, the décor became a cyclorama wall of stained glass reflecting colors on the crinoline of the ascending queen. The orchestra played Schubert and the incredible Josephine sang "Ave Maria"—up up and out—the train last of all. The spectacle defied logic and she defied gravity. (Our own gravity was somewhat impaired.) It was all absurd and sublime. It was Liberace and Radio City Music Hall's East Pageant rolled into one. She announced this as her final stage appearance and when she came forward to sing her adieu, the burden of the song was an account of her responsibility to her village, her castle, her dozen adopted children, and her threatening bankruptcy. She wept on cue at every performance and held out her hands to her beloved public. Men and women—all those bourgeois and concierges streamed down the aisles, weeping loudly and screaming "Josephine, don't leave us! Don't leave us!" Mountains of flowers were thrown on the stage. She hugged and kissed everyone in reach—tears mingled, love crossed the footlights, hovered, and settled. The curtain didn't come down for an hour.

Jo's dilemma was real. Her affairs were in a mess. She had toured, she had begged, she had organized societies, supported causes and committees to combat racism all over the world, she had debts and enemies, endless energy, and an unreliable heart. Her situation was publicized in headlines and editorials to the point of satiety. The world waited for her collapse but the French people couldn't get enough of her and the engagement was extended to a three-month wonder. She was gloriously vivid and sparkling and unpredictable every moment on the stage. The genius was in the extravagance, the panoply, the certainty that you would delight in her as much as she delighted in herself. She read palms, patted bald pates, exchanged back chat with her public. She wore outfits no one else could have carried off. She reigned in glory.

She was tempted to make a real acting venture. Lehár's *Merry Widow* was proposed but she settled for a play with incidental music by Georges Bizet (book by Alphonse Daudet), a pastoral regional melodrama, *L'Arlésienne*. She tried it out successfully on her own stage in her village and she brought it to Paris for a limited engagement. We went to a Sunday matinée at her music hall, the Olympia. The overture was an excerpt from Bizet's familiar "L'Arlésienne Suite." The curtains parted. The décor was a rustic cottage in the landscape of Arles itself. She emerged from the cottage, a simple farm woman in a blouse, skirt, and shawl. The dialogue between her and an ex-member of the Comédie Française came over clearly. Lee and I observed that her accent was much improved and what remained was not that far removed from the regional accent itself. We were in the back of the house but we suddenly felt a gap between the lip movements and the sound. We peered, focused, and sure enough, the performance had been recorded and they were miming to tapes. The illusion was shattered. The whole was out of sync and unbearable. We were certain in advance it was going to be an occasion to tell the next generation about, and so it was, but for those of us who admired her, it would be for all the wrong reasons. We fled to the nearest sidewalk café and consoled ourselves with harsh black coffee. Jo decided acting was not for her. She shelved the whole project but was forced to go on making farewell appearances to pay her debts.

In 1975 she made her real farewell appearance. A smaller music hall, the Bobino, on the Left Bank was redecorated for her. New costumes were designed, a slightly reduced orchestra was put together, the celebrated Folies staircase was more or less reproduced. She paused at the top, dripping with furs over a form-fitting strategically transparent rhinestone belted gown. A four-foot-high fountain of feathers attached somehow to a white turban, all glittering like the Milky Way in a dark sky. Light played about her, the brilliants on her dress dazzled, reflected in our eyes like tiny searchlights. She stood still at the top. The house roared a greeting. She started down the steps. On the landing she paused. The roar rose again, the applause began. She descended to the stage level—a queen's progress. She moved downstage center, flung out her arms, her fingers semaphoring radiant satisfaction. She turned slowly in place displaying a figure untouched by time. She ended up facing front, grinned at the house said, "Not bad for sixty-eight, n'est-ce pas?" The house was hysterical—it wasn't bad for forty, even. She sang, she danced, she changed costumes. She sat astride a motorcycle wearing a white jumpsuit. She sang "Climb up on my knee, Sonny Girl" (perhaps to celebrate the recent addition of two girl babies to her adopted brood). She sang a blues, a spiritual, she sang her theme song, "J'ai Deux Amours," my country and Paris. She sang "Mon Village" and of her twelve adopted babies of all nations who were being raised together to attest to the instinctive brotherhood of man. She presented a tabloid version of her life from a St. Louis ghetto to her triumph in a black revue in Paris, dancing in a belt made of bananas and nothing else, the ensuing notoriety, the liaisons, the marriages, her intelligence work for France during World War II. She talked very little, the songs were meant to carry the story. It was a brisk guided tour, superficial and sentimental. It didn't matter. Her genius for communication and her gleaming vitality were the embodiment of GBS's "life force." Two days after we saw her show that undependable heart failed her. She died in a coma. She was buried with full military honors, followed to her grave by thousands of mourners who had claimed her as their own—one of France's glories like Sarah Bernhardt and Colette.

Marlene Dietrich was already a grandmother in 1959 when she began her world tour with Burt Bachrach at the piano and a small ballet chorus. Every detail of her presentation had been devised as if by computer. Her songs, her patter, her movements were fixed. Needless to say, her lighting, her make-up, her costumes reflected the attention to detail and glistening perfection of a

Hollywood product. "Look me over," she commanded. The façade was flawless. There was some humor written into the script although there was a kind of wry deprecation in this woman that amounted to a challenge to the audience. "Isn't this all nonsense but isn't it packaged beautifully and aren't I clever to stay within my limitations." She sang her almost parodic repertoire—"See What the Boys in the Backroom Will Have," "You're the Cream in My Coffee." Worldly-wise and worldly weary, she sang in German, "Falling in Love Again" and "Warum." She sang those with the warmest identification. She sang a rousing version of "Where Have All the Flowers Gone." She bowed to acknowledge applause. Every hair on her head stayed in place as if it were fibre glass. For her "get-off" number she was in top hat and white tails, the center of the chorus line. She did their routine with them. Arms interlocked, in perfect step with everyone, triumphantly ending with high kicks and a cheering audience. It was a cabaret turn artfully blown-up to music hall dimensions.

Mistinguett, Josephine's predecessor at the Folies, the transatlantic legend, ex-partner to Maurice Chevalier, star of stage and music hall—a symbol "potent as the Eiffel Tower" it was said—made a music hall appearance in the late fifties. She did not attempt to carry the show on her shoulders, and she demonstrated that she couldn't have, in any case. She was born in 1873. The voice and the face were equally ravaged. Her loyal followers were dismayed. The gutter perkiness that was her stock-in-trade was no longer within her grasp. She still was "looking for a millionaire" but there would be no takers. The spirit was valiant but everything else had shrunk away. We had come in on the scene too late and she had gone on too long.

Chevalier, on the other hand, had kept his high-gloss professionalism intact, his body supple and upright, and his charm unforced. We in the United States had always seen him as a sly, Montmartre ruffian, winking with one eye and ogling with the other—our idea of Frenchiness and "ooh-la-la" (the French say "oh-la-la" with quite another inflection, Fifi d'Orsay to the contrary notwith-standing), but in France and in French Chevalier's songs were sharp character-izations of quite different Frenchmen. His celebrated facial mobility was at the service of his acting and not just a "man of a thousand expressions" in a newspaper advertisement. He did a striptease number as his signing-off stint. The percussion in the orchestra tinkled and slithered in striptime, the coat came off, one sleeve at a time with maidenly modesty, the tie was regretfully undone, the shirt unbuttoned, the cuff links unlinked. In the middle of unbuckling his belt with the same concentrated intensity, he stopped, immobile for a couple of seconds, said "Perhaps all the children haven't yet been put to bed," rebuckled, relinked, rebuttoned. With his tie ends still hanging down, he walked to the end of the proscenium opposite a box occupied by two couples. He faced the nearest lady, said exquisitely "If Madame would please look this way," and tied his tie from his reflection in her eyes! A jolting tour de force that made the house stand up and cheer and applaud for ten minutes. He shrugged on his coat, bowed deeply. Pandemonium!

Charles Trenet in music hall was like a bobbing celluloid doll with painted light blue eyes, a mop of straw colored hair, looking like a school boy delighting in his first communion. Like Irving Berlin in America, everyone knew and sang his songs—songs he wrote. We knew them from records in the States: unfailing good cheer, lightly naughty lyrics, an eavesdropping country boy who had just found out about the birds and the bees. The young took him for one of their own—no generation gap.

Yves Montand as a music hall singer reminded us of Olivier. The same painstaking preparation, workouts, perfecting of mime details. He was a Marseille product and worked on his diction as Olivier worked on his dialects. He aimed at spontaneity and high spirits but his earnestness often showed through. The sweat from his warm-up had not always dried before his performance. When he took to acting for the cinema he strove to appear casual and easy but he smoked cigarettes steadily to occupy his hands and mask his tensions. We watched him turn himself into a relaxed and authoritative performer. The earnestness revealed itself in his political stances with his equally committed wife, Simone Signoret. He was the lead in my first French film *The Heros Are Tired.* We were of equal height and almost the same age, but he always called me *fiston* (kid) affectionately. He has become a controversial figure in France, suspected of having political aspirations and harboring ambitions they consider "inappropriate." It is doubtful if he will attain the status of "elder statesman." He is, Hollywood would say, only as good as his last film (a failure) but in Paris he is always in the public eye. His fling in 1959 with Marilyn Monroe in Hollywood brought him more highly charged publicity than his performances in films. He may feel himself too old for the fray now but he will probably coach from the side lines. He is certainly *quelqu'un* (somebody).

But our own Queen of Hearts was Piaf (the Sparrow). Edith herself, with a voice bigger than her whole body, entering from the wings almost hesitantly and grasping the microphone stage center as her lifeline—her one remaining support. She wore a simple black dress that somehow looked a trifle rusty in spite of being styled by Jacques Heim. The orchestra played a medley of her hits—the house was already applauding. She launched her first songs. The "r's" rolled like drums. She slapped out the syllables. The lines were building blocks. The voice throbbed like the engine room of the Normandie. "I wash the glasses behind the hotel bar and this is what I see every working day. Those desperate one-day lovers climbing up the stairs." The lovers commit suicide. She drops the glass she is drying and you hear it crashing to the ground! So much bitterness, so much compassion, so much heartbreak held in check. No tears but no resignation either. "Life is like that. One day he went away. He won't come back. But how we lived and loved when he was with me" and you knew she still felt his arms around her. Piaf songs were one-act plays; none of those self-adoring nods and becks, no arms flung wide and high to announce the end and the triumph. She told the story. She sang the song. She stood with her feet apart like a tree planted by the water. Her strength came up from the ground and that voice was sustained by every inch of that tiny body. She found for almost every song one irradiating gesture. In "l'Accordéoniste," she mimed the gestures of the accordionist's hands—once. At the end, when she is abandoned, one hand came down like a axe-chop. "Stop the music!" She sang about two lovers on their only day off anticipating a whole twenty-four hours of being together. The song was called "Don't Disturb Us." At the song's end she reached out and turned off the light. That was all. She sang a song about a woman who finds herself in a straitjacket and insists, "'suis pas folle—'suis pas folle" . . . "I'm not mad! I'm not mad!" At the end she flapped about laughing madly between gasps like a scarecrow teetering from a pole. The economy of the movements she chose was part of her genius. She looked like an exalted concièrge (Ken Tynan's phrase) yes, but she was classically austere in her act. I had only been in France two months when I went with Hayemi to the ABC, the smallest of the music halls, to hear Piaf. My French was coming along but my comprehension lagged behind. I understood almost every song she sang without straining. She sang "Le Prisonnier de la Tour." The song and the delivery gave me gooseflesh, exactly as Roland Hayes had done with "Little Boy" twenty years before. I grabbed at Hayemi. "What's that song about? I want to sing it." Hayemi, a French citizen, said "I'm not sure." I told *him*: the narrator, Isabelle, told of her lover, imprisoned in a tower—obviously a political prisoner. He killed himself jumping from the window. Isabelle tells her grandmother that they were lovers and all she had or wanted in life was him and that she will mourn for him and tend his grave. Her grandmother warns her that the king will be seriously displeased with her, but, like Antigone, Isabelle swears that she will not be intimidated. The grandmother confesses that it might make the king himself weep because in his youth he loved a girl who was not meant for a king and "I," says the grandmother, "was the girl." Dumas and Rostand—but the song had been written for Piaf in the style of an ancient ballad only some months before. I did indeed learn it and sang it for years in l'Abbaye. It was very popular. Piaf was an inspiring singer. You learned a lot about acting discipline from her.

❧ Doxology

PROBABLY THIS BOOK is not exactly what was expected by my editor. I had no expectations of my own. My fortnightly visits to the American Library in Paris are tinged with wry. "Of the making of books there is no end." Besides—who will care?—except perhaps that handful of people who have seen, heard, loved me, and remember.

I'm sorry I have no public image for this generation to rub this memoir up against—like sandpaper used for wrapping. I am not so deep as a well and I haven't flown that high. What I was and what I did that I cannot recollect will be interred with my bones—rather with my ashes, since I have indicated I want the fire this time. I am past the seventy years the Book of Common Prayer has allotted us—we shall see. I have loved life: it's been—interesting.

❧ Epilogue: Noting Gordon

Richard Trousdell

WHEN I FIRST MET Gordon, at a welcoming party Michael Thelwell and Roberta Uno gave for him, I was struck by how low-keyed he seemed in contrast to the guest celebrity I had expected. His entrance, delayed by a brief tour of Amherst, built dramatic suspense, so that when Gordon did finally step into the room, all eyes turned. Dressed in turtleneck and corduroy jacket and smoking a pipe, he seemed more a professor on sabbatical than an actor on tour. There was a subtle tension in the air as all the officials responsible for bringing Gordon here sized up their star. Another less ducal artist might have sniffed this swelling scene and risen to command it, giving us perhaps a first taste of the kingly role he had come to perform, or making some significant cultural gesture. But not Gordon; he knew what real lions do: they amble on, totally relaxed, turning their huge heads to look with bemused interest at what might possibly feed their curiosity.

Actually, Gordon was making a virtue of necessity. As I found out later, he was exhausted by jet lag and the long drive from the airport, but rather than disappoint us, he was improvising the only kind of party scene he could sustain. As he moved quietly around the group, engaging people in brief conversations, he seemed like a seasoned aristocrat on a walkabout, transforming a public scene into moments of intimacy. As in his art, Gordon was a craftsman who knew how to disguise the effort it took to play the music of the moment to its best effect. When he finally circled around to where I stood he took me in in one long glance, a lion's steady gaze. "So, here were are," he said with a slight smile, conveying both greeting and something of a challenge.

The next day, when we went to meet the student cast for the first time, Gordon was openly nervous about how he would fit in with a group of young people who had already been together in rehearsal for three weeks. He needn't have worried. His long-time friend and collaborator, the choreographer Pearl

Primus, had anticipated his concern and had fashioned a ceremonial dance of welcome by the full cast to bring him suitably into his theater like the king he was about to portray. The beating drums, the costumes, and the gestures of a warrior's welcome took Gordon completely by surprise. But not for long. Quickly and lightly he picked up the beat, and stepping his way between the corridor of swaying dancers, he moved toward Pearl Primus herself, each beaming at the other with delight and pride. Moments later, we all sat together for a first reading of the play. When Gordon spoke the old king's first lines, the quiet manner of a bemused professor was completely gone. In its place were the ringing tones and full emotion of an accomplished actor in engaged performance. The waking lion roared, and we all felt his power.

❧ Afterword: Getting to Know Gordon "An altogether most sufficient man"

Ekwueme Mike Thelwell

PARIS WAS particularly lovely in the spring of 1986. I was there—on my way home from Africa—because James Baldwin, in many ways the single most important intellectual influence of my young manhood, was to be "elevated to the rank of Commander of the Legion d'Honneur" by the French government. The ceremony in the Elysée Palace was something I had very much wanted to see.

But that was not to be. I had gotten to Paris, very tired, the day before the investiture—four days later than we had agreed. I was late because when I arrived in France, sans visa via the Calais channel boat, I had not been allowed to land. An inflexible, inexplicably hostile immigration official forced me to return to England. Back there, I learned that this had become an increasingly common occurrence for blacks arriving in France by boat from England. (On an earlier visit, when I arrived by air from New York, no official had given my visa-less papers more than a cursory glance.)

In Paris, Jimmy had more bad news and was quite visibly upset. He had just been informed that I would not be able to attend the ceremony after all. I could not be admitted to the Palace because for some unexplained reason my name "had failed to receive security clearance" and there was "no time for the decision to be reversed." The ambiguity of the language was troubling, but I was more immediately concerned by Jimmy's evident agitation.

I certainly did not wish to be the source of any discordant note on what was otherwise so happy and triumphant an occasion. I reminded him that I had wanted to be present mainly to tell the French president and/or press that their initiative was appreciated by black people in the United States, who saw the tribute as a source of honor to France and of shame to America. Now, after the Calais experience, I was no longer sure I wanted to say even that much, so we laughed and agreed to let the matter drop. And that is how it happened that I spent the afternoon of the investiture re-meeting Gordon Heath.

↩ AFTER LEAVING Jimmy, I visited the Village Voice, the remarkable bookstore-cum-café, owned by Odile Hellier, which was being compared in the French press to Sylvia Beech's Shakespeare & Co. as the contemporary center for American literary activity in Paris. Odile was an old friend from Amherst, Massachusetts. The store was especially impressive in its offerings of black authors. Still puzzled and a little troubled by the security clearance incident, I was only half listening as Odile reeled off the names of African-American artists and writers for whom the store was a gathering place and communications center where they could collect their mail and leave messages. The list was long and most of the names that I recognized prompted not, as Odile had expected, an urge to renew contact, but quite the reverse: "So that's what happened to that sucker, huh? Best thing he could do for black people's struggle in America is to stay in Paris."

Then a name I had scarcely thought of in twenty-four years snapped me to sudden and excited attention.

"Did you say Gordon Heath?" I shouted. "I know him."

Odile was surprised as much by the shout as by my sudden animation. "Yes," she said, "Gordon Heath the actor, you know him, yes?"

"Yes . . . no . . . I mean, I was in a play with him. . . . He'd never remember me." But before I could explain exactly how inconsequential the encounter would certainly have been to him, she was on the phone.

"Odile, please don't . . ."

"Alo, Gordon. Alo. A friend of yours is here . . . a man who says he was in a play with you . . . years ago . . . he's a friend." She handed the phone to a very embarrassed visitor, full of apology and plagued by a sudden stutter.

"Mr. Heath . . . I'm sorry. . . . Odile shouldn't have. . . . I didn't mean to suggest. . . . I was only a student, an extra. . . . Yeah, Howard University . . . Marlowe's *Dr. Faustus.*"

The voice was deep, resonant, and quite obviously gently amused by my embarrassment.

"Oh yes. *Dr. Faustus.* . . . Dear, dear Owen."

By the end of the conversation I'd regained a measure of composure and we'd agreed to meet in his local café at noon the next day for lunch. That meeting would evolve into four of the more interesting afternoons of my life.

* * *

Exactly twenty-four years earlier, in the spring of 1962, I was in the final semester of my junior year at Howard. The only course I can specifically remember from that semester was one in playwriting offered by the irrepressibly theatrical Owen Dodson, chairman of the theater department and master of the Howard Players.

One morning he fairly sprang into the classroom, the picture of a man consumed by glee and excitement.

"Chilluns," he glowed, "*I've got it.* Ooh, this is going to be *grand. Grand chile!* Oh Lawd *today,* we're gonna be so fine. *So fine.*" We all knew by then that whenever Mr. D. went "deep folk" something interesting was about to happen.

Mr. Dodson struck the pose of a man inspired, raptly gazing into the distance above our heads like a devout visionary, his entranced eyes fixed on the New Jerusalem emerging shining out of the desert sands. As one, the class turned, following his gaze but seeing only the upper quadrangle through the window. So we asked.

"Why *Dr. Faustus,* chile. *Dr. Faustus* by Christopher Marlowe, that's what. It's rarely done anymore, and never well. But the Howard Players will resurrect it. Yes, indeedy. Gordon Heath as Faustus. Lee Payant as Mephistopheles. We'll bring them from Paris. Can't you *see it?* Oh we going be so *grand,* chillun." His artfully projected excitement, exactly as intended, was infectious.

He devoted the rest of that class to introducing us to Marlowe's "neglected masterpiece," and, for the first time, a highly dramatic version of the Gordon Heath legend: Broadway star at twenty-seven in *Deep Are the Roots,* and later as Death, in *Death Takes a Holiday* (at a time, he reminded us, when black folk couldn't even sweep them theaters, chillun); the voluntary romantic exile; major figure on stage and screen in French and English, in Paris and London; the BBC's great Othello, the whole schmear.

When Mr. Dodson told us for the umpteenth time how *grand* it would be, I had excellent reason to believe him. He had for some years been tending more and more toward the spectacular. To this end, he would pare down the department's production schedule so as to concentrate resources on a major annual production, usually a classic and usually directed by him. For this production no short cut was envisioned or tolerated. In the grand manner it was theater technology gone mad: costumes, scrims, elevators, smoke machines, bolts of lightning, *deus ex machina* where indicated, elaborate sound effects. It was nothing if not *grand.*

The previous year, I and a few football player-types had been drafted into a production. We stood at parade rest in front of a temple façade (complete in all details) for the duration of a very long *Medea.* We were attired in the full dress armor of Greek soldiers, complete with plumed helmets, gleaming breast plates, pleated miniskirts, knee-high sandals, and lethal-looking spears. In painstaking authenticity we stood, so many mute, inglorious Hellenes, awaiting our single great moment of high drama when we barred, with crossed spear shafts, Medea's entry to the temple. That was all. But we were grand.

So I was more than a mite leery when a beaming Mr. Dodson cut me off as I was leaving the classroom. He glowed with the self-satisfaction of a man about to bestow a grand benefaction.

"Mike, it's all cast and guess what? I've got just the part for you!"

"But Mr. Dodson. . . ."

"Oh hush, chile. . . . You are going to be the *cardinal!*"

"But Mr. Dodson. . . ."

"The cardinal, chile, the *cardinal!* A prince of the church! You're going to be so grand."

〜 TRUE TO HIS word, the prelate—at least in his elaborate vestments, insignias, and theatrical poses—was grandeur made manifest, but he was also mute as a log. Mr. D was clearly not disposed to entrust a single line to my thick Jamaican intonations.

But, thus I had license to stand at the back of the stage and observe closely as one of the great classic actors of our time thought and worked himself— gradually, purposefully, incrementally, completely—into a challenging role. Or more accurately, as he gradually *transformed* himself into Dr. Johannes Faustus, scholar of Wittenburg. Ironically enough, if I hadn't been cast for this role (which I had not been allowed to refuse), I could not have witnessed this because, when word spread across campus about this extraordinary thing daily unfolding on the stage of the Ira Aldridge Theater, the ever-growing throng of observers in the back of the auditorium became so intrusive that rehearsals had to be closed to all but cast and crew.

So I watched Gordon Heath, with Lee Payant as Mephisto, engage each scene: as Gordon's uncommonly resonant yet flexible and controlled voice explored all the possible meanings, rhythms, nuances, and subtleties of his lines; as his fluent and expressive movements explored the geography of the scene; as he discovered the psychic dynamic, the human composition of each scene played against his lover, friend, and partner, a Mephistopheles of no small effect and subtlety. One saw Gordon feeling, testing, discarding, selecting (tone, inflection, pitch, gesture, expression): *thinking* and *understanding* his way into the character and the scene. And one day the watcher realized, with shock and considerable wonder, that the goal had been achieved and that in a kind of miraculous fusion, actor and character had become one, and that a new entity, seamless, organic, indivisible, had been created. Then it all appeared natural,

Mike Thelwell as the Cardinal
in *Doctor Faustus,* Howard
University, 1962

even effortless, unless one had seen it abuilding and could remember the brute work, the meticulous attention to detail, the repetition, the experimentation, the *intelligence* of the construction. But that transformation was more than technique and control, driven by a finely discriminating intelligence and taste. At the moment of fusion, the performance, though born of these elements, was greater than the parts, and it was beautiful and chastening to see.

Gordon, then about forty-five, seemed at the very height of his form, a master of his craft. His mere presence was breathtaking; the noble, almost sculpted, head; the mature face, very handsome and elegantly boned yet strong and virile withal. He was also physically impressive; his lithe, tautly muscular athlete's body gave him a regal bearing that made him appear taller than his six feet and more powerful than his 170 pounds. In motion he had the controlled effortless-seeming grace of a panther in total and easy harmony with its body and the enveloping space.

Rough and untutored though I was, I came to understand very clearly that I was witnessing an acquired virtuosity, the reward of technique and discipline. Here was a master craftsman and he himself a "perfect instrument" through which his craft found splendid and sensitive expression. The full range of his voice, eyes, hands, and posture was disciplined, finely tuned, governed (indeed choreographed) by intelligence and available to his art. It seemed to me that this was acting in a different, older tradition, one calling into play completely different aspects of an actor's being than the "method" then the fashion in American theater. It was the difference between artifice and feeling, between

Lee Payant as Mephistopheles and Gordon Heath as Faustus, Howard University, 1962

taste and passion, mind and viscera. I summed it up with the word *cerebral,* the dominance of technique governed by intelligence and judgment.*

But that was not, of course, the whole story. For there was a point in performance where mind, will, artifice, technique disappeared or were subsumed into something transcendent and full of mystery. Two incidents will help to try to illustrate this mystery.

*In the memoir, Gordon remarks Owen Dodson with students: "Teaching them at the same time how *gesture could focus emotion and illustrate words.*"

Toward opening night—the character was well evolved by then—my friend, the late Helmar Cooper (Helmar had a speaking part) cut one of Faust's lines. In this particular scene it was very much the intemperate Faustus—the arrogant seeker and devourer of knowledge and experience. When Helmar cut his line, Faust leaned closer, his face utterly demonic, and hissed in Helmar's ear (only he and I could have heard), *"Cut my line again you miserable whelp, and I cut your throat."* Helmar almost fainted. My eyes must have popped. Then Gordon smiled kindly at the student, flung an arm about his shoulder, and said ever so gently, "Not to worry kid, we'll take it from the top." The thing was so intense and so quickly over that I doubted what I had seen and heard. Finally, what I realized was that while it was Gordon who had settled and reassured the young actor, it had indeed been Faustus who had threatened violence and fully meant it.

The second incident involves the only time I actually spoke to Gordon. (I later discovered he was very shy.) But even that one time was mightily instructive.

During a final rehearsal I took a phone call for him while he was on stage. The scene was ending so I asked the caller to hold and waited at the apron of the stage. (What then happened is hard to re-create with words. You will have to try to visualize it, remembering that it was very, very quick.)

As the scene ended he was facing away from where I stood, so I said timidly but loudly enough to get his attention.

The phrase expresses precisely what happened in the scene that made the greatest impression on me then.

It was early in rehearsal, the scene was a confrontation between Faustus and Mephistopheles, which ended on an impassioned concluding speech by Faustus. On the surface the speech was intellectually aggressive and defiant, yet with undertones of self-doubt and self-justification, and it concluded with a semirhetorical question which boldly projected the one, while revealing or at least suggesting the other.

The actor elected (or was directed) to deliver the lines while pacing the stage, approaching his antagonist, and to conclude with a little bound to another level, the leap and final posture punctuating the question while illustrating the character's ambivalence. Hence, the tone, pitch, and cadence of the words, the balletic elements of the bound, and the concluding posture all had to be complementary. And it was not quite what the actor wanted.

We watched him repeat the sequence—question, bound, concluding posture (which ended with a small gesture of the right hand, half challengingly interrogatory, half supplication) at least six times. Each time was subtly but visibly different, and each time the variation in delivery precisely matched and reflected the difference in motion and gesture. It was uncanny. But no combination quite satisfied him. I remember watching and marveling at the infinitely subtle variations in the gesture of the right hand, because each time it matched so precisely the change in timing and inflection of the words.

Then it was right. The actor felt it, and we who watched could *see* it. There was a spontaneous smattering of subdued applause from us. The actor paused as if reviewing it in his mind's eye, nodded to himself, and did it exactly the same twice more as though to imprint it and store that sequence in his muscular and psychic memory. Thereafter, in performance, that sequence drew applause each night, and each night it seemed so inspired, so perfectly natural, so *unrehearsed*.

"Mr. Heath?"

He whirled, obviously still in character, looked, and took a few steps toward me while booming in a stage voice carrying to the back rows.

"WELL, YOUNG MAN, WHAT? . . ." and caught himself. Then there was in that brief moment of transition—Faustus having departed and Heath not yet arrived—a sudden vacancy in his eyes and face, something slightly akin to panic as his voice attempted to find a normal tone and pitch. Yes? Yes? *Yes?* as though flipping through a repertoire of tone and volume to find an appropriate conversational voice and a normal persona. This was in the space of two strides, by which time the kindly, smiling face of Gordon Heath looked down at me and asked in his rich, cultivated voice:

"Yes sir, what is it?"

"You have a phone call in the lobby."

"Thank you so much."

But I had seen that moment . . . and never quite forgot it.

*   *   *

In 1962 I was recently removed from the culture that had formed me, and exactly half Gordon's forty-five years. I was at an age which, although one does not necessarily understand this, and certainly not in quite this way, one is very definitely in search. Of what? For the terms of engagement: those values and positions from and by which one will attempt to define one's presence in, and against, the world in which one finds oneself. I had arrived from Jamaica, as I thought, pretty much formed; quite comfortable, by imprint of family, education, culture, with the man I imagined myself to be, or was at least capable of becoming. But what is true in one culture, does not necessarily apply in another, at least not in the same way. In Jamaica I was seen by others simply as a promising young man. I had never been denied food in a restaurant. Once I stepped down from the aircraft, into what Baldwin would call, "this dismal republic," I was seen by many only as a "Negro boy."

Three years later, by the time I watched Gordon Heath work at his craft, I had already learned that much. I had not really entered *that* republic, but, happily, another rather more complex and culturally enriching terrain known as black America. By the time of the play, I was passionately involved in the Movement, had already met and been inspired to the very core of my being by James Baldwin's writer's example and by his eloquent and uncompromising affirmation of his own—and by extension our—black integrity. And equally by Brother Malcolm's private warmth and kindness and by his flinty public dignity and fearless, totally unapologetic affirmation of our common blackness. What splendid, supremely self-confident *black* men they were! And though I scarce knew it then, they were for me—nothing quite so pedestrian as role models—but exemplars, bright, shining beacons whose lights enshrined themselves indelibly in the heart and spirit of a youth looking for honorable ways to be a black man in this country. They illumined for me the possibility of excellence and pride in self, for as Gordon's Barbadian father, in a much different context, said in these pages, "What man has done, man can also do." And miracle of miracles, these were *black* men!

My five weeks observing Gordon introduced into my small pantheon of beacons another potent, apparently very different, light. Watching him as Faust, I had no idea of his politics, or of whether he even had politics at all. Nor did his persona *appear* to speak, as Jimmy's and Malcolm's did, directly out of the rich cultural legacy, bitter social experience or the powerful traditions of political struggle of black America.

This persona seemed rather to be anchored in the style, sensibility, and classic cadences not simply of Europe but of its "Great Tradition," European high bourgeois culture. And that was something with which, given my own colonial education, I had not only passing familiarity but also a deep and instinctive need to reject, or at least transcend.

But what Gordon held in common with my other two exemplars was simply excellence. Like them he had that consummate, visible, effortless quality of being infinitely superior at what he did than any representative of the "master race" yet to present itself to my ken. (True in 1962; even more so today.) I felt that Gordon's appropriation and mastery of their terms, techniques, style and discipline must, indeed had to, conceal a force of will and a proud militancy in blackness as deep and fierce as Jimmy's or Malcolm's; that the evident mastery of craft, the dignity and graciousness of person were themselves a most profound and evident affirmation of black possibility.

I had tried to explain some of this to Odile by way of justifying my uncharacteristic excitement at the sound of his name. She, bless her provident heart, managed to unearth a lone copy of my novel, *The Harder They Come,* from somewhere in her bookstore, and the next day I was off to meet the man.

Odile had said, and Gordon confirmed, that he was "not well." She had also said that he had recently appeared to age drastically. How so? Well, she had seen him a week or two ago and his hair, unlike the prisoner of Chillon's, had gone completely white, almost overnight.

I went with a mixture of curiosity and trepidation. How does one meet an icon of one's youth? My memories of the man were those of a twenty-two-year-old undergraduate. Now having seen much and done some, I was approaching the end of my fifth decade. I was a mature man. What changes would those years have wrought? In my perceptions? In him? By my calculation he must be nearing seventy. On the phone the voice had been deep and strong, ageless. But he was said to be infirm? Time must surely have impaired the "perfect instrument" of my recollection. Would I find in its place an enfeebled, aging "star"? What would I now make of him? And he of me?

Nervously clutching my novel—part self-justification, part tribute—I found the café, entered, and looked for him. Unless time had whitened much more than his hair, he was not there. "I must be early," I thought; "Have a beer and wait." But the proprietor came over and very solicitously asked if I were looking for Mr. 'Eath.

"Today é is not so well. É wishes you to go to him, yes." He gave me directions and a message of solicitude for "Mr. 'Eath."

At the top of four or six long, very steep flights of stairs I found the apartment and knocked.

"Come in, it's open."

The apartment was tiny, as small as the ship's cabin it resembled in the efficiency and meticulousness of its organization. (I learned later that after the death of Lee Payant a few years earlier, he had disposed of their Paris apartment, closed l'Abbaye, and returned to New York with the intentions of resuming life there. That scene proved incompatible and so he returned to the Paris he loved.) Gordon reclined on a long narrow bed running along one wall. He seemed to fill the space completely. He raised himself on an elbow and extended a hand.

"You must forgive me. . . . Today, I am not so strong. . . . It comes and goes."

Except for the dramatic whiteness of hair and beard against the dark skin, the powerful face, unmarked by time, was that of a distinguished man in his prime who took good care of himself. I stared. (Now, on reflection, I wonder if his position and gesture, consciously or otherwise, might not have been a little staged.) In any case, still breathless from the climb and forgetting whatever it was I had prepared to say, I took his hand and embarrassed myself by blurting something like, "Oh, wow, Mr. Heath, you are even more handsome now."

He smiled, but not unkindly, shrugged away the compliment, and said, "Tell me about yourself. What brings you to Paris?"

I thanked him for receiving me and promised not to overtax his energy by staying too long.

"I'll tell you about myself in a minute. But I want to tell you about the effect your visit to Howard had on me when I was a student." I went on in some detail. He seemed intrigued—at once pleased and a little embarrassed at the same time.

"Enough." He motioned me to stop, "Tell me about yourself."

"But you should know this," I insisted, and went on about the importance of his presence and example to me and other students at Howard. He told me his version of the *Faustus* production. He told me about Owen Dodson and their last sad meeting in Denver; about his life in exile, the club l'Abbaye, Lee Payant; about the theater group they had formed; about a visit he had made to Jamaica in the fifties. He seemed interested in my experiences in struggle, and I was fascinated by his in art. We laughed a lot.

His was a cultivated intelligence. He was highly literate in music, art, and, of course, theater, well informed in politics, and very sensitive and knowledgeable on black culture—African, Caribbean and American. His conversation was witty and clever, but always judicious and his judgments, sophisticated and subtle and always authoritative. We seemed to have been talking for about an hour, when I asked, "Are you getting tired yet?"

"Yes. I think you must go now, my friend. Perhaps you will come back tomorrow, yes?"

It was only then I realized we had been talking for nearly five hours. I was late for a reception that the American cultural attaché was giving for the Baldwins. I apologized.

During our talk, I had given Gordon the copy of my novel that Odile had unearthed. The English edition had come into the world encumbered by a garish, irredeemably tasteless jacket, obviously representing some English designer's idea of Jamaican popular culture. And the binding was in so lurid and bilious a shade of yellow that the ugly jacket could not be discarded. He accepted the book, I thought, somewhat gingerly and quickly opened it as though to avoid having to look at the jacket. I had seen the merest flicker of a pained expression. Then he looked at me, smiled warmly, and warned, "I shall read this very carefully, you know."

"Do," I said. "I believe it can hold up, even to your meticulous scrutiny." He smiled.

When Gordon had asked what brought me to Paris, I'd mentioned the upcoming French edition of my book and the ceremony for Jimmy. I expressed surprise that so prominent a figure in the African-American artistic community would not be there.

"I would have expected that you and Jimmy would certainly be friends," I ventured.

"Yes, but we haven't been close recently. In fact, I haven't seen him in years." There was an undertone of regret in his voice.

We then talked about Jimmy and his career. I gathered that when Jimmy first arrived Gordon and Lee had befriended and "looked out for him." It was clear that he knew Jimmy well, foibles and all, and there was a kind of avuncular fondness and exasperation in his voice.

"Jimmy, Jimmy! You'd invite Jimmy to dinner and he'd show up three days late, wistful, smiling ruefully, and with an explanation so outrageous it could only be true."

"So what happened? You guys should be close now, allies, be looking out for each other," I insisted.

It was a long story, obviously not to be explained fully to me, except that it was simply a misunderstanding. Before we left the subject, I sought permission to try to effect a reconciliation.

"Clearly you love Jimmy, too. You should be friends and allies again. May I try?" He did not forbid it.

*   *   *

The reception in an immense, ornate apartment belonging to the American government and people was festive and crowded with elegant Parisians. Jimmy seemed emotionally drained after the ceremony. He and his brother David described the day's events. Jimmy asked how I'd passed the afternoon.

"You'll never guess who I spent the afternoon with."

"Who?"

"Gordon Heath."

The sound of his name brought the brothers to full attention. Jimmy sat bolt upright almost as I had done in the bookstore.

"*Gordon,* my God. How *is* he?"

"He's having trouble with his legs, but he seems fine otherwise."

"My God, Gordon! Where is he? Do you have a number?"

"No, but he's at 45, rue de Sèvres."

Jimmy seemed lost in the past. "Ah yes, I remember that apartment." "It's been years," he mused, "I met Lucien there." (Next day, Gordon said, "Jimmy always forgets; it was in the other apartment that he met Lucien.")

"I'll go see him. I'll go tomorrow."

"I think so, man. I got the impression that there had been some kind of falling out. . . ."

"Oh that . . . a misunderstanding . . . I know now that lies were told . . . unfortunate, unnecessary. I'll go see him while I'm here."

"Great. You two are kinda heroes of mine, you know. And it's obvious that he respects and cares for you. . . ."

"And I, him. No. I'll definitely go. I want to."

There was no question that Jimmy meant it. But I had seen the crush of publishers' flacks, journalists, and hangers-on that surrounded him. It would not be easy for him to get away.

＆ Next afternoon Gordon seemed pleased enough at my enthusiastic report, but not entirely convinced.

"Well," he said, "we shall see."

I distinctly recall being warmed by his greeting when I arrived on my second visit.

We talked about his Barbadian relatives and a visit to Jamaica he remembered fondly. At one point I interrupted his description of a place on the north coast.

"Hey, that's in the novel. When you have a chance to read it, you'll see. . . ."

"I've read it," he said.

"How? When? Had you read it before?"

"I devour books," he said. "I read it last night."

"But I thought you were sick. You'd have had to have been up all night."

"I was," he said. (When I received a copy of the manuscript which is this book, I returned the compliment.)

That afternoon as we discussed books, I discovered another facet of this remarkable man. When he showed me a couple of novels—I think the Barbadian Paule Marshall's *Brown Girl, Brownstones* was one—the jackets of which he had designed, I fully understood the fleeting, pained look I thought I had seen the previous afternoon when I handed him my book. His designs were models of elegant simplicity, entirely consonant with the spirit of the cultures depicted in the novels.

I told him about my twelve-year-old Jamaican nephew Ali and the cover of a German edition which featured a golliwog-like caricature. Young Ali had stared at it for a long time and then said slowly, "Uncle Michael, you wan' know what I think?"

"Very much Ali, what you think?"

"That these people don't have any regard at all, at all, for *us*, y'know?"

"But they don't know us, Ali, how can they have *anything* for *us*?" I probed.

"I don't mean for you and me, Uncle Michael, I mean for *us*, . . . our . . . culture." A very thoughtful kid was young master Ali. Then it occurred to me.

"*Hey!* Do you think . . . I mean it would be such an honor. . . . I'm seeing the French editor tomorrow. . . . Are you up to it? Would you design the French edition?"

"I'm up to it, and I would," he said.

"Let's call them now." In a delirium of sudden excitement I made the call, with no French, unable at first to make myself understood. Finally Madame Lilenstein, the publisher, grasped what I meant. I handed the phone to a much calmer Mr. Heath and they made a deal.

I shall always remember the feeling of euphoria with which I left that afternoon: a sense of unexpected and undeserved good fortune. It seemed entirely too felicitous, somehow symmetrical that any work of mine should have chanced into such an organic association with this idol of my youth. I was prepared to cherish whatever might result but I was not to appreciate fully the extent of this good fortune until what seemed an impossibly short interval after I returned home. In about two weeks an eye-catching package addressed in boldly elegant calligraphy arrived. The accompanying letter, on note paper of Gordon's design, framed by his engraving of a wood carving of a Mandingo Madonna, was couched in the understatement that I had begun to recognize as typically Heathian, viz:

My Dear M:

Enclosed is my idea for a mock-up for a book jacket. It is comparatively crude as executed and the photo has falsified—slightly—the basic color which is browner and warmer, but the photo is not a deformation. Odile and your Mme. Lilenstein profess to like it a lot. I like it myself. The figure is built up from one of the small African masks you admired *chez moi*. . . .

From which, and because of the very short time, I expected a preliminary sketch. However, what revealed itself was, as far as I could see, a jacket brilliantly conceived and fully executed in every detail. Most remarkable and pleasing, especially given the crude cultural insensitivity of the European designs, was its tasteful yet powerful evocation of the spirit and resonance of the novel's culture. The composition of its elements, the image, calligraphy, and colors, made it a thing indeed to be cherished. My greatest regret at the nonappearance of the French edition (the beleaguered translator apparently having been defeated by the Jamaican patois) is that Gordon's design has never seen the light of publication.

At our last meeting in Paris I very tentatively raised an idea that seemed at the time to border on fantasy—and sentimental fantasy to boot. I'd learned from Odile that Gordon had appeared on stage as recently as that year, though he had withdrawn from the production before the run was completed, possibly, she thought, for reasons of health or perhaps in despair at some ineptness in the production.

Encouraged by this information and inspired by the memory of the impact of his performances on my generation at Howard, I mentioned a production of Wole Soyinka's *The Lion and the Jewel* being planned in Amherst. It was to be a collaboration of our New World Theater and the university's theater department and Gordon's old friend and collaborator, Pearl Primus, would be its choreographer.

So if he were still acting, and if the "competent authorities" there agreed, as they certainly must, and if his strength permitted, and if we could afford his fee, would he possibly consider. . . . He smiled pensively.

"The Lion," he mused, "the *kabeyesi* himself . . . what an amusing idea."

"You mean you're interested? I'm not sure we could afford. . . ." Now his smile really was bemused.

"First let me look again at the part. Then, you see if they want G. Heath. That will be time enough to see if they can 'afford' him, eh?"

Far from dampening my enthusiasm, that practical good sense was more encouragement than I'd dared hope for. That such a thing could be accomplished had seemed wildly improbable. In the first place, for the theater department at the university the production was a ground-breaking venture into the uncharted waters of an alien theatrical culture. For an actor-director of Gordon's wide experience and legendary status it must certainly appear an excursion into the remote provinces. Still, there had been no condescension detectable in his manner. And, with visions of *Faustus* dancing in my head, I was driven by a sense of the immense treat in store for the community and the professional example for our student actors, if only the thing might be accomplished.

That prospect dominated my thoughts on the way home, as did more general reflections on those unexpected afternoons in the presence of this man who'd fleetingly touched the periphery of my life twenty years earlier and then literally disappeared from sight and concern. But that chance encounter had all but displaced some recent experiences with people and places that had been central to my interests and concerns throughout those same twenty years. I refer to various political, cultural, and personal meetings in Kenya, London, and, now, Paris that touched important areas of my emotional and professional life. All instructive, all in different ways very moving, they were by any measure a psychic overload: entirely too much was competing for immediate assimilation. Yet, to my own surprise, above all loomed the image of the stranger, the enigmatic presence of Gordon Heath, which easily succeeded in dominating my memory of this visit. For his had been a considerable presence: a profound serenity that was saved from austerity only by frequent flashes of an irreverent humor, in turn impish or with a wickedly ironic sense of the absurd that was always without meanness. In appearance, he was physically impressive, in fact robust, yet he was said to be ill. Even so, the vigor of his intellect indicated a mind of uncommon range, depth, and complexity. He exuded an overall sense of calm withdrawal from the world, suggestive of a kind of peaceful spiritual semi-retirement.

On first going to meet him I had some trepidation and no idea what really to expect. Fully aware of the increasing politicization of my response to people and events over the years, I recognized the extent to which a prism, if not of race then certainly of cultural politics, had come to color all my perceptions of the world and my judgments of people. I could manage less and less tolerance or patience for those precious black "artists" who affected to "transcend" race and historical realities and our rich cultural inheritance in order to attain a realm of "pure art."

So I'd worried. Would there indeed be common ground with this legendary exile, the magnificent actor of my memory, exemplar of black excellence? It proved the most unnecessary worry of my life. There was in Gordon Heath not a hint of the isolated, alienated black artist who felt victimized and embittered by the stifling of his talent and career by "racism."

There was nothing deracinated about him. Co-existing with the urbanity of the sophisticated Parisian was the calm, unpretentious self-acceptance of a conscious, deeply rooted black American. He radiated a wonderfully engaging quality for which I could find, at the time, no words. I recognized what I felt only recently in an unpublished memoir by Leslie Schenk, a friend of Gordon's Paris years, who knew him much better than I: "Gordon, of course, the most superlatively achieved human being most of us are ever likely to have met. . . ."

At the time, I had only the vaguest sense of his European career. As for most of my American generation not deeply involved with theater, he had not been a presence in cultural discourse. Somewhat later I would begin to understand the dimension of his achievement in Europe.

Even so, it was impossible to avoid a comparison of the meaning and lessons in the careers of the two celebrated exiles: Baldwin and Heath. For while there were obvious similarities in their choices and in the consequences of those choices, the careers represented in sharp counterpoint and an almost sublime irony, the opposite sides of the same obdurately racist coin.

On one side Baldwin had—so went the received wisdom of his countrymen—unwisely elected a militant and uncompromising engagement of art with politics, to the inevitable detriment of both. While this had produced a transitory fame, the "art had been sacrificed to politics" so literary America moved on, leaving it to the less artistically discriminating French to recognize the enduring value of Baldwin's witness.

On the opposite side was the course elected by Mr. Heath. Also rejecting the deformation of his talent by the constraints of American racial attitudes and social practice, Heath had chosen simply to disengage. He decided instead to find an environment relatively free of vulgar racial politics in order to master—with considerable success—the very same artistic excellence that Baldwin was said to have abandoned. Both formulations are facile, simple-minded, and, therefore, inaccurate. However, the results, as far as their countrymen were concerned, were in effect the same: an exclusion in one case, an expulsion in the other, from the text of national culture.

That last is, of course, my reading. Neither man ever expressed any such sentiment in my hearing, perhaps because the one quality that they held most in common was a kind of grace: a resolute, uncomplaining acceptance of the consequences of their very different choices. As I reflected on these two men whom I found so admirable, the one possibility that never remotely occurred to me was that within a few years these luminous presences would be dead, without ever having overcome the differences that they both had come to discover were without basis.

The other information I did not then have—the details of Gordon's career—came when he sent over a file from which we were to fashion publicity materials for the production. I mention some of this now because it illuminates a period which he was not granted the time to cover in his memoir, and also because there are aspects of his achievement he would have been too modest to mention himself.

For example, it seemed no more than a year after his arrival that he mastered the French language and was appearing on the professional French stage with most critics particularly praising the excellence of his diction. He was in demand for dubbing foreign films into French. Leslie Schenk recalls in this connection:

> The actors Gordon directed were not Oliviers or Brandos for the most part, yet Gordon's analytical faculties permitted them to get inside their roles as they never would have been able on their own. As great an actor as he was (on the level of Olivier, I would say) he was an even greater director. It may sound frivolous to say, but the films he dubbed, or directed the dubbing of, were infinitely more dramatic, underlined three times, than the usual dubbed merchandise.

Similarly, I read for the first time of the albums of folk songs and spirituals that resulted from his singing at l'Abbaye. There was the information that he had been sufficiently accomplished a singer to be selected for the lead in an opera, an accomplishment he dismisses, one suspects, rather too lightly in his account.

I read that he'd appeared on stage and in film in London and Paris, in 1968, for example, with Katherine Hepburn in *The Madwoman of Chaillot*. And so it went. The Studio Theatre of Paris (STP) experience was intriguing, hinting as it did of a public as well as an artistic involvement during the sixties. He spent ten productive years as creative director of STP which presented American plays in English to Paris audiences. These were serious theater and he directed many of the productions.

In one case he stepped in after a "disastrous" French production of Arthur Miller's *After the Fall* and, with the playwright's permission, directed a highly successful resurrection of the play. The material around the STP and its related activities situates him at the center of a group involved in important American theater and in other public activities as well—artistic and political events during the intellectual and political foment of that decade.

I found the single most arresting item in the press packet to be a panel of images showing the actor in fifteen of his most important roles from 1945 to 1985. This was not exactly a photomontage since the dramatic pictures were black-and-white duplicates skillfully enhanced by the hand of the artist and composed into a kind of tapestry of the career.

They show an extraordinary range, covering the full historical sweep of Western theater. We see him as Oedipus, as Faustus, as Hamlet, Cassius, and, of course, as Othello. We see him as the poet Langston Hughes, as Brett Charles, and as a powerfully imperious Henri Christophe. There is, interestingly enough, no picture of him as the Emperor Jones, a part for which some of his admirers felt he had been obliged to "thicken his speech, [and] vulgarize his mind."* He appears as the proletarian rebel Kolhass, as Hamm in Samuel Becket's *Endgame,* and with guitar as the folk singer in *The Madwoman of Chaillot.*

One is struck immediately by the variety. These are not pictures of an actor in costume, but are studies of characters. Each single image manages to suggest an entirely different character, complete and unique, each a new incarnation of the actor's genius.

From among the notices one line leapt out provocatively. During the *Othello* tour of the British Isles in 1950, it was perhaps inevitable that reviewers would invoke Paul Robeson's name. And so it was. One writer predicted confidently that Mr. Heath was "poised to inherit the mantle of Robeson." I read this to mean not merely the role of Othello, since that was a fait accompli, but instead, the towering international stature and public presence, the leadership and devotion once commanded by the great Robeson. In 1950 this must have seemed not just predictable but inevitable, given his remarkably rich endow-ment of mind, talent, discipline, and character, which all seemed every bit as impressive as Robeson's.

But his ascension, which must have appeared automatic in 1950, had not happened? Why? The evidence suggested a very distinguished multifaceted career, but one that seemed to unfold quietly, almost privately, for the eyes of select groups of *cognoscenti* and away from the glare of the mass media. Was that by choice or from necessity? The familiar "art versus politics" conundrum again, or something more interesting and complex?

Not much further on in the reading, the sentence from Clive Barnes's *New York Times* review of *Oedipus,* with which Doris Abramson ends her introduc-

---

*This idea occurs in a very insightful comparison of Heath's Othello with Olivier's: "In contrast to Olivier, he used his inherent urbanity to underline the aristocratic quality of Othello's nobility. It was when he played the Emperor Jones that he had to act himself out of that urbanity, thicken his speech, vulgarize his mind so to speak, in short do everything Olivier had done with Othello" (Leslie Schenk).

tion, kept teasing at my attention. It was with a rush of recognition that I read Barnes's praise. Surely the writer had apprehended not just Gordon's stage presence but his essential character. But where could this classic anachronism, the natural nobility, come from? From training, a kind of osmosis in which an actor, perhaps even subliminally, internalizes and comes to embody as a way of being? In this case the stoic reserve and balance, that greatness of soul that was the Aristotelean ideal, the golden mean? Whatever the provenance, that certainly seemed to be his spirit.

If so, what place was there really for such a spirit in the cut-throat vulgarity, the publicity-driven mendacity of the modern "industry." One could hardly envision such a figure producing sound bytes and photo-ops in a know-nothing rabblement of fast-taking agents, flacks, promoters, and hustlers. And even less so, as a public standard bearer for one or other of the partisan ideologies of the times. That mystery only served to sharpen the eagerness with which his arrival in Amherst for the play was anticipated.

* * *

He admitted that the flight had been exhausting and his ankles really painful. And in truth, his tread was slow and he seemed wan. Beneath the shock of white hair, his face seemed drawn, the eyes tired. And the day was not over; he still had to cope with a ninety-mile car ride and a reception in his honor. But in the car he relaxed visibly and seemed to rest as he listened—for a while most intently—to a British production of *Othello* which I'd thought splendid. Then he asked that the tape be stopped, trying with precision and admirable patience to explain to my wooden ears exactly why he had found the actors' rendition of the poetry and meaning of Shakespeare's language so jarring. Finally, but with good spirit, he gave up on me.

As he approached the reception which would introduce him to the company he was to work with, he seemed to gain energy. A spontaneous curiosity and sense of occasion or simply a willed effort to rise to expectations? I couldn't tell, but once inside he seemed rejuvenated, gracious and warm without any affectation or projection of rank, and he genuinely seemed to draw strength from the people's excitement. One instance of his perceptiveness and sensitivity comes to mind.

He was seated surrounded by a small, very animated group, mostly actors, all young, all black, and all quite uninhibitedly staking claim to him. His new director, Professor Richard Trousdell, the lone white, lingered on the periphery, looking at this paragon he was to direct and quite possibly wondering just what he'd let himself in for.

Gordon noticed but said nothing until,

"Will you," he commanded suddenly, fixing him in a gaze, "stop looking at me as though you'd invented me?"

The stunned silence was followed by inclusive ice-breaking laughter. The circle had attained a new member and a new ease, and Gordon a new friend and admirer.

☙ THE NEXT DAY, when he came to the first reading, he was surprised and visibly moved by the Yoruba royal dance of welcome with which he was drummed and danced into the company. He saluted Pearl Primus who had choreographed the greeting and even managed a few appropriately kingly steps on his painful ankles.

As soon as that marvelously resonant, flexible voice delivered his first lines at the read-through, people knew that they were in the presence of a master. I recognized then how much preparation he must have already done and remembered the magical virtuosity he and Payant had displayed from the *very* first moments of *Faustus*. (I must admit to a slight feeling of outrage coupled with recognition when I read in these pages how *that* illusion had been accomplished. "Dummy, you should have known they had to have been rehearsing before they got to Howard.")

But that was where the similarity ended. As rehearsals progressed it was clear that these students would also be graced with an uncommon experience, but it would be entirely different from ours at Howard. Time and illness had indeed eroded that perfect instrument.

Where there had once been the appearance of unfettered freedom and infinite possibility, there was now the reality of limitation and constraint. Instead of an effortless virtuosity commanding inexhaustible physical resources, there was now an old pro, a wily veteran carefully inventorying diminished stocks, husbanding what remained so as to deploy them most strategically, substituting what was available for what was gone, so artfully that the audience never suspected.

The legs were gone and memory was not always completely dependable, so the base had fallen to the enemy. But the extraordinary presence remained, as did eloquent gesture and, of course, the great voice, and the skill to deploy them, strengthened by an intelligence honed and seasoned by experience.

The struggle had been at once harrowing and inspiring to watch. Harrowing because one knew the price of failure to this proud man; inspiring because of the determination and courage with which the old pro willed and maneuvered the characterization onto terrain his forces still commanded. By opening night he had constructed an apparently organic, dramatically convincing character out of the options left him. It was masterly and impressive, especially because

Gordon Heath with Celia O. Hilson (*right*) and other members of the cast of *The Lion and the Jewel*, University of Massachusetts, 1987

the role did not really offer the challenges of complex characterization and subtlety of language which would have fully engaged his abilities. I think he knew it was the last splendid go-round.

While onlookers at rehearsals sensed something of his struggle, part of his success was that none recognized how really weakened he was. Few knew, for example, that on many days he did not, in fact could not, leave his apartment except to present himself on time and fully prepared for rehearsals and that he then returned exhausted to sleep all the next day.

Some admitted to a certain disappointment that Mr. Heath was not more socially present. They had nurtured visions of sitting at his feet to be regaled with theater reminiscence, insider insights, and those weighty opinions informed by a lifetime in the profession. They wanted "to learn more" from him, scarcely recognizing that the most valuable lessons he had to impart were offered nightly during rehearsals.

Troubled by his monkish regimen, I wondered if he mightn't welcome some social invitations. He smiled and admitted that those would be nice, but that what energy he had needed to be husbanded and very carefully rationed. He didn't have to say that his responsibility to the part received all that energy and his total concentration. That it wasn't Broadway or London's West End, but the main stage of a provincial university in a small New England town was a distinction that did not seem to exist for him. And this was not, I felt sure, evidence of the egotism of a star, but of honor: a proud professional integrity, a personal code that seemed out of another, better age.

Not once did he complain, reveal his physical difficulties, or seek or accept treatment any different from the rest of the company. This quality of character was more than professional. Anne Halley and Jules Chametzky were his Amherst hosts. Jules complained one day:

> He's almost too perfect a guest, so very careful not to be any trouble. Yesterday he was going into town, and I offered to drive him since his ankles seemed very tender. But he claimed he looked forward to the walk. When I followed in the car there he was limping along painfully. Then, óf course, he couldn't decline.

At this point, I thought I had begun to glimpse something more of that core of values which informed the being and guided the choices of this centered, principled man. A fundamental element of which can be illustrated by an incident.

One day, before opening night, he learned that the sculptor and master printmaker Leonard Baskin lived nearby and would be pleased to receive him. His eyes lit up and his entire countenance quickened, but he postponed going until after the play had opened and the role fully established.

The Baskin estate is a remarkable place organized around the making and displaying of beautiful things. During a tour of the workshops—various studios for painting, engraving, carving, and one housing the ancient hand-press where Gehenna Press art books are produced—Gordon's acute interest was evident. He had an informed and detailed knowledge of the process and of its fine technical aspects, especially of block-making and printing.

Then we arrived at the high-ceilinged library which housed an extensive collection beginning with Baskin's own work in various media and the Gehenna Press volumes, and including a large number of rare, ancient, and beautiful books and a collection of esoteric etchings and engravings from unknown masters, which appeared to recapitulate the entire history of European printmaking.

Suddenly, Gordon was transformed, rapturous. I watched as a pleased Baskin produced one treasure after the other, and the two men immersed themselves in exploring and admiring the intricacies of the works and in involved discussions of the arcane mysteries of technique and methods of artists whose names I'd never heard. Gordon seemed to gain sudden energy and did not tire until very late that evening. His transformation was almost magical, as was the intensity of his concentration and the unaffected purity of his pleasure. There was a perceptible light that seemed to come from him.

It was not simply that for him the aesthetic experience was paramount, being more fully and completely received than with most humans. He also brought to it an acute analytical intelligence, a critical faculty that was as fascinated with the process, stratagems, and techniques of creation and performance as by the end result. And from this came the imperatives that guided his life and his important choices.

Toward the end of his time in Amherst, Bruce Wilcox, director of the University of Massachusetts Press, requested a meeting. He was eloquent and persuasive. Gordon Heath was a veritable receptacle of theater lore and history . . . surely it must have come up? . . . the life and career of such interest . . . did he ever think to? . . . Gordon smiled enigmatically. Yes indeed, that had been said . . . the subject had been broached, yes . . . he had indeed thought . . . but there were important considerations. . . .

When it became apparent—to Mr. Wilcox's great and visible relief—that these "important considerations" did not involve large sums of money beyond the means of a university press, he shrewdly brought out a number of the more impressively and tastefully produced of the Press's books. Gordon examined them in some detail, his expression inscrutable. Then he smiled.

"I will try," he said, "time and strength permitting."

The two men shook hands and the deal was made. The result of it is this book. There was no discussion of contracts in my hearing.

Back in Paris, Gordon turned to the memoir with his usual determination, but the work was intermittent, with frequent lapses into illness. "The book," he once wrote me, "proceeds in leaps and lurches." I can well visualize the effort of memory and will he must have mobilized toward meeting his commitment to leave us this record.

He sent installments periodically in a sequence that seemed to follow thematic rather than chronological imperatives. Once they arrived on two cassettes with his great voice reading from his text. Our appetites had been whetted and folk prayed for the completion of this last project. The presentation of each section was quintessentially Heathian. Although the typing was rough, the marginalia—pen-and-ink drawings and copies of photographs of places and people mentioned, all artfully placed—gave the manuscript something of the appearance of an illustrated medieval text that cried out to be published in facsimile. The quality of the writing indicates that he might easily have had a career in that medium. His description, for example, of the Harlem church service is among the very finest rendering of this much described aspect of black culture that I have read anywhere.

But he was not to complete the account as he had planned. We can be grateful for what he was able to give us, which is considerable. However, it is because he could not finish the account of the middle and later years and to reflect over his larger career, that I have written at the length I have. I hope he will approve or at least understand.

Jules Chametzky who also met him in his later years and also came to admire him without reservation, accurately, and, I think, best captures the essential Gordon:

In 1989 we walked slowly (his feet gave him much trouble then) around St. Germain des Près, past the site of the Old L'Abbaye and Les Deux Magots, and Gordon remarked that for more than twenty-five years he had known just about everyone on these streets, but now he knew almost no one there. I searched his face for any sign of regret or self-pity as he said these words, but I could discern none. Was there none? Or was he displaying the composed and stoic mastery, "the natural authority of a classic hero" as Clive Barnes so aptly put it in the review of *Oedipus?* The mastery was there, as well as the self-discipline and inner strength of a man who had made certain decisions about how he was to live, lived fully, experienced life deeply, and transmuted his experience into something unique and precious.

Truly, we shall not see his like again.

Pelham, 1992

❧ Index